PHOTO WISE

MASTERCLASS

EXPLORING BLACK AND WHITE PHOTOGRAPHY

PHOTO WISE

MASTERCLASS

EXPLORING BLACK AND WHITE PHOTOGRAPHY

By

PAUL GALLAGHER

RHE MEDIA LTD

www.RHEMediaPhotography.co.uk

This book was first published in 2016 by:
RHE Media Ltd
5 Pennsylvania Crescent
Exeter
EX4 4SF

ISBN 978 1 910226 45 2 (Paperback)
ISBN 978 1 910226 37 7 (fixed layout eBook)

British Library Cataloguing in Publication Data
A catalogue record for this book is available from the British Library.

Print and bind by Short Run Press Limited, Bittern Road, Sowton Industrial Estate, Exeter, Devon EX2 7LW UK

RHE
MEDIA LTD
www.rhemediaphotography.co.uk

CONTENTS

FOREWORD

Ever since Kodak started the mass production of colour film in the 1950s, critics have been predicting the demise of black and white photography. Yet it continues to appeal and, in fact, it is enjoying something of a Renaissance, due in no small measure to the many students and young people who are rediscovering the joys of analogue photography. What the devotees of monochrome are discovering is that by reducing the image to just its tonal values, one is able to unearth a mystique that is missing when presenting the image in full colour. Few photographers are able to achieve this better than Paul Gallagher.

Having had the pleasure of assisting Paul on one of his many landscape workshops, I am patently aware that he is a natural teacher. Enthusiastic and empathetic, he is capable of instilling the same passion for photography in his students that he currently enjoys. One of the key skills when teaching is to understand the students' needs and to design a programme that positively moves them on. *Exploring Black and White Photography* truly is a 'masterclass' in this respect. As a teacher, he gains so much pleasure when he is able to help one of his students improve, and it is clear that he has approached this book with the same generosity and enthusiasm.

Much as I admire Paul's abilities as a teacher, it should not be overlooked that he is a highly accomplished photographer. Aside from his many personal exhibitions, he has written several other very successful books on the art of black and white photography and is respected both nationally and internationally.

This publication is one from our PhotoWise collection, so there will be an assumption that the reader has had some experience of photography; the principle aim is to move the reader on to the next level. Paul intelligently reinforces key camera craft issues that some may have overlooked such as composition, the appropriate use of filters and, most importantly, how best to convert your digital file into monochrome. With his many years working in the darkroom, he has a unique expertise that has proven invaluable to those now wishing to step up to digital monochrome.

In *Exploring Black and White Photography*, the author has struck the right balance between offering technical advice and helping the reader to respect the importance of personal input. Paul understands that photography is not just a science; it is also an art and, therefore, one should be encouraged to pre-conceive the image even before pressing the shutter and then work positively in the lightroom to bring this to fruition.

Working on the principle of leaving the best till last, the author has added a truly inspirational Gallery section, which not only showcases his

own personal work, but reveals the thinking behind his photography. If you have any doubts whether this publication merits the strap-line 'Masterclass', then this truly impressive portfolio will convince you otherwise.

Tony Worobiec, July 2015

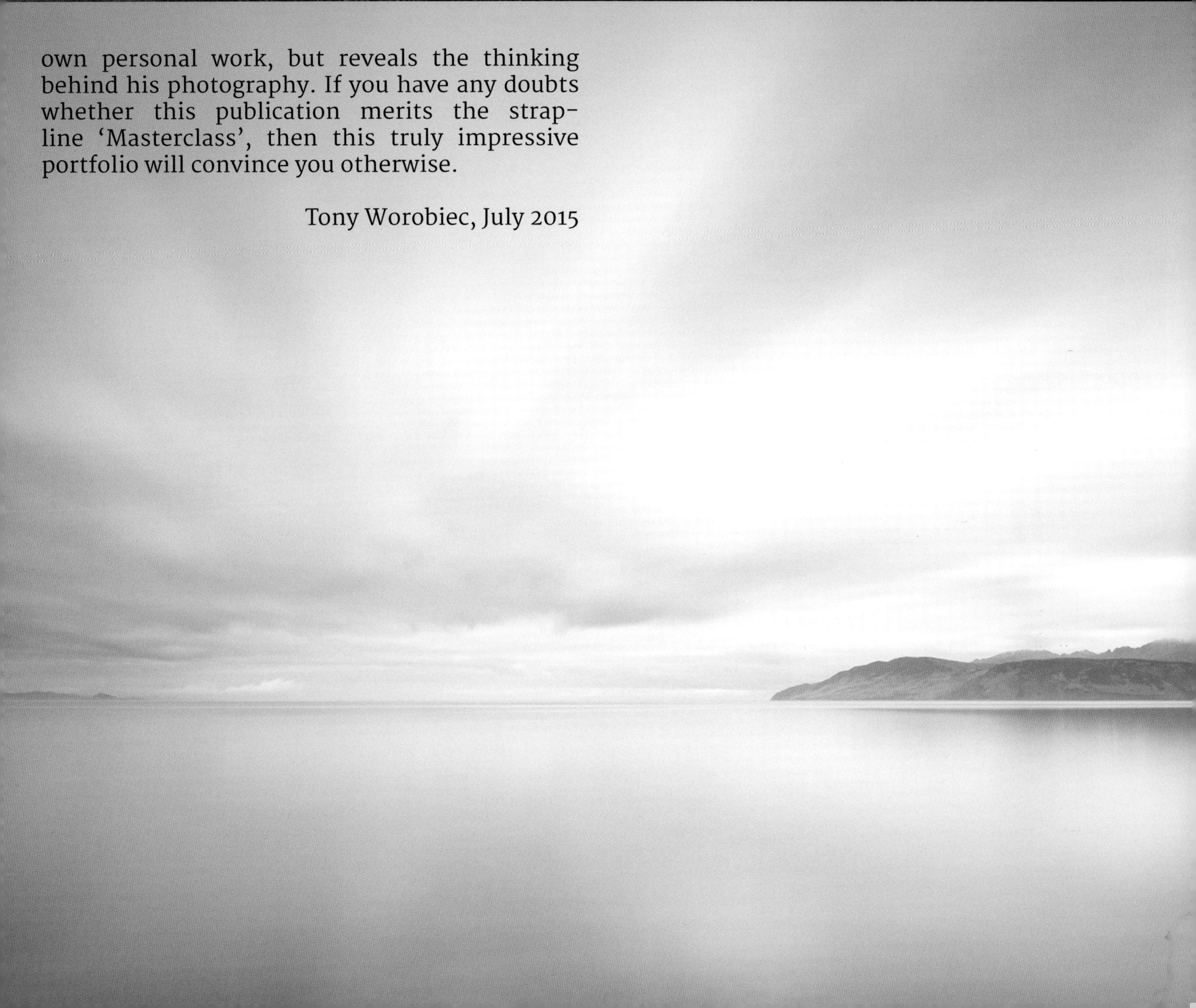

BENNAN HEAD, ISLE OF ARRAN

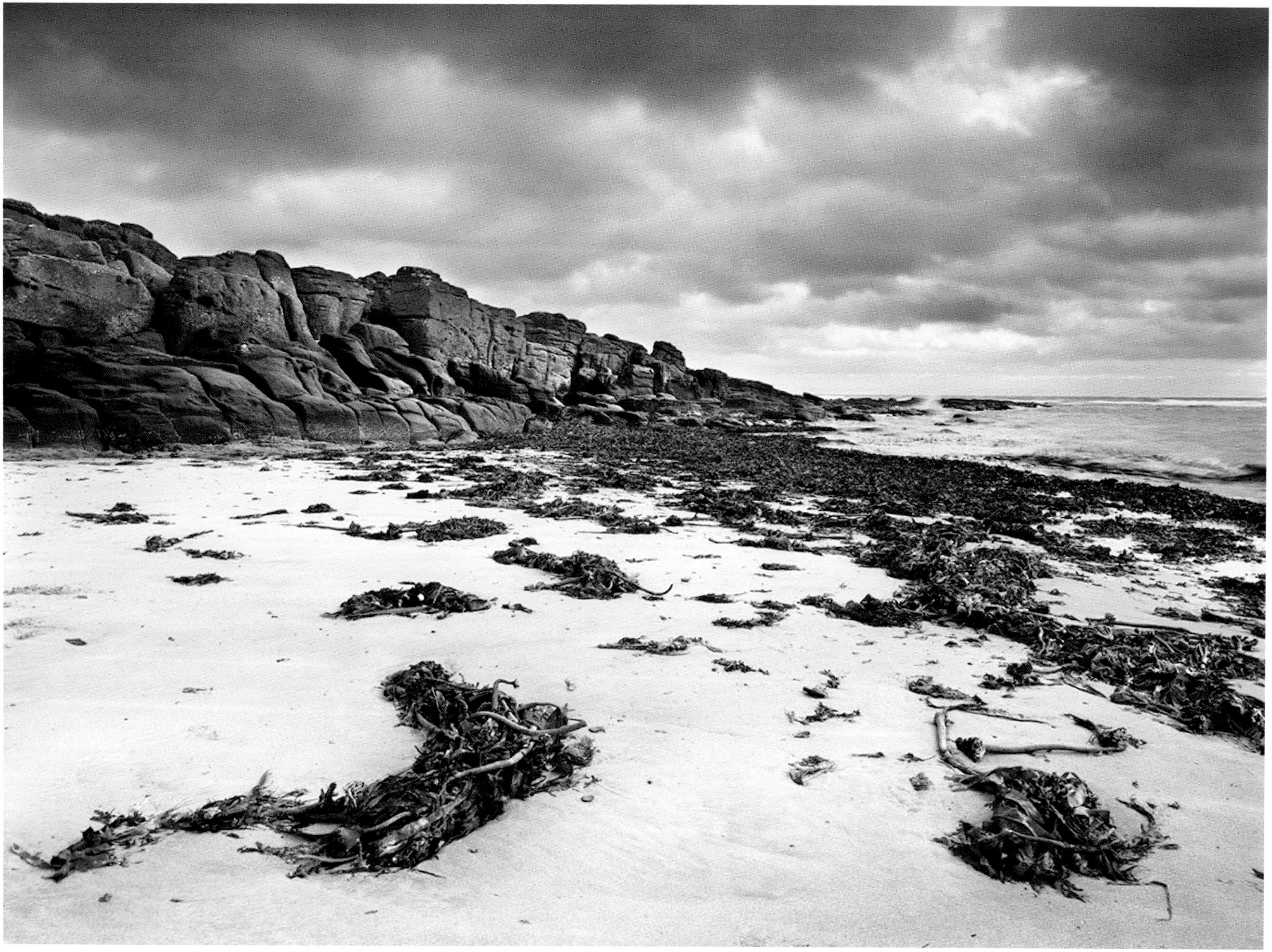

A bad day with poor light but the drama of the moody skies makes the image powerful. Taken on the south coast of the Isle of Arran with an impending storm brewing. *Ebony 45Us large format camera, 90mm lens, f22, 1 sec.*

My beginning

From my very early introductions to photography as a graphic design student I was always attracted to black and white photographs. In the early 1980s colour photography was very popular and black and white was regarded as somewhat 'old-hat' for many of my peers. I clearly recall visiting the college library and sifting through so many titles, and I always seemed to sit down at a table with a pile of books by Ansel Adams, Edward Weston, Wynn Bullock and Paul Strand. Their photographs resonated in me with beautiful tones, depth and amazing compositions. To me, these photographers were breaking new ground even though many of the photographs I was looking at had been taken decades before I became a photographer. I also think that as a graphic design student at the time, I was faced with projects that involved the use of shapes and space on a daily basis and this seemed to be an ever-present consideration in the works of these masters. It soon became apparent that these simple parameters would become the skeleton behind all of my work and the principles to which I would adhere for the next 30 years.

Can we consider black and white photography to be the true foundation of photography?

This is a question that I often ask students. If you look at the history of making photographs, the very first photographers only had black and white materials to work with and managed to produce some of the most beautiful photographs ever made. Today everybody is capturing moments in time with all manner of devices, although I suspect that many of these are not dedicated cameras at all, but multi-functional handsets such as iPads and mobile phones. Even modern-day digital SLR cameras capture everything in colour and when you look at the display screens on the back of your cameras you see a colour image.

Although we are surrounded by colour photographs all day, every day, there is still a passion and pursuit for making black and white images. Why is this? I feel the reason is that black and white images convey the world in a different way to colour images. Many of us see everything in colour during our day-to-day lives, so a colour photograph, unless it is exceptionally different, presents to us something of a 'record' of the scene, something that is a 'literal' statement. If you are presented with a black and white image of something you are familiar with, then it is likely that you will stop and take the time to look because it is different.

When colour photography became almost the norm in the early 1970s, black and white photography was relegated to niche markets, but it was never lost or entirely replaced by colour. Black and white lasted and many masters

of photography remained true advocates in the monochrome world, even while the majority of professional photographers embraced the commercial advantages of colour.

Is black and white photography alive today?

It is without doubt that black and white photography has had a strong place in the world of image making since its inception in the 1800s and I suspect this will always be the case. If you consider the photography magazine market, which is a very competitive environment indeed, there remain several titles throughout the world that are entirely dedicated to the celebration of black and white photography. When you take a look at social media, or conduct a web search on the subject, you are inundated with societies, forums and groups who are in constant conversation about a subject that was 'apparently' superseded in the early 1970s.

Lastly, the giants of the photographic industry have not left black and white behind either. Virtually all cameras and capture devices have some form of monochrome setting to enable the photographer to peer into the wonderful world of black and white, allowing them to see what they had seen in full colour only moments ago represented in a series of tones of grey. Almost all image manipulation software and printer manufacturers that are dedicated to the post-capture segment of the photography market have also assigned time and money to ensuring that photographers have access to exploring their photographs without colour. So why is this?

A different world

As a photographer you capture moments in time with your camera, which collects light from that moment and presents you with a representation of reality. When you elect not to use the colour in your photographs, these representations depart from your world of reality a little more. In doing so, you are exploring the world about you from a slightly different viewpoint. This is an exciting exploration and one that allows you a freedom to express yourself that can become rather addictive.

Why I still love black and white

Although I do photograph in colour, I still consider myself to be, predominantly, a black and white photographer. This is because it is through this medium that I can leave the colour world behind and dive into the infinite tones of grey between black and white that have always fascinated me. Throughout this book, I intend to show you the wonders of black and white and convey to you the basic ways of embarking on your

own journey of photographic self-discovery. I will take you through the foundations of what will get you closer to a quality black and white photograph. I will start with basic camera considerations and controls that are at your disposal, look at what you should try to train your eyes to 'see' and which subjects you should consider when you are out there with your camera. Along with this I intend to offer you a set of simple principles to follow, which are, I feel, the foundations of black and white photography - from field craft to exploration in there with your camera. Along with this I intend to offer you a set of simple principles to follow, which are, I feel, the foundations of black and white photography - from field craft to exploration in the digital darkroom. Having been through virtually all of the black and white processes during my career, I have sought to simplify these steps for you and to cut out as much confusion as possible to make your journey and exploration a pleasure.

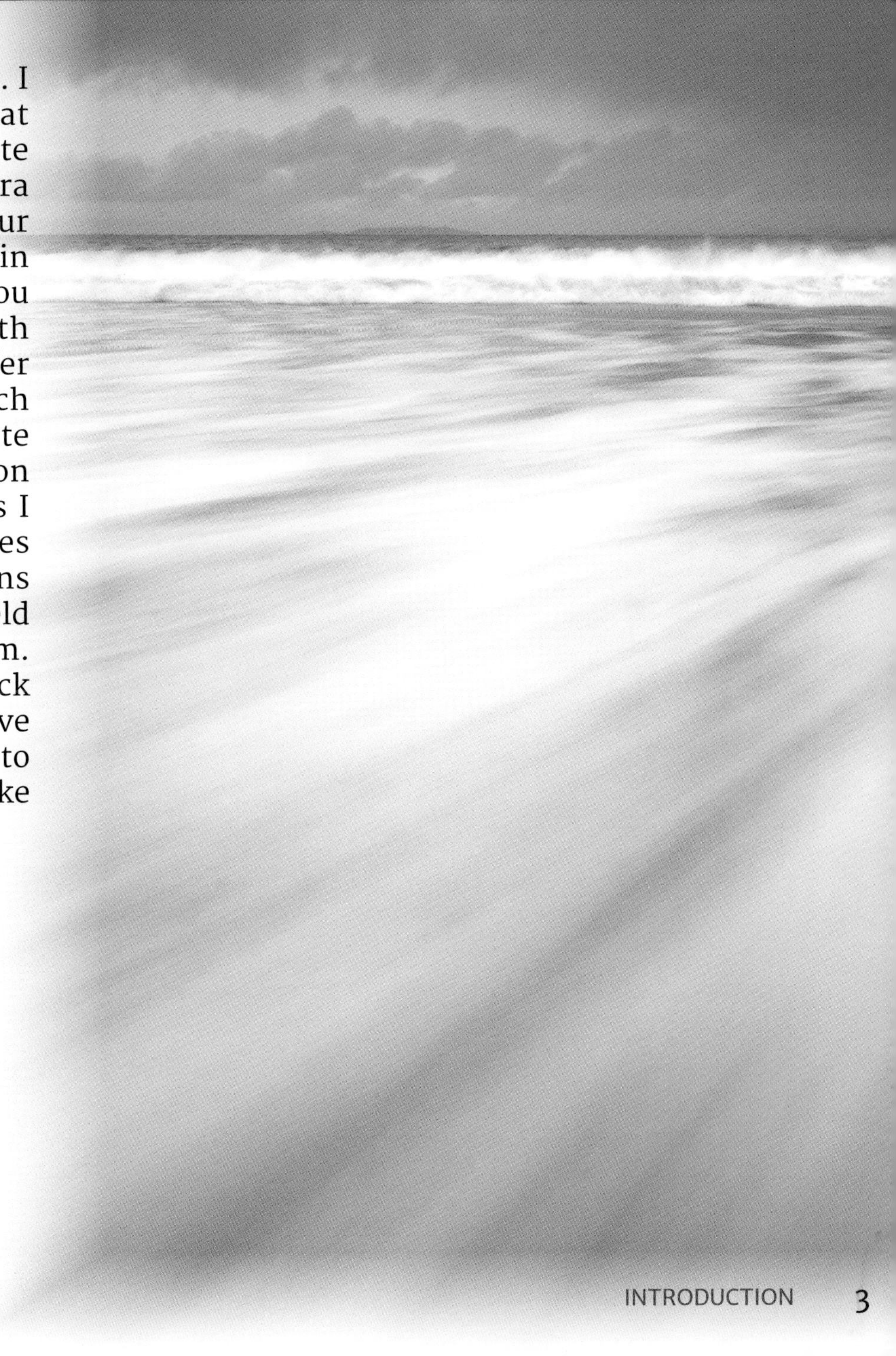

BUACHAILLE ETIVE MOR

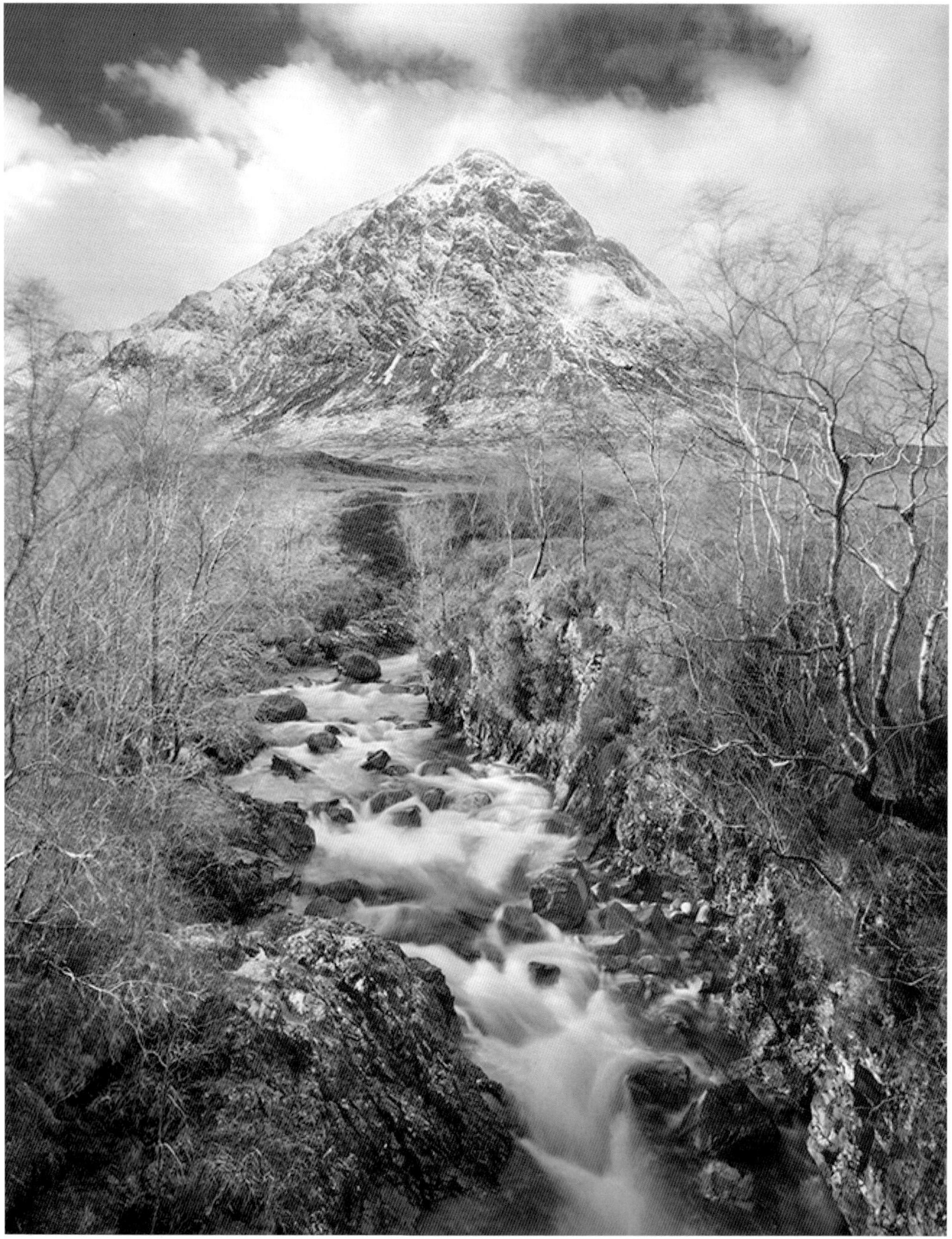

A break in the snow storms and a flash of light brought the scene together. A commission from the BBC for Glen Coe. First light after a snowy night. *Walker Titan large format camera, 90mm lens, f22, 1 sec.*

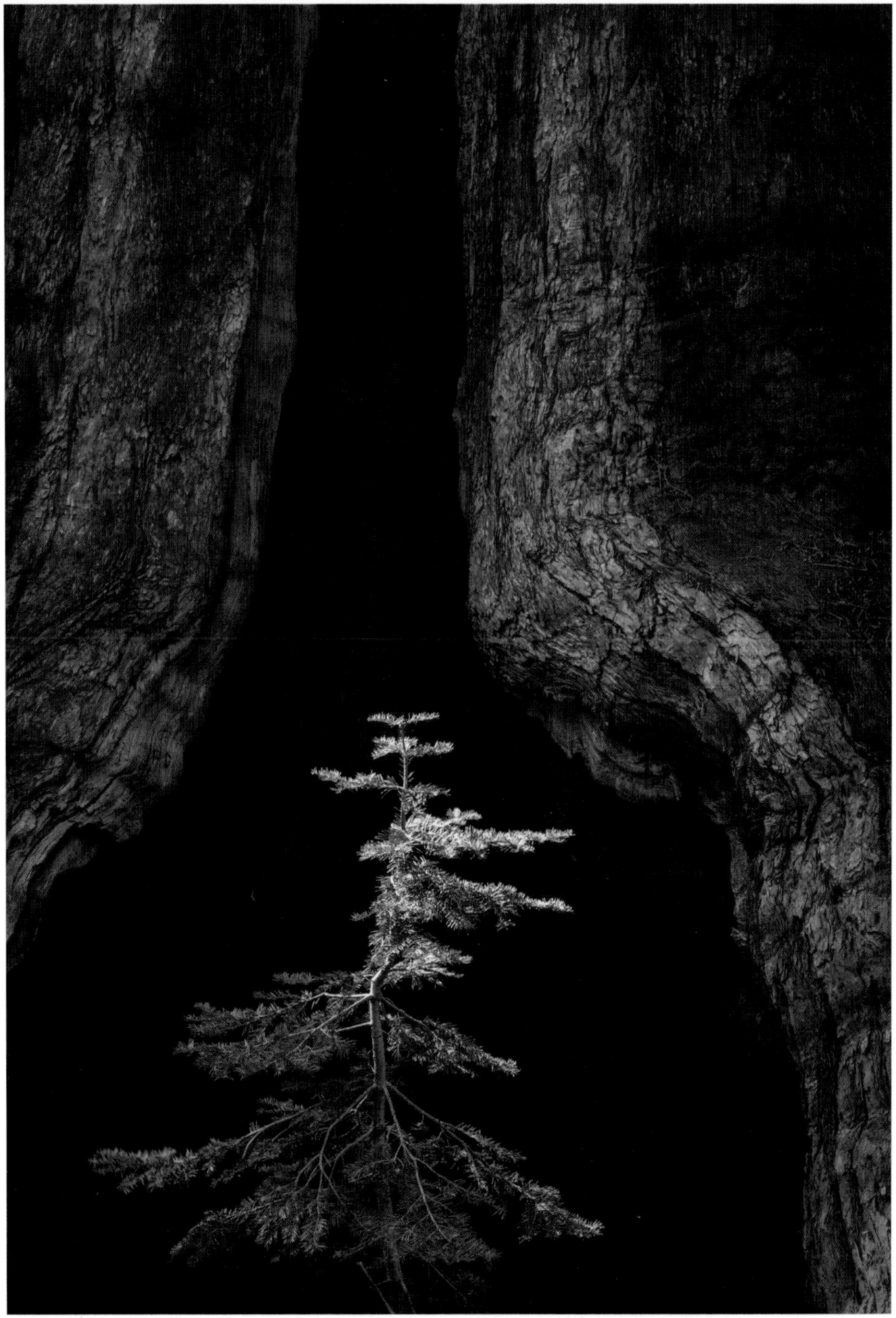

Last light of the day catching the sapling set against the foot of a giant! *Nikon D800e, 70–200mm lens, f16, 0.8 secs.*

2. WHY PHOTOGRAPH IN BLACK AND WHITE?

Do you really need colour?

I feel tempted to say 'Why not?' or 'Because you can'. It may be better to start with 'Do you really need colour?' It would be fair to say that certain subjects clearly need colour information to work. There are particular situations, such as flower photography, where the absence of colour may be somewhat detrimental to what the photograph is trying to convey such as, for example, the beauty of the flowers' colours in full bloom. That considered, the same flowers photographed in black and white would convey a different message entirely and the experience for the viewer would also be different. Black and white is the true foundation of photography as all you are dealing with is light and nothing else. If you have not already tried to make images in black and white then it is worth the effort as the results can often be outstanding.

Seeing in tones of grey

I think it is good for all photographers to try to 'see' things in tones of grey. The act of 'seeing' is not as simple as it sounds. It is hard work at first but the rewards can be huge. Black and white is different from colour because you are forced to look for rhythms, patterns and shapes. Also, shadows become more important as they add to the overall balance and tones in a photograph. Black and white photographs often add drama, but black and white photographs that display a simple 'high-key' tonality can also capture the eye. I often say to students and clients, 'Go out and play with the light'. The reason for this is that light is the only thing you need to look for and, without colour, it is something that is both challenging and fascinating to do.

The versatility of black and white

Black and white photography is so massively versatile. You could be photographing a wedding or portraits, be out there in the urban environment making images of buildings, on the street taking candid photographs, or working in a forest or valley in the landscape. The choices are limitless. However, if you compare this with colour photography, there are certain limitations to what you can do to get the same appeal in a colour image. The reason for this is that colour is what you see all the time, and if colour tonality is adjusted too far colours look over-saturated and false, and can quickly become ugly.

BARCALDINE FOREST – SUBTLE LIGHT & HIDDEN STRUCTURE

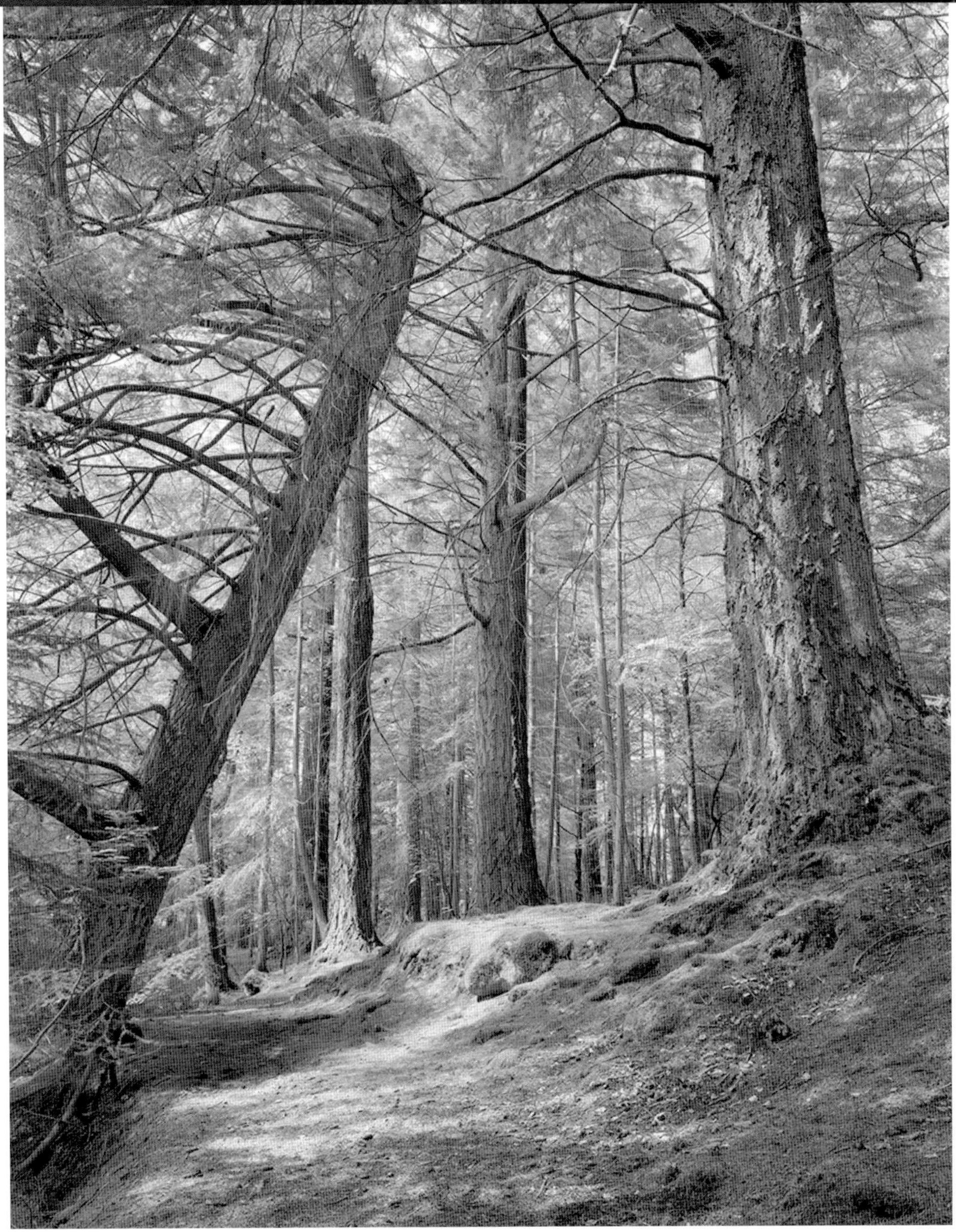

Have a look at 'Barcaldine Forest' as this is an example of where black and white photography comes into its own. It was early spring and the foliage was beginning to form on the huge conifers. This was the type of day that many photographers exploring the landscape would not venture out because the skies were hazy with a strong yellow sunlight and it was in the middle of the day. When I entered the forest I was staggered by the 'milky' sunlight pushing through the canopy high above and the gentle shadows that were cast upon the forest floor. If you look at the composition it is really simple. I positioned one of the three main trees of the composition in the centre of the frame so that it was perfectly vertical, leaving the other two giants to lean inwards, so framing the scene. It is an image that uses three dominant structures and it is brought to life with dappled sunlight.

Ebony large format camera, 90mm lens, f22, 1sec

OLDSHOREMORE – OPEN SPACE AND PALE TONES

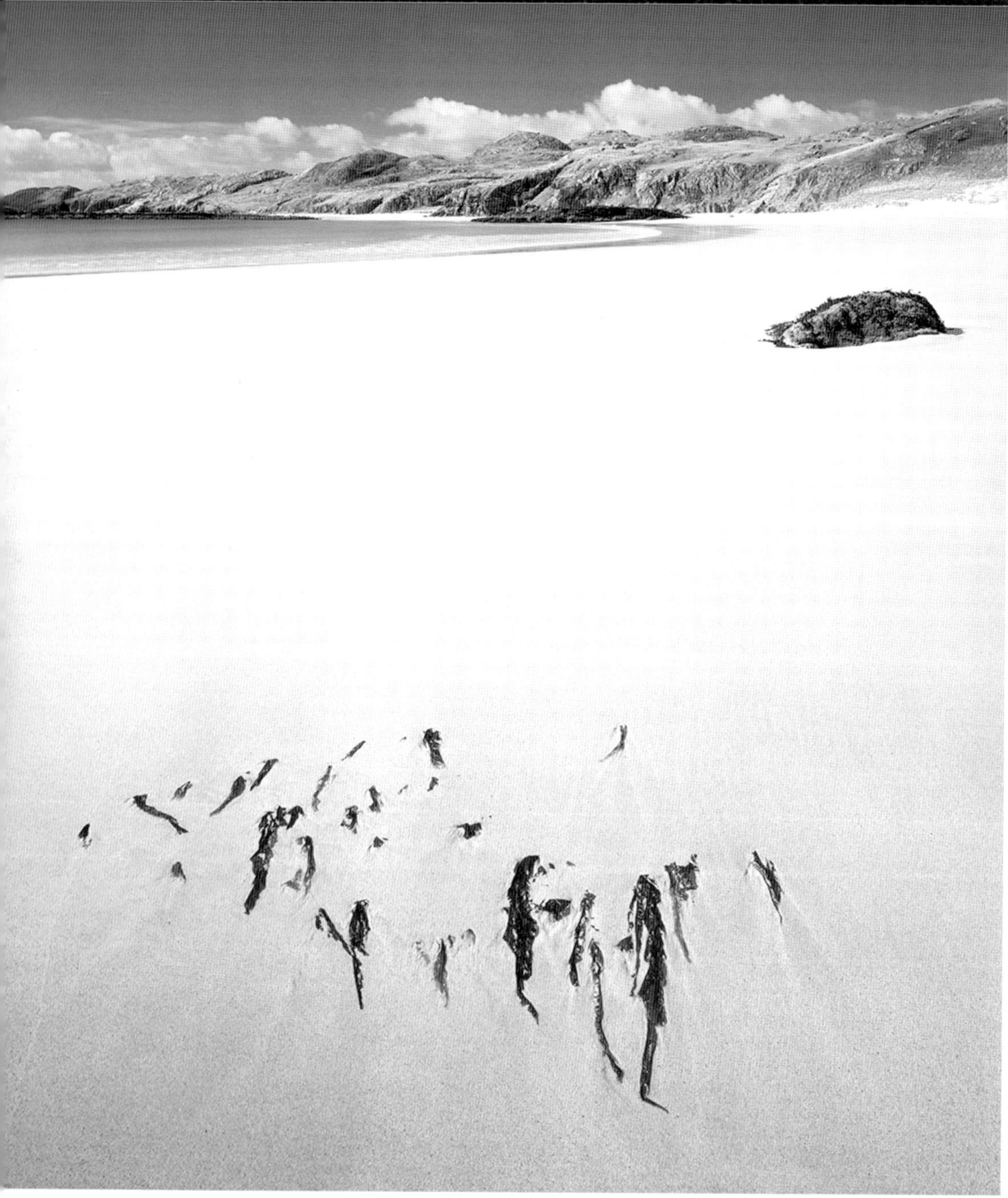

The opposite of Barcaldine Forest is this image 'Oldshoremore'. Once again, this was taken in early spring, in Sutherland in the far northern highlands of Scotland. The sun was very direct and harsh but this made perfect lighting conditions for the subject matter. Visualising in black and white, I could see an image of strong contrast embracing this light. The black seaweed occupies the open white swathe of sand in the foreground and the upper single boulder leads the eye towards the distant headland with an almost clear blue sky. If this image was presented in colour it would look awful and resemble a 'record shot' or postcard image, but because there is no colour and only tones of grey it works well and the simple components are brought together without yellow sand and harsh blue skies.

Walker Titan large format camera, 90mm lens, f22, 0.5 sec., 0.6 Neutral Density Hard Graduated Filter.

LOW SUN, GLEN COE – MOOD AND POWER

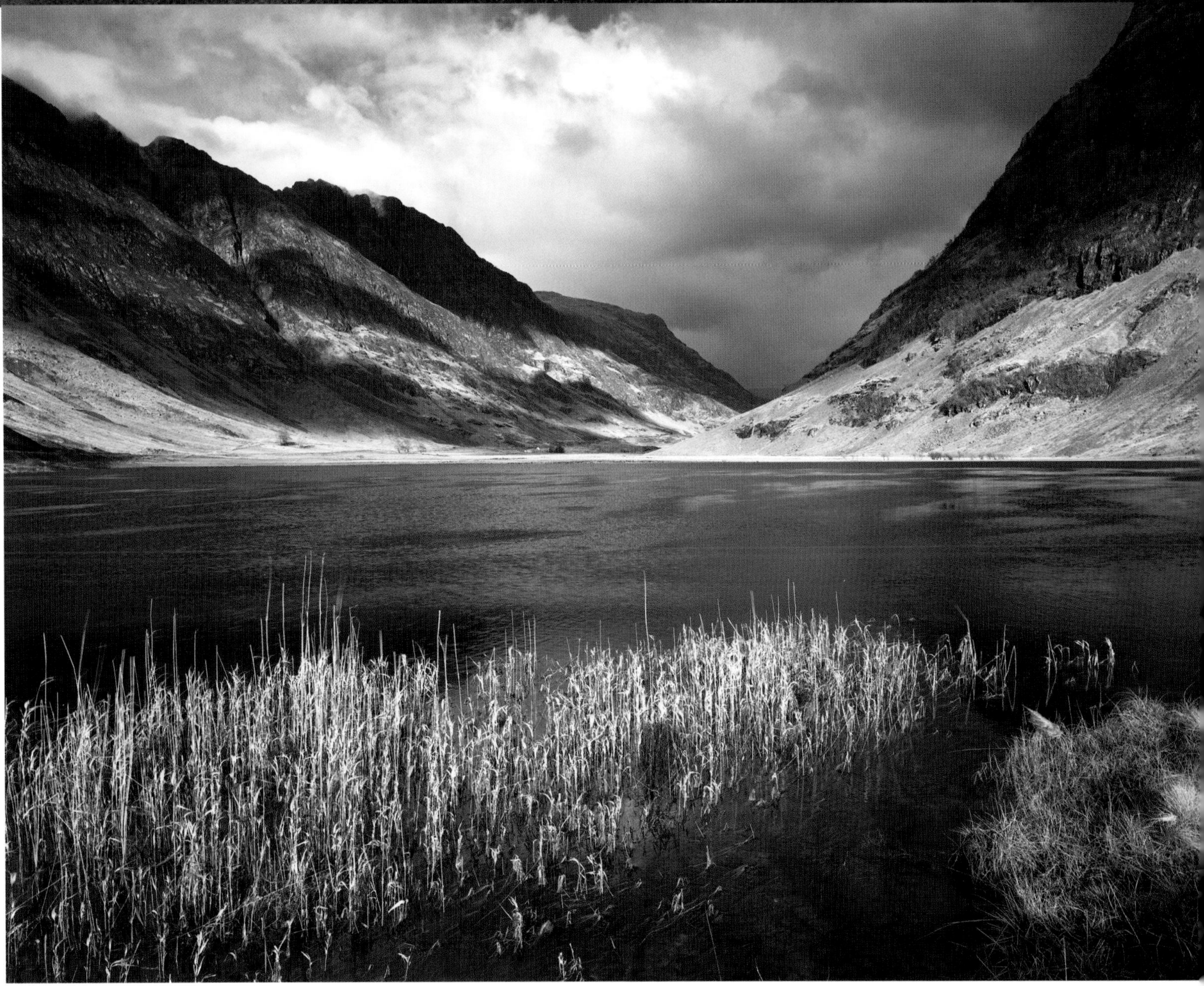

Ebony large format camera, 90mm lens, f22, 1 sec., Lee 0.6 Neutral Density Hard Graduated Filter.

Low Sun, Glen Coe

It is without doubt that black and white photography is astonishingly effective at portraying drama, and the image 'Low Sun, Glen Coe' depicts this perfectly. I was standing at the edge of Loch Achtriochan with a storm approaching from the upper part of Glen Coe and Rannoch Mor. As the building cloud modulated the light it sent shadows down the flanks of the mountains and lit the reeds at my feet. The play of light represented in a series of dark shadows and glistening light grey give the composition depth, and the structure of the clouds convey exactly what it was like when I was stood there with my camera. For me, it is a classic black and white situation to be in and conveys far more of the mood of the moment than a colour representation. Simplicity is also a powerful tool for black and white photographers to use at will.

Trees in Snow

'Trees in Snow' is an example of the use of simplicity taken to extremes and a style of black and white I enjoy immensely. The landscape was a white canvas after a recent blizzard and the thin trees soon lost their coating of snow in the prevailing winds, leaving them standing in the landscape as a stark, dark contrast to the white background. All I had to do was decide the position of my camera to establish a separation between the trees and to position them in the frame. Mist can also offer similar circumstances and this is well worth bearing in mind.

TREES IN SNOW – STARK CONTRASTS

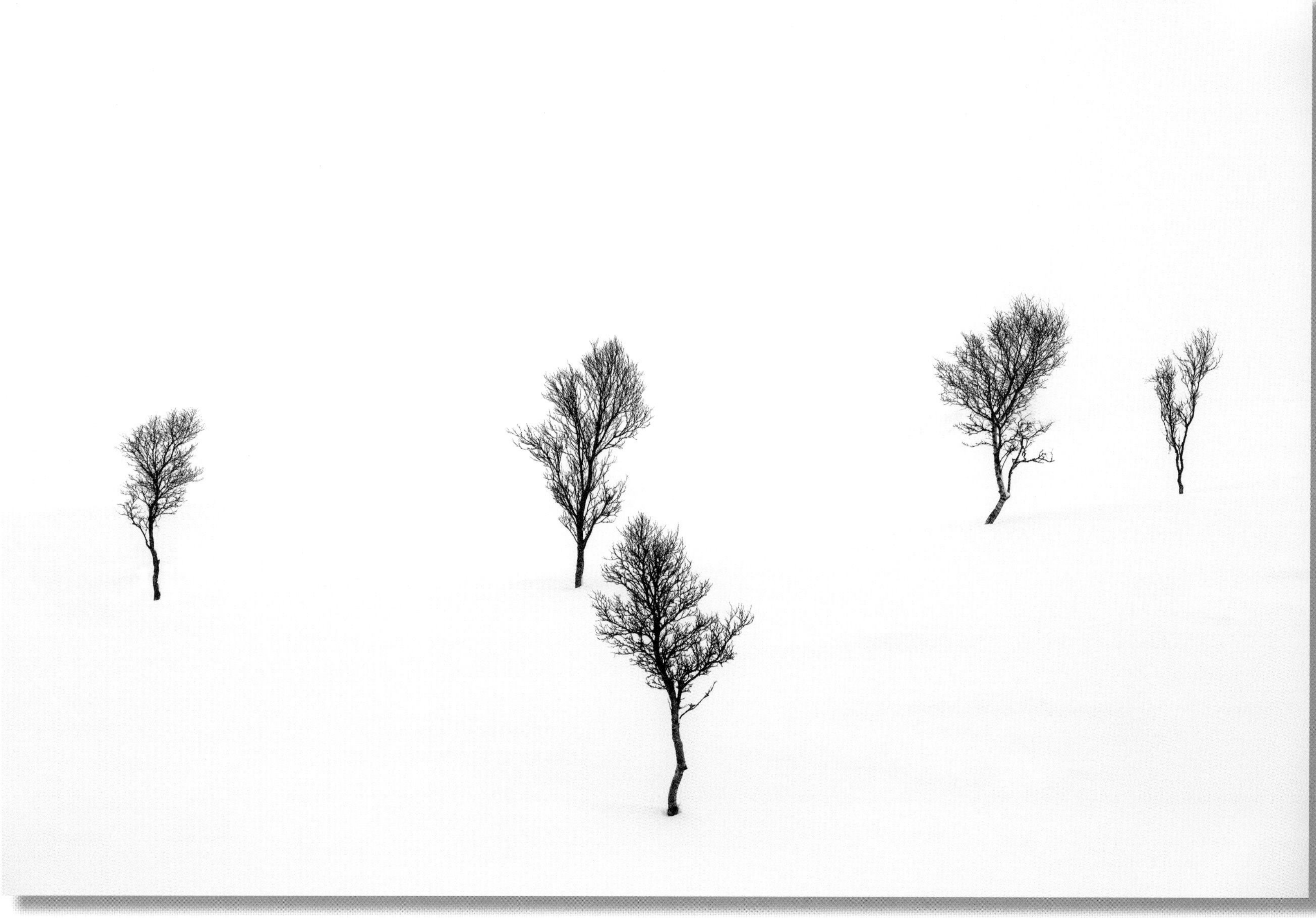

Nikon D800e, 70-200mm lens, f16, 1/125 sec.

HODGE CLOSE – PROMINENCE

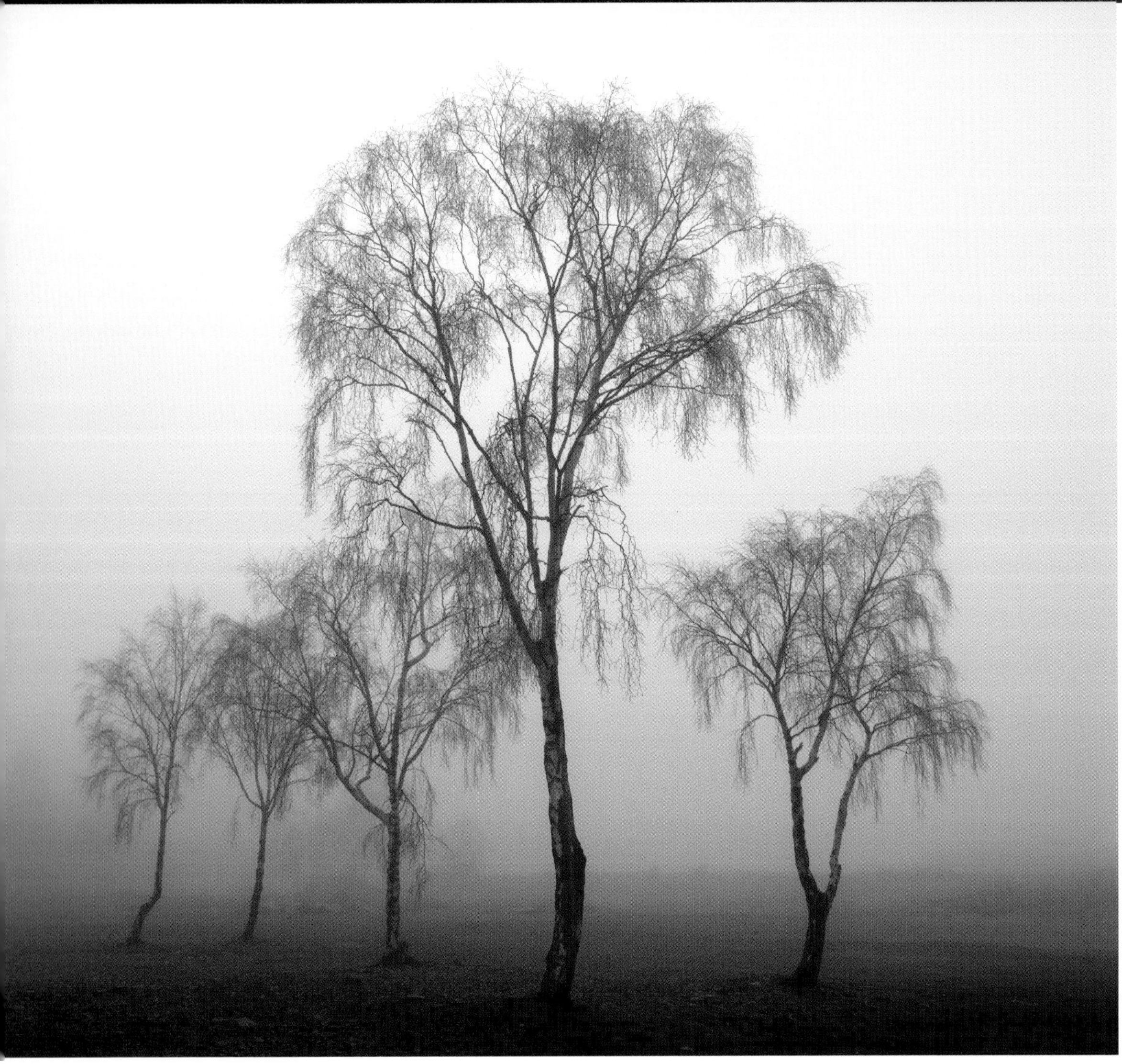

Lastly, looking at 'Hodge Close', this was a stand of trees I had seen on many occasions before I visited on this day, but the back-drop to the trees is a cluttered mix of old slate workings and the flanks of a Lake District mountain called Wetherlam in the distance. While I was there a thick mist encroached on the area and placed a veil over the landscape behind the stand of silver birch, making their arrangement prominent and quite profound without any distraction. Although I had to work quite quickly, the resulting photography is one of simplicity once again, taken in conditions that would almost prove to be ugly in colour landscape photography.

Nikon D700, 24-70mm lens, f16, 30th of a sec.

Conclusions

What you can see from these images is that the variation of light and conditions can all be considered as contributing factors to making strong black and white photographs. You have seen mist, snow, harsh and hazy sunlight, and storms. With all of these conditions considered, you can venture out and embrace what the elements of nature are presenting to you, and the resulting photographs can convey these elements beautifully, without a single colour present.

Light and surfaces

When you photograph in black and white and you are not considering colour information, you only have luminosity to use, which is essentially light reflecting off surfaces. This may sound limiting, but it is actually a great way to understand light and how, when reflected back at you, it can transform subjects and the way in which you see them. When exploring black and white photography, a way of getting used to not using colour is to start by looking at surfaces and the little areas of shadow and highlight that define them. You do not need direct sunlight to do this; in fact it can be a rather overcast day with very little sunlight at all.

If you now look at 'Branch and Leaves', it is clear that there is no strong light striking the woodland floor and the photograph was taken on a rather overcast day in dense woodland. What I relied upon on this day was the simple reflective and silvery nature of the surface of the dead branch and the fallen leaves that surrounded it. The simple difference between the smooth texture of the branch set against the many fallen leaves separates the branch and accentuates its shape and 'line'. If you train your eye to see these areas of light, shadow and texture, this opens up a whole new world in which black and white works beautifully. This comes with time and practice, and exploration of subjects such as this will enable you to understand that subjects that would look rather dull as colour photographs actually come to life in a series of greys.

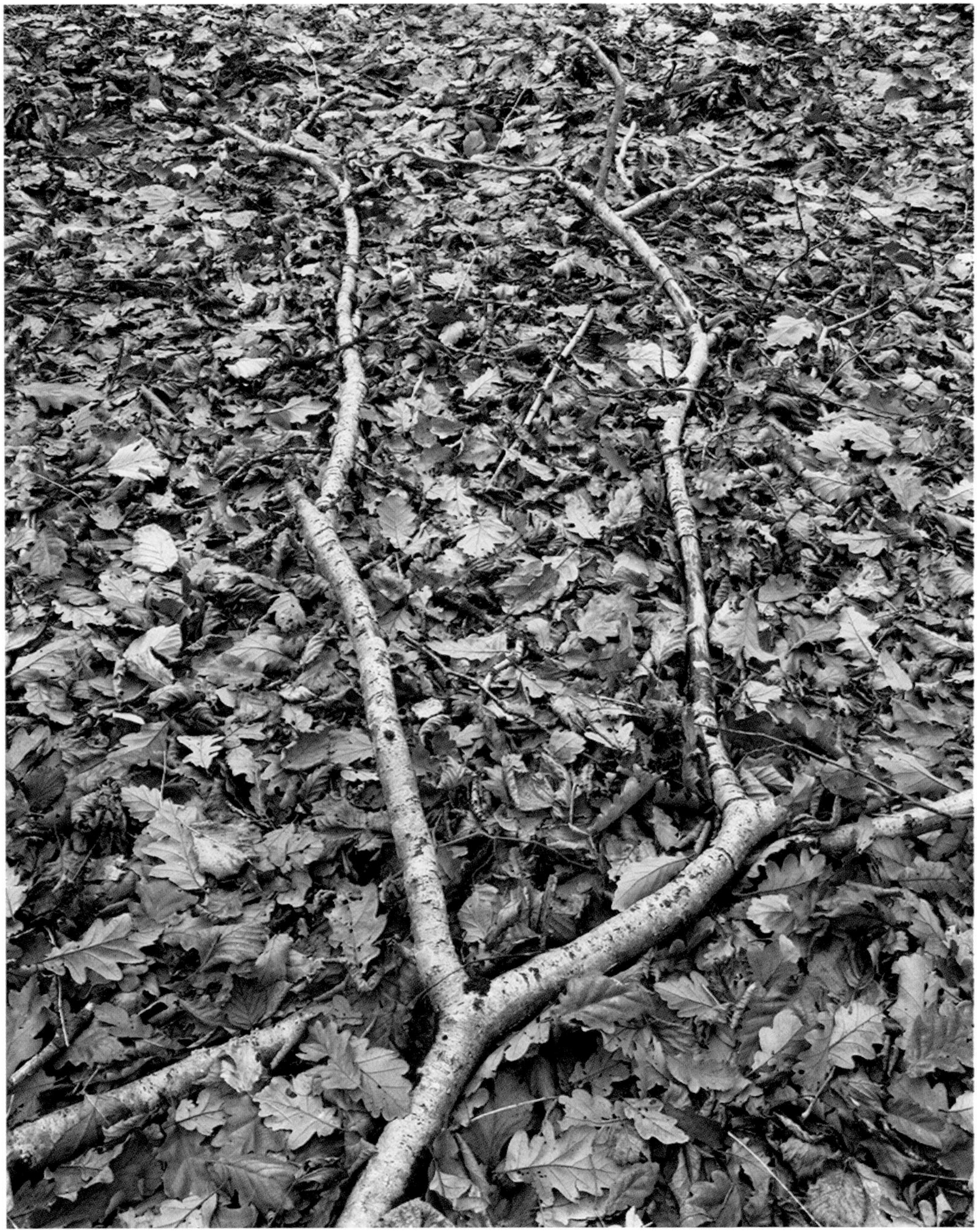

Walker Titan Large Format camera, 120mm lens, f32, 2 secs.

MESQUITE SANDS, DEATH VALLEY – RHYTHMS AND SHAPES

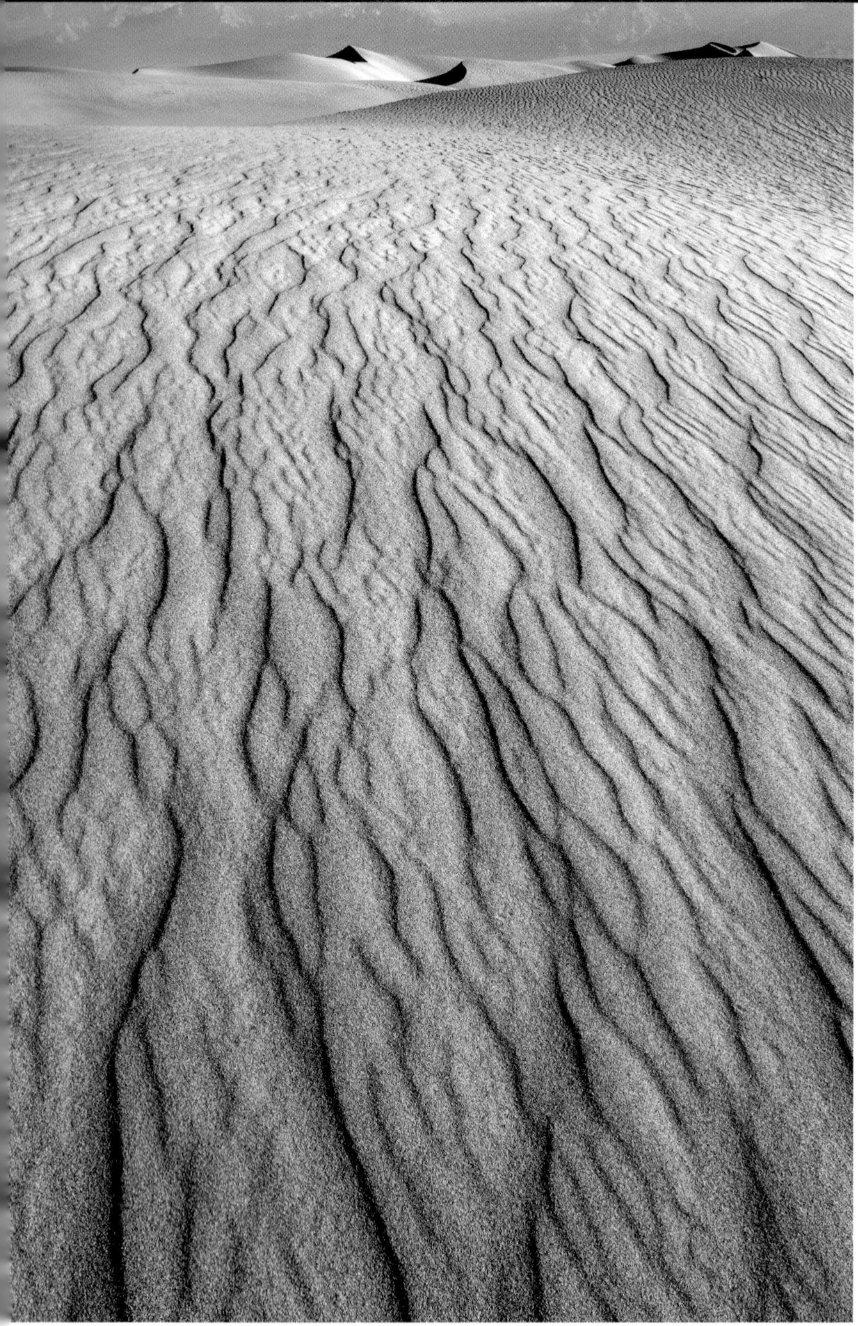

Using form, lines and textures

The use of form, line and texture has always been a good way to begin exploring subjects without colour. If you explore subjects in direct sunlight then the form, line and texture are accentuated – the textures introduced by the sunlight hitting the subject provide far more contrast, the light areas become lighter and the shadows cast are much darker.

If you first consider 'Mesquite Sands, Death Valley' you will be struck immediately by the strong foreground sand patterns and shapes that occupy a large portion of the image. I might have been tempted to make a more open view of the sands by using the camera in a landscape format (i.e., not having the camera set to vertical) and taking in more of the surroundings. However, on this occasion I knew that the strong, low and direct sunlight would accentuate the sand patterns and I selected this as the main part of the composition, with the distant sand dune shapes and textures occupying only ten per cent of the photograph. My camera was pointing down at a sharp angle so the patterns are exaggerated even though they were only a few centimetres deep and wide. Sometimes some shapes may be apparent and others may not and you have to allow your 'mind's eye' to see what you can create in making an exposure.

Nikon D800e, 24 mm PC-E lens, f13, 3rd of a sec, 0.6 Neutral Density Hard Graduated Filter.

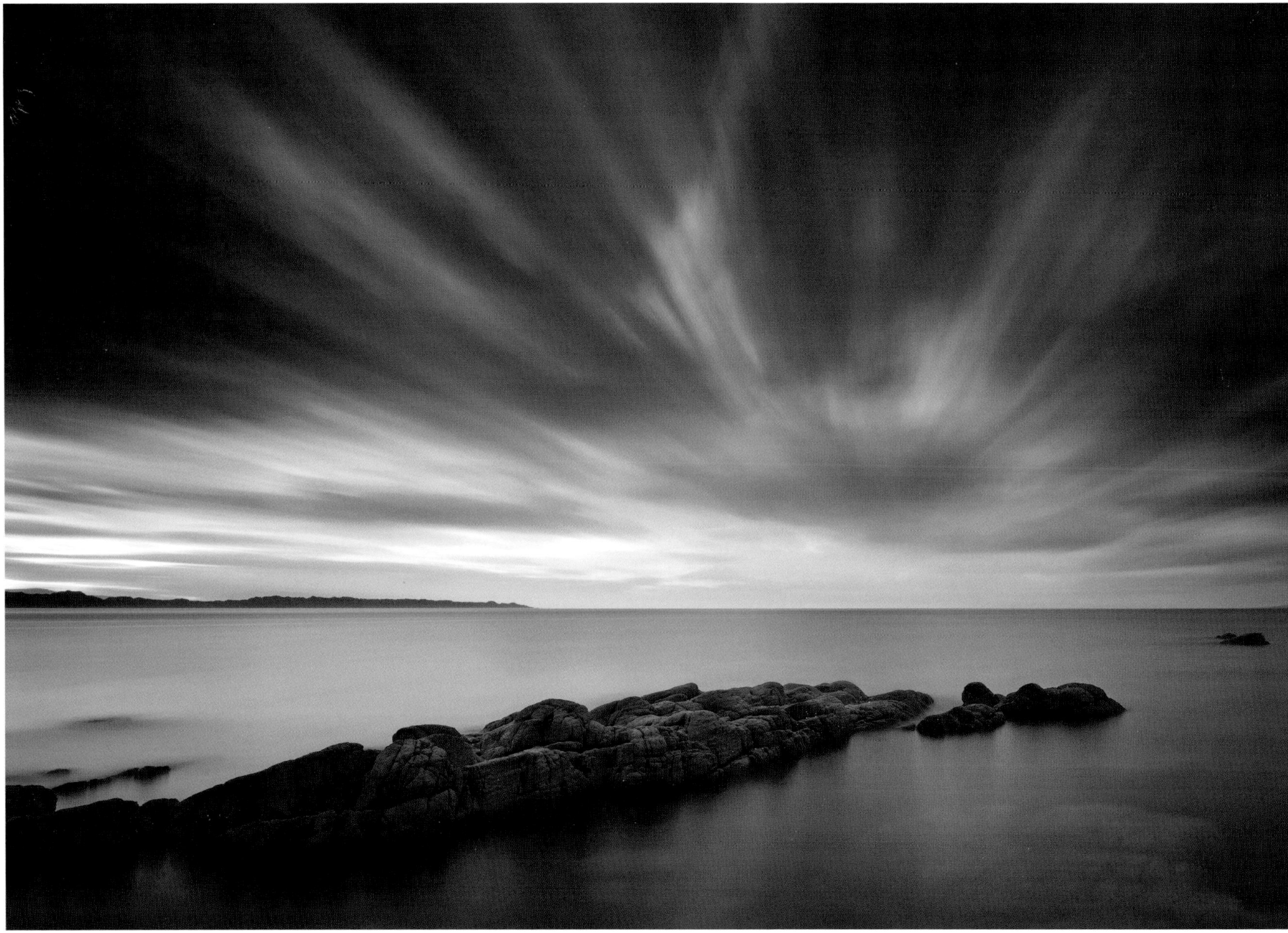

Nikon D800e, 24mm PC-E lens, f13, 7 minutes, 0.6 Neutral Density Hard Graduated Filter, Lee Big Stopper.

With the image 'Lonbain, Applecross', the composition consists of two strong lines – the line of rock in the sea and the streaking clouds in the sky – which bring the two halves of the image together. It was clear to me when I stood there that the outcrop of rock would jut out across the composition from left to right, but it was only when I allowed my eyes to judge the direction of the cloud movement that I knew these would appear as lines shooting upward in the final image. After I decided that this would make a strong photograph, the only way to bring out the cloud structure was to make a long exposure. The final image shows the meeting of the two lines almost at the horizon, which was what I was hoping for. However, as I will explore in another section of this book, you sometimes have to wait and hope the wind does not change direction, thus also changing the direction of the cloud, which would result in a failed image.

In woodland areas the exploration of form, line and texture can be taken to its limit. The reason for this is that trees present you with many intersecting lines, the bark of trees is full of texture and the overall form of trees is beautiful. The image 'Beeches and Pine Plantation' was not only an exploration of forms and lines, but also of the tonal contrasts that are always evident in woodland and which can sometimes be tricky to deal with. On this occasion I was firstly fascinated by the tonal differences between the almost white trunks of the beech trees set against the dark and dense pine plantation. After I established that I wanted to use this as part of my composition, all I needed to do was make some order out of the chaos of the woodland, which is often easier said than done. As I walked about I noticed that in one particular position in the woodland I was able to get a separation between the beech trees but also to place them against the darkest part of the pine plantation. To further accentuate the forms of the beech trees I placed them running vertically through the frame. Using forms, lines and textures in woodland often requires the photographer to be somewhat ruthless in making compositions. This is because the more of the beautiful environment that you leave out of the frame the more the finished photograph becomes understandable and digestible to the viewer. My last example is one considering shape alone, as it explores the absolute total simplicity resulting from leaving much of the surroundings out of the composition.

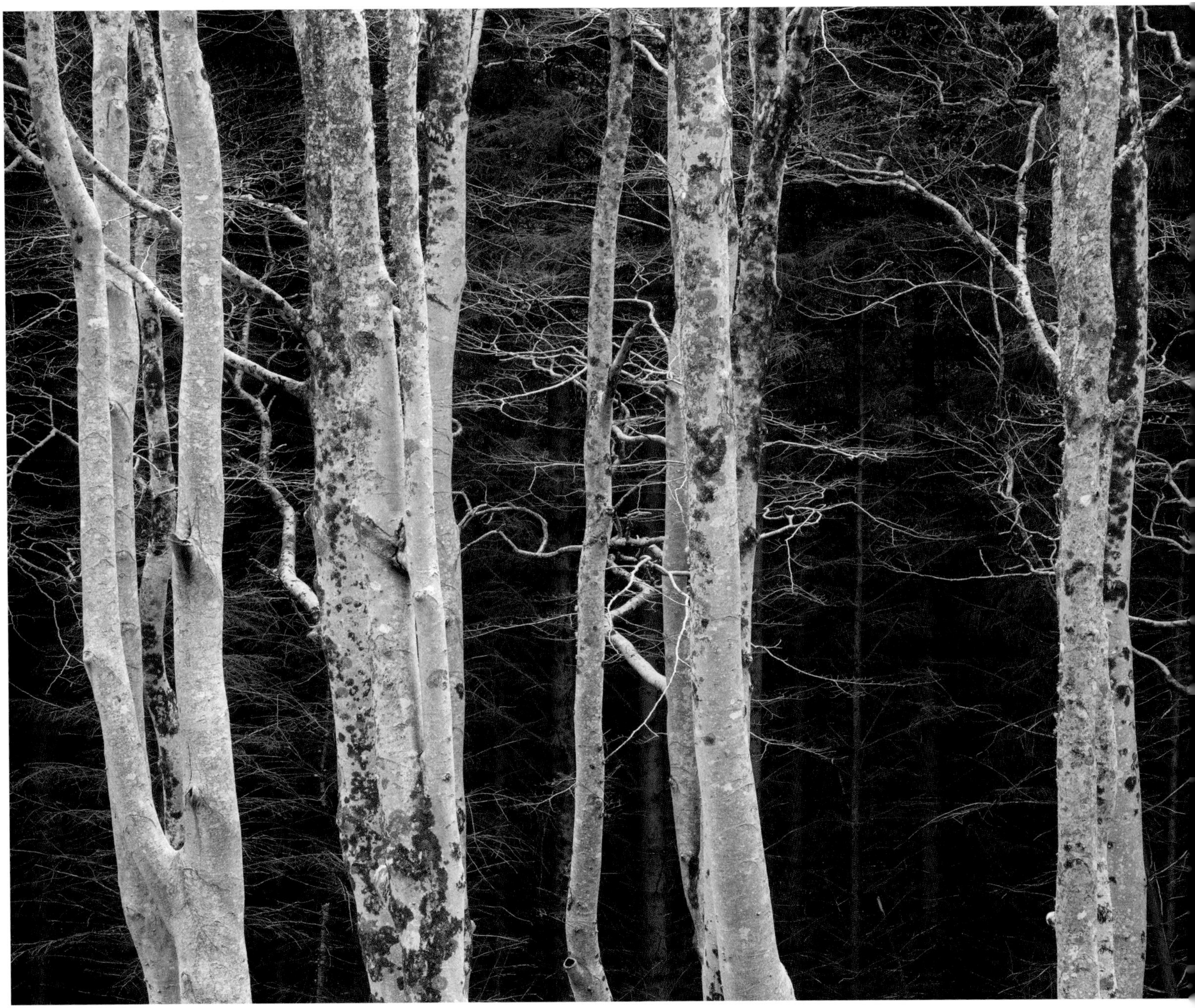

Nikon D800e, 70–200mm lens, f16, 0.8 sec.

PLANTS IN SNOWDRIFT – LESS IS MORE

Nikon D800e, 70-200mm lens, f16, 1/125 sec.

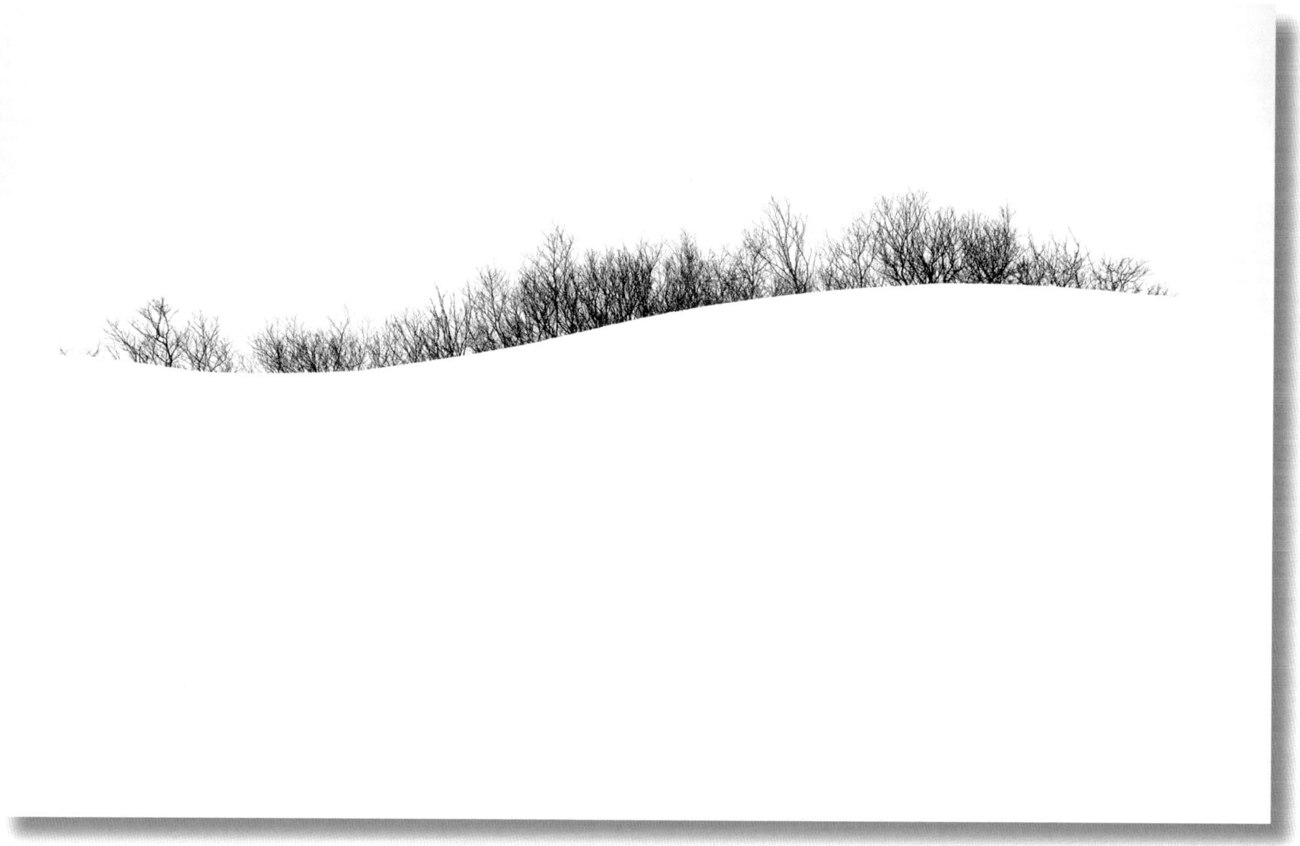

'Plants in Snowdrift' was taken in Lofoten in Arctic Norway. I recall being with some fellow photographers who were complaining because they could not 'see' a composition. We were walking through fields that were deep in snow with only the occasional shrub poking out of the drifts. My initial thoughts concluded that the plants alone were not strong enough subjects to photograph and so I began to look at the relationship between many of the plants and the shapes that the drifting snow had made, which were beautifully formed like large waves by the prevailing winds. I also knew that the only feature that would depict the wave shapes would be the plants as there was nothing else in the fields. After allowing myself some time to think about the forms of the snow, I found a position close to the ground that set the curve of the snowdrift against the plants behind and my composition came together.

Whether you are shooting for colour or black and white, getting the exposure right is the most important thing you need to master. If you get this part wrong then sometimes there is little you can do when you get back home and want to refine your images on your computer. In the days of film you had to rely on the use of your camera's internal light meter and, after you had exposed your film, you would then send it away to be processed and just hope for the best. At least today technology allows you more control over the final image.

Using histograms – what the camera has seen

One of the best things about modern digital cameras is that nearly all of them have a screen that can display a histogram. This is equally useful in black and white and in colour photography and should be used in all circumstances as this is the camera showing what has actually been captured, which is often different from what your eyes see as you can see more than is detected by digital technology. Using histograms may sound technical but it is really very simple indeed. The histogram has two axes, one on the left and one on the right. When you take a picture on your camera and look at your histogram you will see a 'wave-like' shape between the two axes, which is the data that the camera has collected. The portion of the 'wave' on the left-hand side of the histogram represents the dark areas of your image such as the shadows. The middle of the 'wave' represents the mid-tones and the portion of the 'wave' to the right of your histogram represents the highlights of the scene you have photographed. Each time you make a picture the shape of the 'wave' in your histogram will change as the shadows, mid-tones and highlights vary in the scene. The most important thing to remember is that you want to try as much as you can to prevent your 'wave' from running up either the shadow side of the histogram, or the highlight side of the histogram. The reason for this is that if this happens it means that those areas of shadow or highlight will be solid black or white and will contain no data so you can do nothing with them back at your computer.

Examples of histograms

I will now look at three examples of the same simple image and take a closer look at the histogram.

1. In Exposure Example 1 you can see that the histogram wave is placed mostly in the middle, with neither the dark or highlight ends of the histogram touching either end of the histogram axis. This is an example of a well-exposed image file.
2. If you now look at Exposure Example 2 you can see that the histogram is 'bunched up' to the right-hand axis of the histogram. This means that this image file is over-exposed.
3. Lastly, if you look at Exposure Example 3, you can see that the histogram is pushed mostly to the left-hand axis, and the resulting image is very dark and therefore under-exposed.

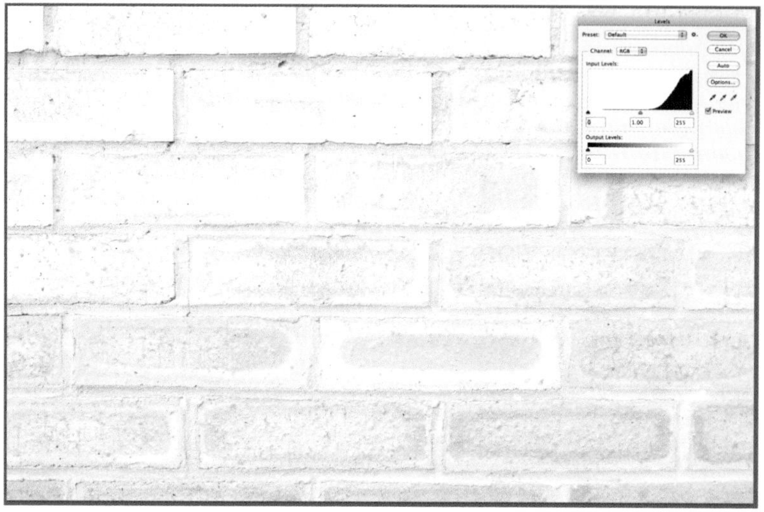

Exposure Example 2

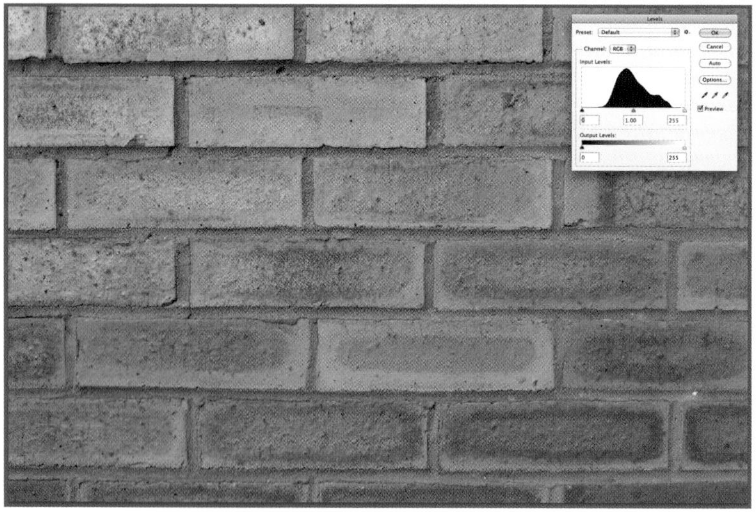

Exposure Example 1

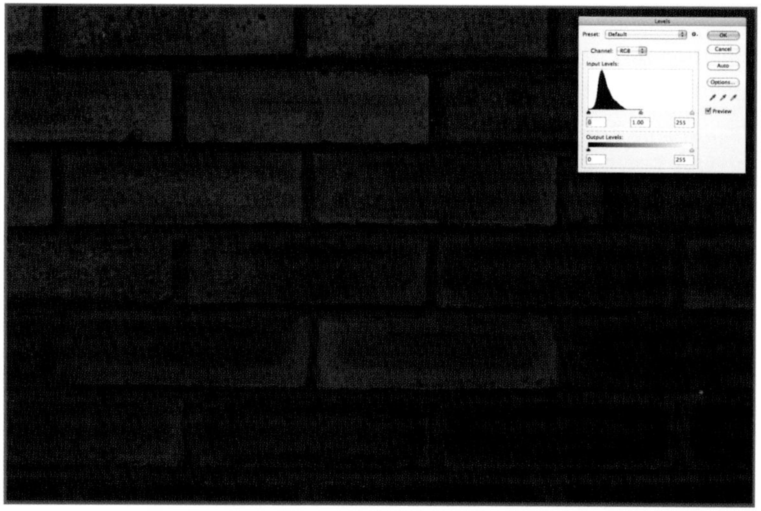

Exposure Example 3

Dynamic range

It is easy to assume, with the most up-to-date modern DSLR cameras, that they can cope with anything, but they can't. Certainly, in most landscape situations, the difference between the highlights in the sky and the darker areas on the ground is often far beyond the dynamic range that the camera can cope with. What I mean by this is that, whereas our human eye can see both the shadows and the highlights almost wherever you look, the camera does not have this capacity. Therefore, when you make photographs in these lighting situations you will either be left with highlights that are known as 'blown-out' or shadows that are known as 'blocked-up'. This means that either the shadows or the highlights of the scene that you have photographed will contain no data at all, and so these areas of the image will either be solid black or solid white, which can ruin a picture. This is where filters come in handy.

Do you really need filters?

If you are in a situation where you are faced with a scene that has deep shadows and harsh highlights, and your resulting histogram shows both blocked-up shadows and blown-out highlights, then the only way to remedy this in the field and in-camera is to use filters. Some photographers opt for taking two identical images of the same scene, one exposed for the highlights and one exposed for the shadows, and they then blend the two images together back at their computer. While there is nothing wrong with doing this, there can be problems when the two images do not match and movement has occurred between the two exposures. Also, I believe that it is almost impossible to do this with long exposures as movement in this case is highly likely. Therefore, in my opinion, you need to get it right in-camera rather than hoping things will match up back at your computer.

Blown-out highlights

If you look at the image 'Blown-out highlights' and its associated histogram you can see that there is a lot of the histogram wave that is 'bunched-up' to the right-hand axis. This represents the brightly lit snow in the waterfall photograph and, because all of these highlights are over-exposed, they will contain no tonal variations at all.

Blocked-up shadows

In comparison, if you now look at the image 'Blocked-up Shadows' you can see the opposite effect. This image has been under-exposed and, as a result, the histogram is now 'bunched-up' on the left axis, which means that the shadows will contain no information at all and will be represented as solid black with no shadow tonal variation.

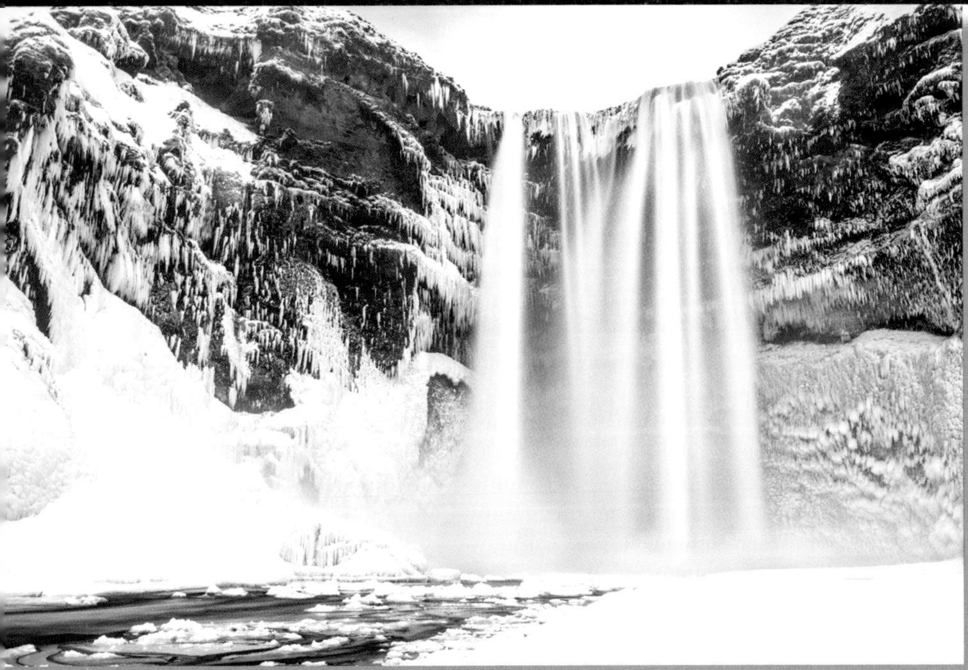

Blown-out highlights.

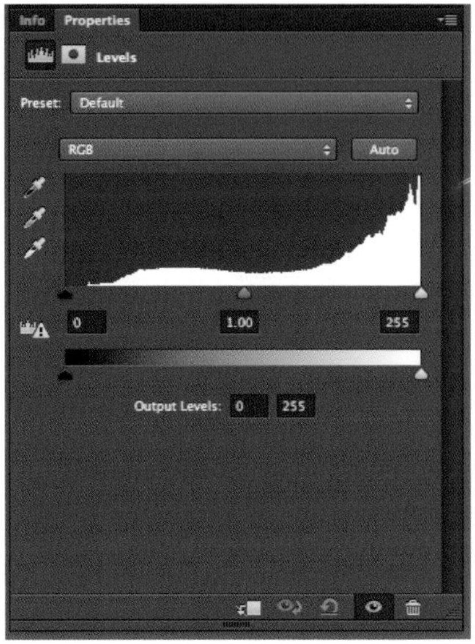

Blown-out highlights histogram.

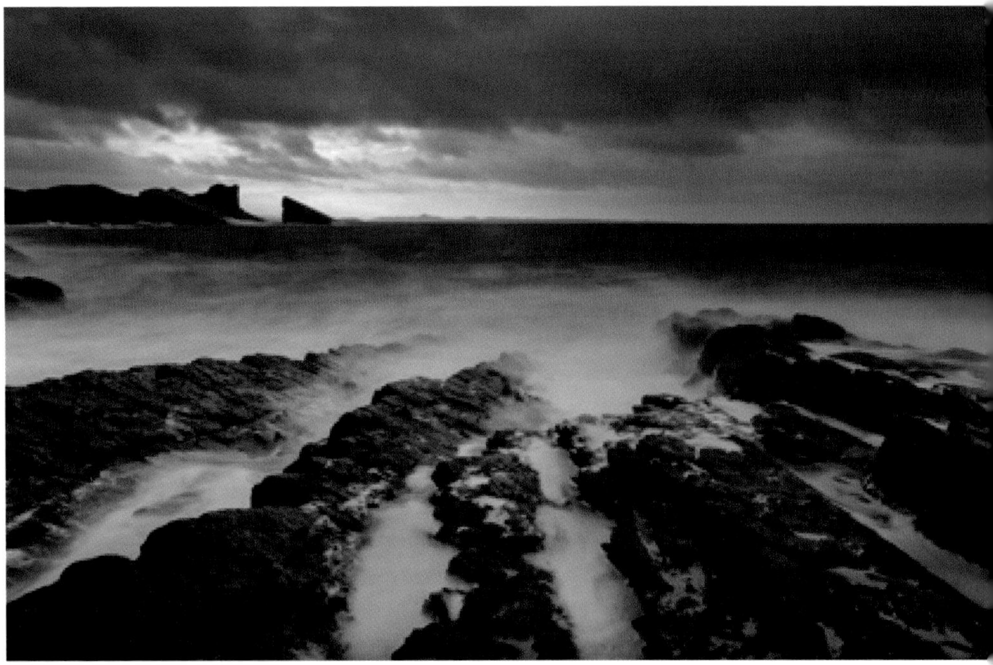

Blocked-up shadows.

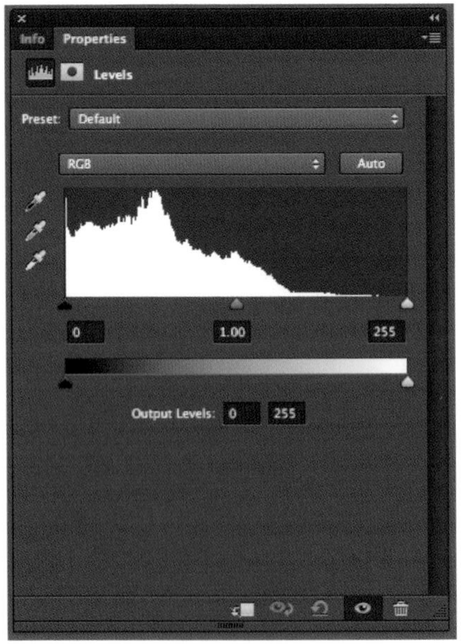

Blocked-up shadows histogram.

Using filters in black and white

Filters do many different things but all of them adjust or cut out light that is entering your lens. I am making specific reference here to Neutral Density Graduated Filters that, in appearance, are filters that are clear at the bottom and then mid-way they begin to become darker, which continues to the uppermost part of the filter and this transition from clear to dark is graduated, hence the name. There are several types of neutral density graduated filter and the first difference is the variation of densities or darkness at the top. They are numbered 0.3, 0.6 and 0.9, which translates to 0.3 being a density that cuts out 1 stop of light, 0.6 that cuts out 2 stops of light and 0.9 that cuts out 3 stops of light (see Exposure Example 4). Secondly, there are two main graduations available, 'hard' and 'soft'. Hard and soft refers to the area of transition that graduates from clear to the darkest part of the filter. Hard graduated filters have a far shorter transition from clear to dark than do soft graduated filters.

All of the above sounds rather confusing but, in practice, the entire process is very straightforward. When faced with a scene that has a bright sky you simply place your filter into your filter holder and slide it down to where the line of transition begins (normally to horizon level), at which point the darker part of the filter is covering the brightest parts of the sky, which reduces those brightness values and the camera can then 'see' what our eyes see, and the resulting histogram will not show signs of 'blown-out' highlights. Let's look at my three examples:

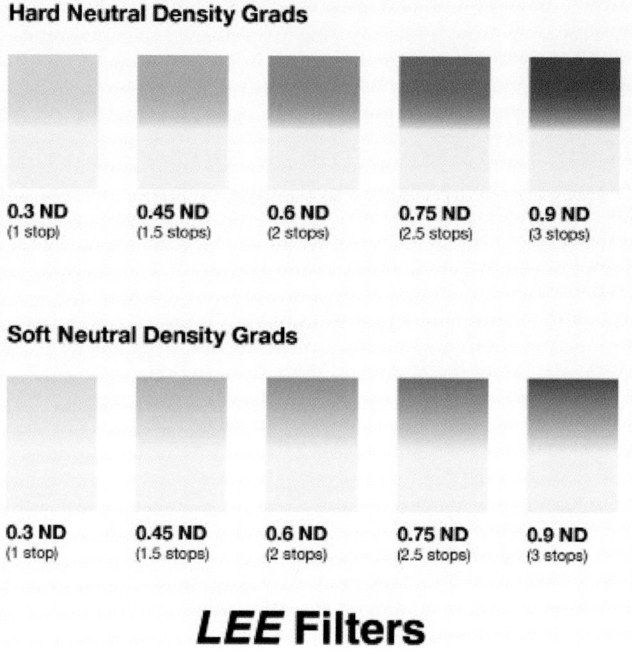

Exposure Example 4.

1. Exposure Example 5 shows the use of a Soft 0.6 (2 Stop) Graduated Filter to control the highlights in the clouds above the trees. A soft graduated filter was used because of the undulating middle ground and so not to darken the trees too much.

2. Exposure Example 6 shows the use of a Hard 0.3 (1 Stop) Graduated Filter to help with the highlights in the skies above the sea, and ...
3. Exposure Example 7 shows the use of a Hard 0.9 (3 Stop) Graduated Filter to calm the very bright light from the setting sun, enabling a finished photograph that has both subtle highlight details along with strong shadow detail, just as our eyes see it.

Lastly, on each of the examples you will notice a red line across the picture. This line denotes the approximate transition in each of the graduated filters from clear to neutral grey.

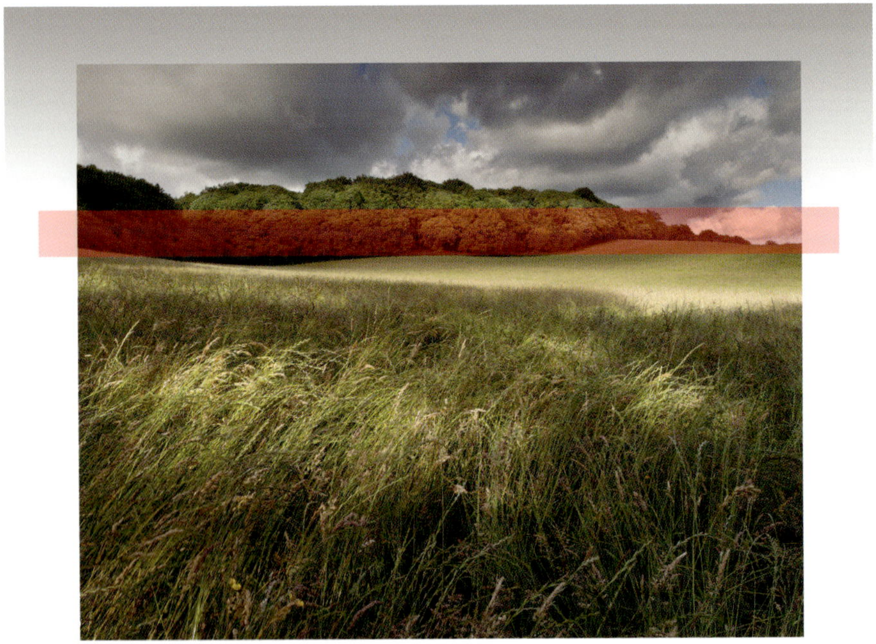

0.6 or 2 stop soft grad

Exposure Example 5.

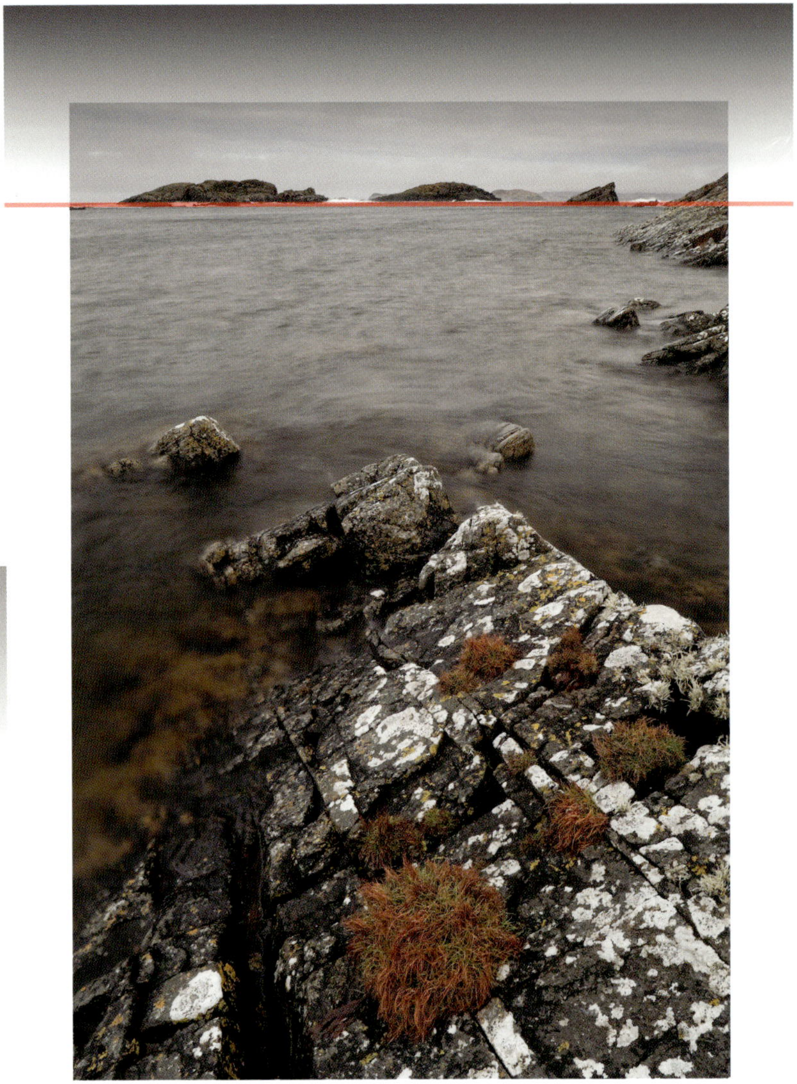

0.3 or 1 stop hard grad

Exposure Example 6.

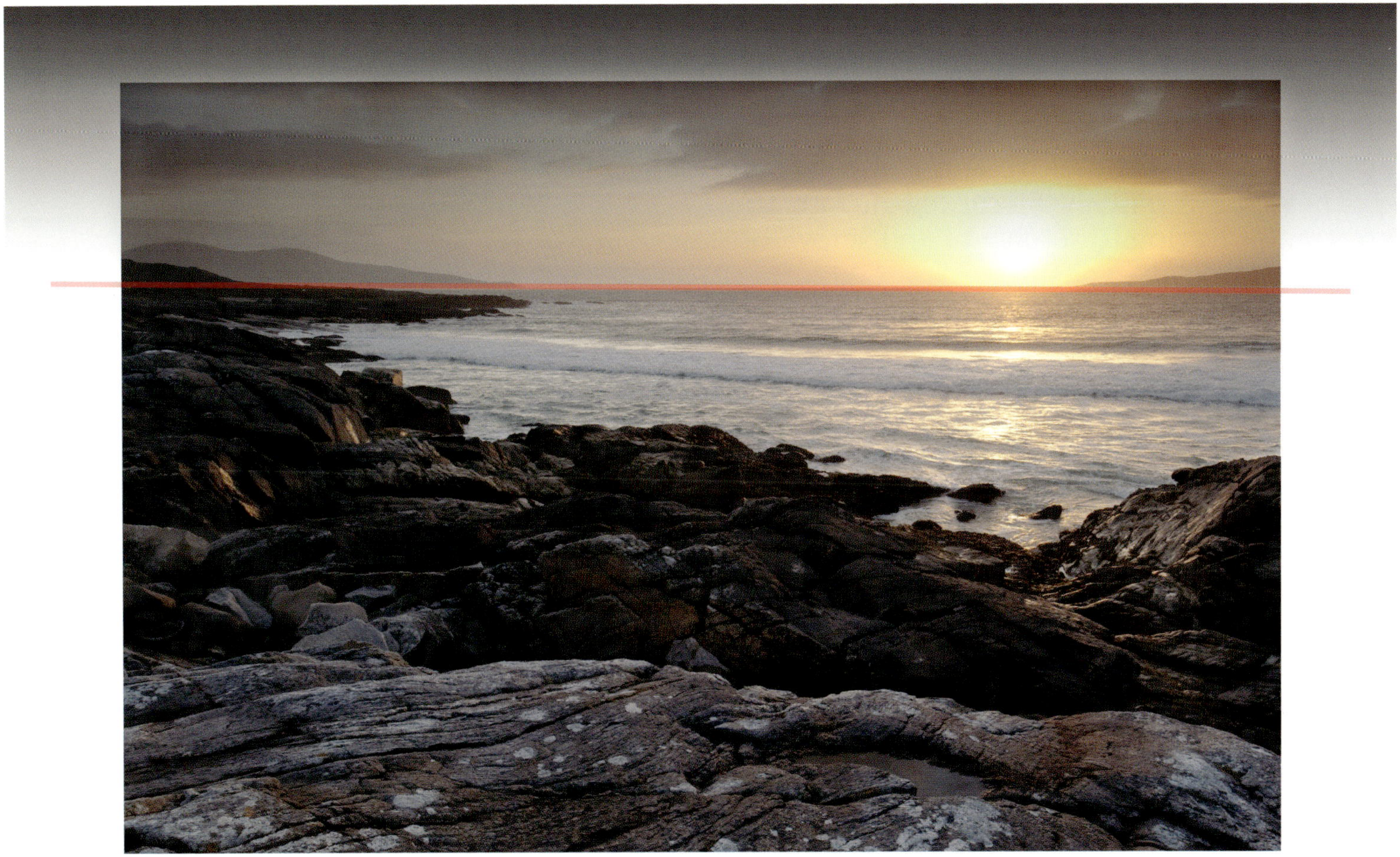

0.9 or 3 stop hard grad

Exposure Example 7.

Choosing filters

Over my career I have had the opportunity to use many different makes of filters, some of which perform well and others that have performed very badly and have given strong colour casts in my colour work. The first filters I used were the screw-on type that attach to the front of your lens. These were quickly discarded due to the frustration of having to screw-on and screw-off each time I made an exposure.

The most convenient filter set to use is one that comes with a filter holder that has slots that can hold two or three filters at the same time such as, for example, a neutral density graduated filter and a ten stop neutral density filter. On the market today there are filter sets like this from many manufacturers, the most popular of which are Cokin, Formatt-Hitech and the Lee Filters System. The Cokin filters leave a lot to be desired in my opinion as they tend to give awful colour casts and, in most situations, the neutral graduated filters are too short so the bottom edge of the filter can appear in your finished photograph if you have a small amount of sky. The Formatt-Hitech are a better size and do not show in your finished photograph, but they can introduce colour casts in colour images. Although this may not seem important to black and white photography, you will only want to buy them once so get a set that will perform well for both black and white and colour. The only filter system I have used to date that has ticked every box for me is the Lee Filters System. They are neutral (do not introduce colour casts) and many are available in Pro-Glass, which is ideal for high performance digital cameras. In short, you get what you pay for.

Long exposures and neutral density filters

If anyone has been a keen amateur black and white photographer over the past six years they will, without doubt, have seen pictures taken with long exposures. This trend has been mainly attributed to camera filter manufacturers producing very strong neutral density filters. Without strong neutral density filters the only way to achieve long exposures is to set your camera's ISO to its lowest setting and stopping down the aperture on your lens or, quite simply, photographing when there is very little light such as at twilight or even at night.

Working with neutral density filters

As previously discussed, filters cut out some of the light that reaches your camera sensor, therefore requiring you to prolong your exposure to differing degrees. So, when very strong neutral density filters are fitted to the front of your camera, they cut out a large amount of light and the resulting exposure time can run into minutes.

The resulting images are somewhat ethereal and 'other-worldly'. This is because if there is any movement at all in the subject matter you are photographing, it will be rendered as very smooth or even vanish completely. There are two main effects on a landscape image as a result of using this type of filter:

1. If you have water in your composition then this will become almost 'milk-like' in appearance with no surface texture. As you can see with the image 'Loch Torridon', here I used a Lee Little Stopper 6 stop neutral density filter and my exposure was 15 seconds at f16, which has smoothed the sea water out but retained cloud structure.
2. The second effect is evident in skies. Although water will begin to look smooth without a particularly long exposure, skies are totally transformed – clouds streak and become very dramatic. If you look at image 'Kilbrannan Sound' you can see that the sea water is very smooth and so are the clouds that have streaked across the skies. For this image I used a Lee Big Stopper, which is a 10 stop neutral density filter, my lens at f19, and my exposure time was 3½ minutes.

Another great effect of using this type of filter is in urban situations where there is movement of people or cars. During the exposure time everything becomes blurred, only the parts of the image that were static in the first place will remain sharp and people and cars will almost disappear.

LOCH TORRIDON

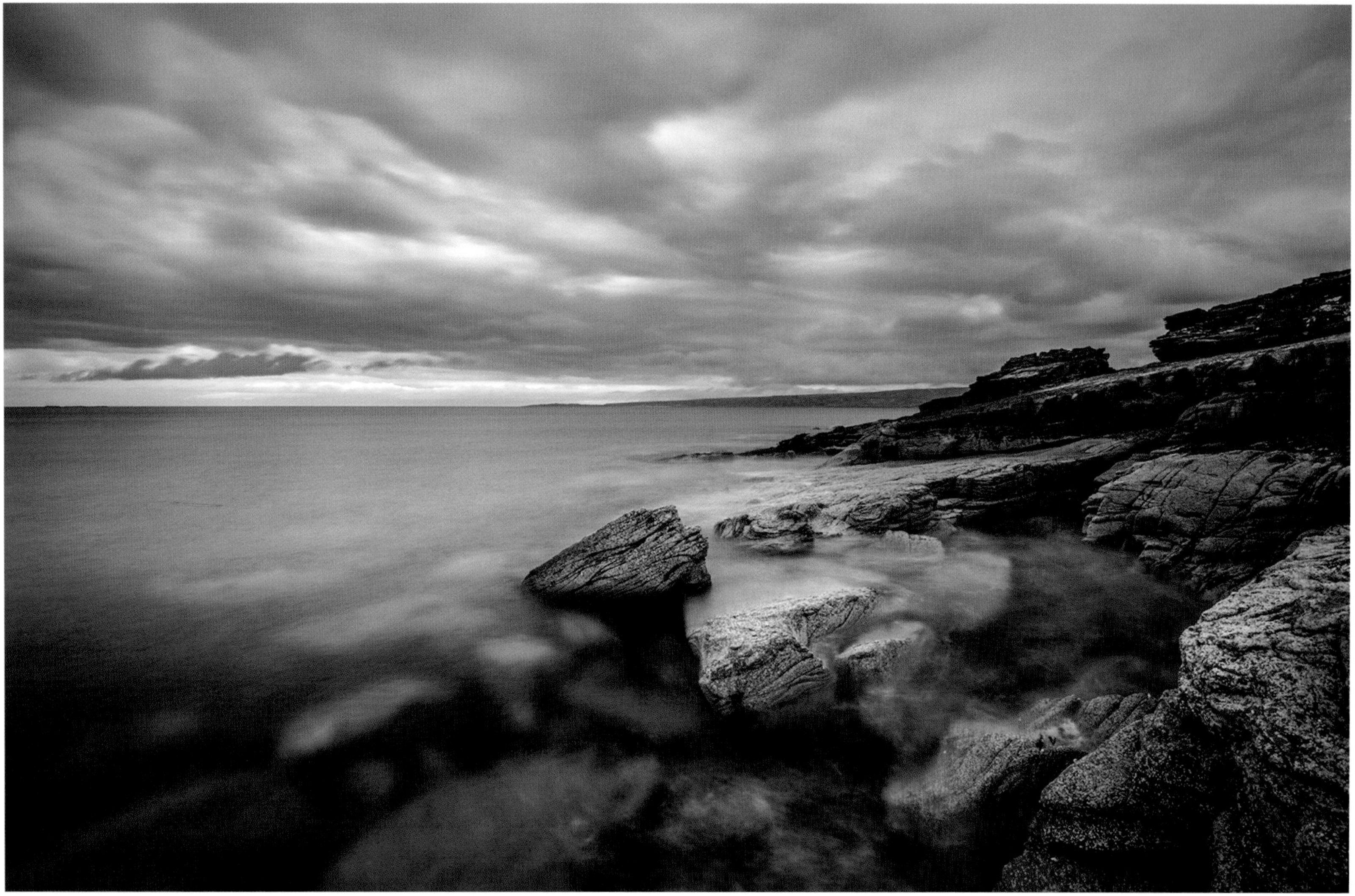

Nikon D800e, 24mm PC-E lens, f13, Neutral Density Hard Graduated Filter, Lee Little Stopper.

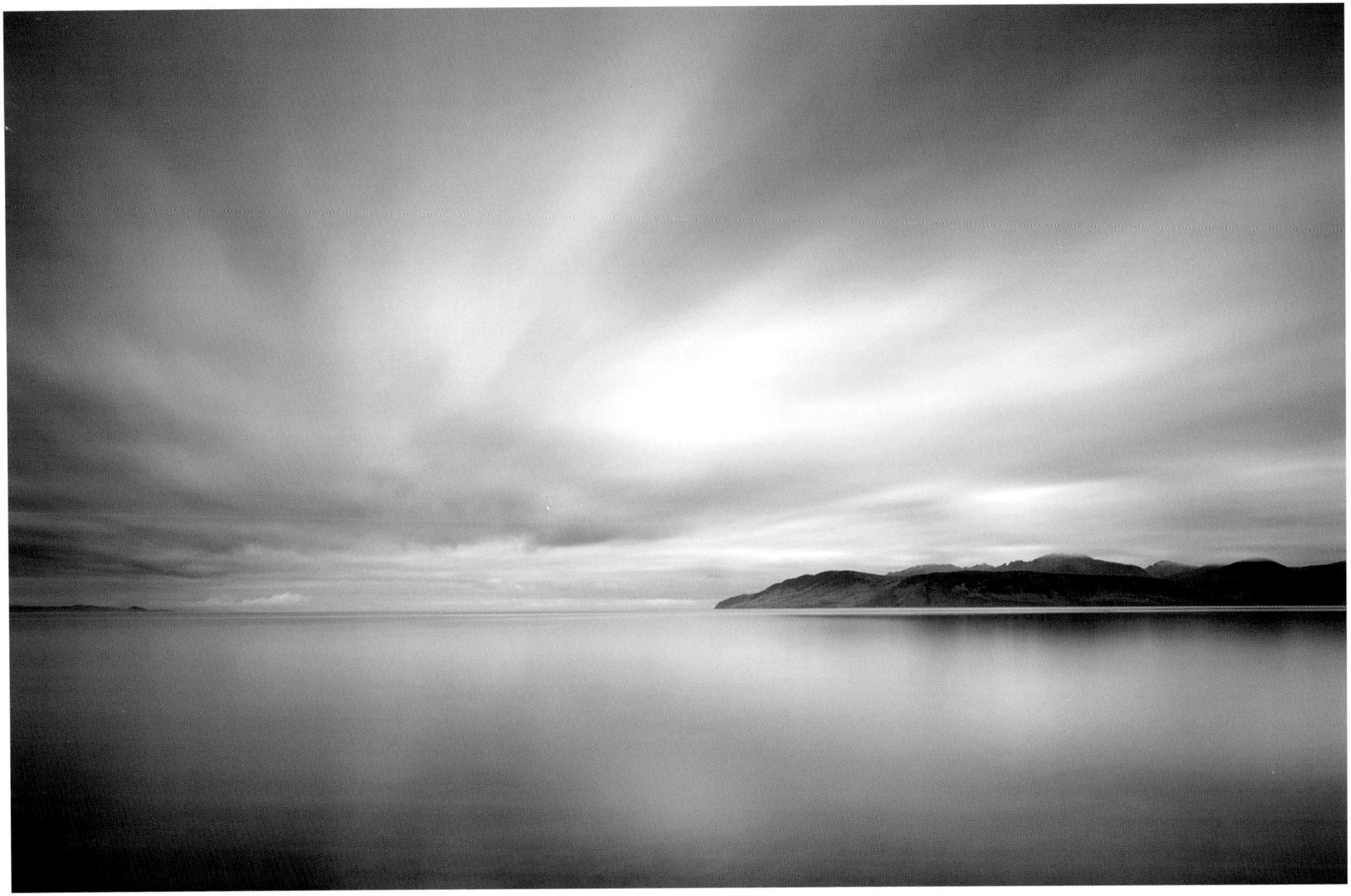

Nikon D800e, 24mm PC-E lens, f19, 3.5 minutes, 0.6 Neutral Density Hard Graduated Filter, Lee Big Stopper.

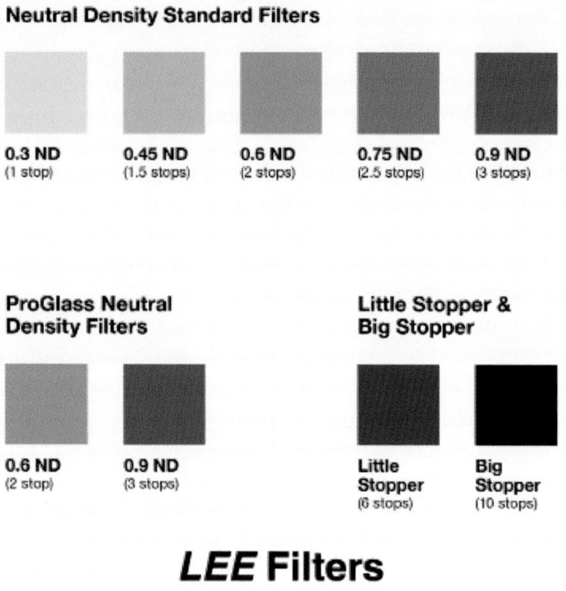

Long Exposures Example 1.

Six-stop and ten-stop neutral density filters

The two main filters that fall into the strong neutral density category are the six-stop and the ten-stop neutral density filters. It will become apparent how dense these filters are when you first hold them up to your eye and try to look through them. The six-stop filter will allow you to see detail if you let your eye adjust and peer though the filter for a few seconds. A ten-stop neutral density filter is almost totally opaque and you will be left wondering how it will ever let any light though it at all. There are also other, less dense, neutral density filters that perform in a similar way but do not lengthen exposure times to the same degree (see Long Exposures Example 1). Needless to say, the use of these filters takes some practice and time to get used to them, so the system that should be followed is:

1. Calculation of the exposure is often done using an exposure calculator card that comes with the filter, but what you have to do first is to make a composition and set an ordinary exposure time without the neutral density filter fitted to your camera. Bear in mind at this stage that to keep your exposure from blown-highlights you may have to use a graduated neutral density filter to control the brightness range of your image.
2. When you have done this, and you have achieved a good histogram without any blown highlights or blocked-up shadows, then you can take this exposure time and refer to your manufacturer's exposure calculation card, which will give you the correct exposure for when the neutral density filter is in place.

Other tips for long exposures

Sturdy tripod

There are other important things that you need to have in place when making long exposures. A

sturdy tripod is a must. You have to bear in mind that even the slightest camera movement will show up clearly in your final image. This is because a lot of your image will display smooth textures due to the long exposure time and, in contrast, other portions of the image will be sharp. If your camera has moved during the exposure then this camera movement will be clear to see.

On the subject of tripods, it is useful to try and avoid using the centre column of the tripod. If there is any vibration at all, then the centre column simply amplifies it and, once again, you could get camera shake.

Use the 'Bulb' or 'B' setting

You will need to use the 'Bulb' or 'B' setting on your camera (see Long Exposures Example 2). Most DSLRs have their longest exposure setting at 30 seconds; beyond this you will have to select the 'B' setting. The 'B' setting enables you to manually open and close the shutter of your camera so you can set any exposure time you want, for as long as you need with long exposures. This often involves pressing your remote cable release once to open your shutter, then once again to close your shutter, often locking it open for the entire exposure time.

Use a remote release

When using the 'B' setting you will need to use a remote cable release. The reason for this is that

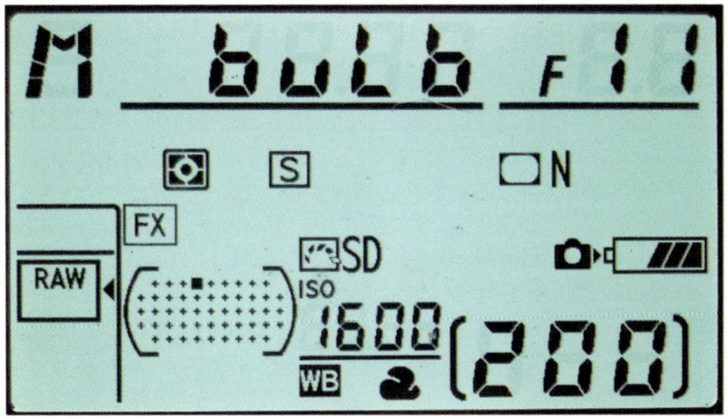

Long Exposures Example 2.

you will not be able to touch your camera during the long exposure as this will almost certainly introduce camera movement, no matter how steady your hand is. Using a remote cable release will enable you to open the shutter of the camera without actually physically touching it. A remote cable release is usually screwed or plugged on to a socket on your camera body and has a trigger at the other end that can lock open the shutter for the desired period of time.

Cover your camera eyepiece

Another important thing to remember when making very long exposures is to cover up your camera eyepiece (see Long Exposures Example 3). This is because during the time of the exposure very small amounts of light 'leak' into the camera and bounce onto the sensor, which leaves a purple streak on the finished file (see Long Exposures Example 4). Although this may not seem critical to a black and white image, it is,

as this artefact is very visible and usually ruins the image. On some cameras there is an eyepiece shutter that can be closed using a lever near the eyepiece itself, and on other DSLR models you are provided with a rubber eyepiece cover, attached to your camera strap, which you slide over the eyepiece.

Wind direction

It is always wise to keep an eye on the direction of the wind when setting up any long exposure. If rain looks likely then there is little use in pointing your camera into the wind as the rain may arrive during your exposure and there would be little you could do to protect it. Also, during long exposure photography, use your body as a shield between the prevailing wind and your camera. Although you may have a sturdy tripod, one small gust is all it takes to shake your camera that tiny little bit and you will have wasted your time.

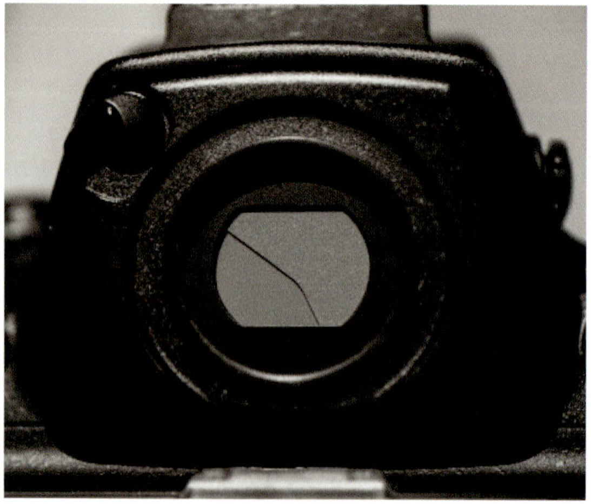

Long Exposures Example 3.

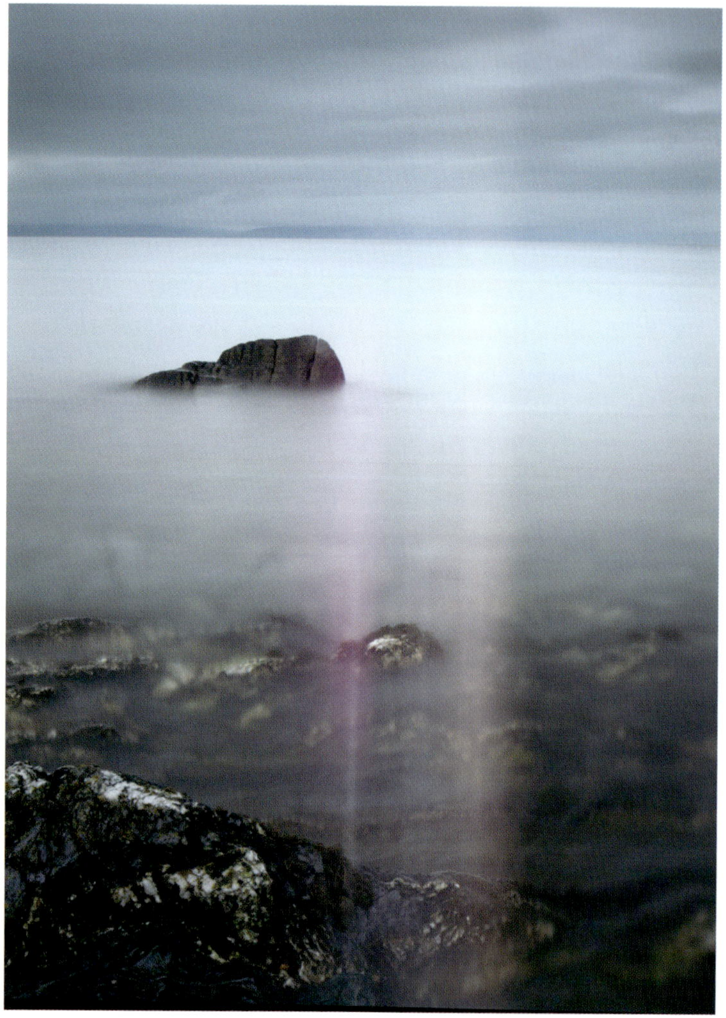

Long Exposures Example 4.

ABANDONED FISHING STATION – LOFOTEN, NORWAY

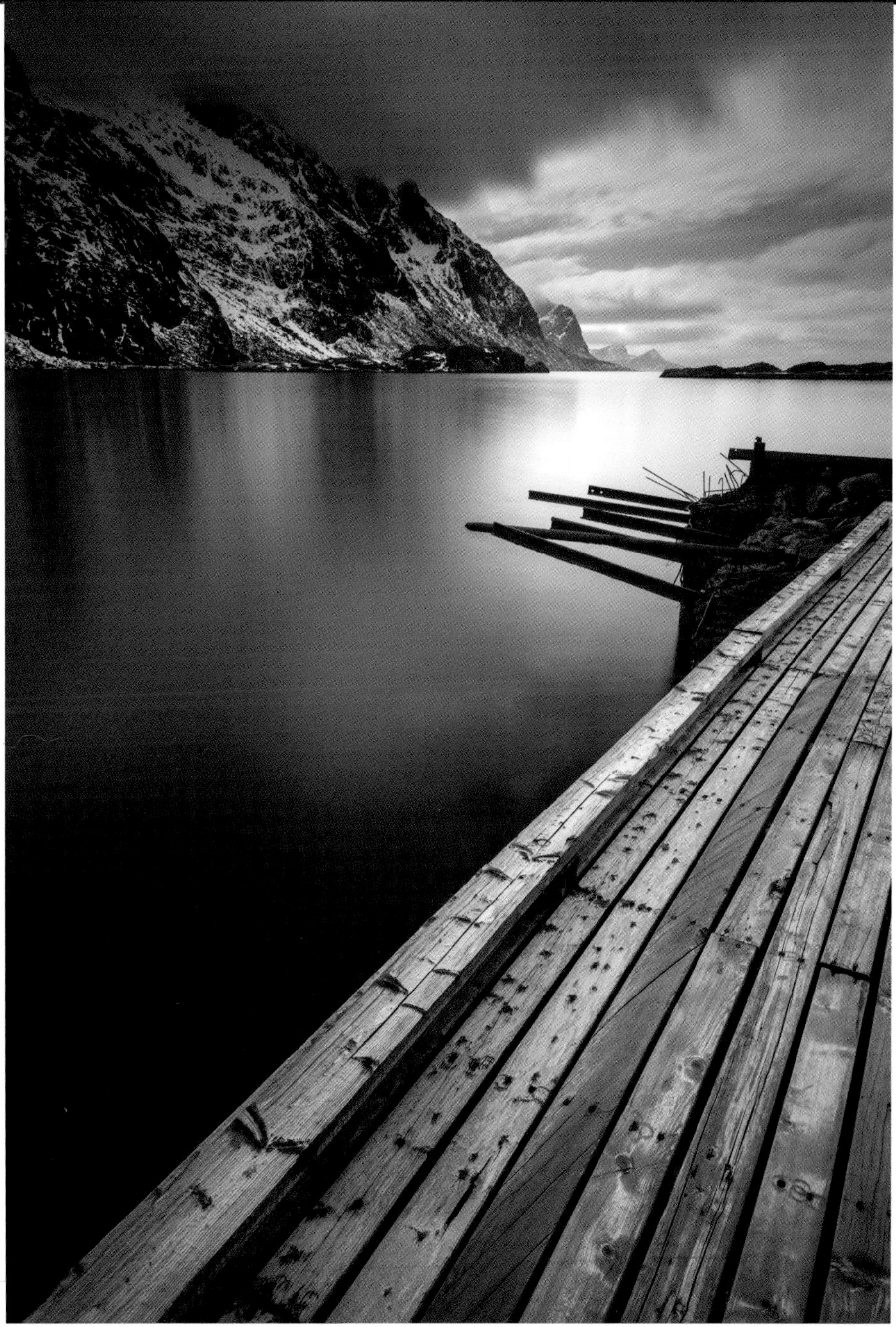

A long exposure on this occasion smoothed out the water beneath the boardwalk and introduced the reflection of the mountain in the fjord. *Nikon D800e, 24mm PC-E lens, f13, 74 seconds, Lee 0.6 Neutral Density Hard Graduated Filter, Lee Polariser, Lee Big Stopper.*

BLACK BEACH – ICELAND

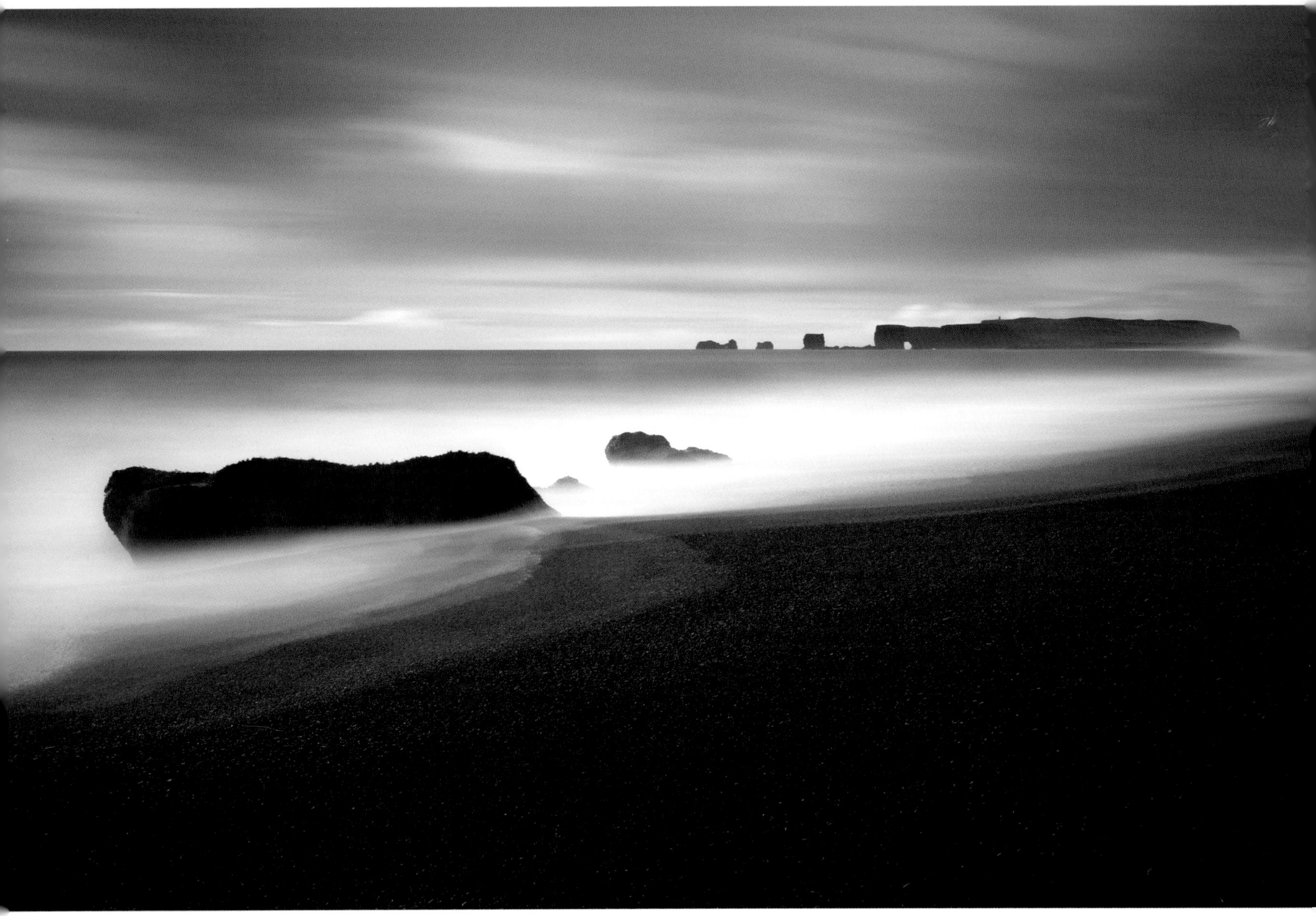

For this image the prevailing winds were pushing the clouds rapidly across the dark sky. This cloud movement with the movement of the water on the black sands brought the composition together. *Nikon D700, 24–70mm lens, f16, 90 seconds, Lee 0.6 Neutral Density Hard Graduated Filter, Lee Big Stopper.*

WESTER ROSS – SCOTLAND

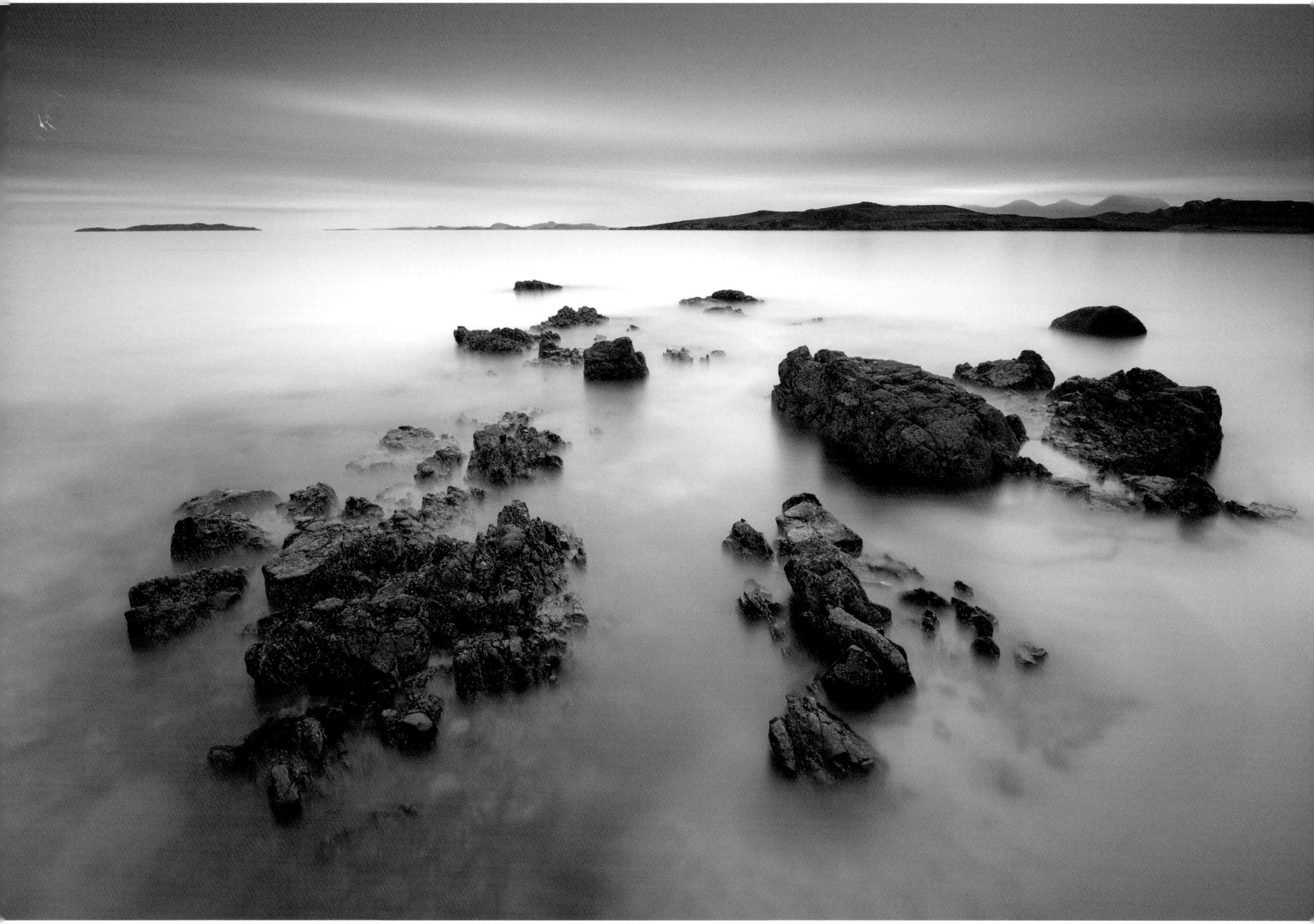

I used long exposure here to make the foreground rocks stand out. The long exposure has made the sea silvery and the skies smooth over the distant peninsula. *Nikon D800e, 24mm PC-E lens, f13, 180 secs, Lee 0.6 Neutral Density Hard Graduated Filter, Lee Big Stopper.*

6. UNDERSTANDING YOUR CAMERA AND WHICH SETTINGS TO USE

In the modern digital world one thing you do not have to worry about is committing to buying a certain type of film. Before digital capture you had to decide whether or not to expose colour or black and white film and, when you had made this decision, you were committed until that roll of film was used up. The way you use digital cameras for black and white is much the same as photographers have always used cameras in the past, but there are certain things that can help you get the most out of your equipment to enable you to make really good black and white photographs.

Shoot using Raw

The first thing to consider is whether you shoot in camera Raw or choose to shoot in jpeg. This might sound a little confusing but a lot of digital cameras nowadays give you this choice. The main difference between the two is that:

- A camera Raw file is exactly what the camera sensor has collected when it was exposed to the light when you took your photograph or made your exposure, with nothing altered.
- A jpeg (or Joint Photographic Experts Group) is a compressed file that has been created by your camera's on-board processor.

There is nothing terribly wrong with using jpeg files but there are certainly benefits to shooting in Raw when it comes to refining your images later on at your computer. As I have just mentioned, a jpeg is a processed image file that has been created by your camera's mini-processor. If you consider the power of your computer processor, you clearly have far more power there to decide how you want the image to look. Probably the most important thing is that a camera Raw file can record a far greater brightness range, which is often one of the problems photographers have to grapple with.

If you are faced with a scene with dark shadows and bright highlights, then a Raw file will give you the best chance of recording all the detail in both, and you will see this clearly when you are post-processing. Lastly, the detail recorded in a Raw file is far greater and it can easily be teased out later on whereas, if you tried the same treatment with a jpeg, the image would soon begin to look pixelated and 'crunchy'. If your camera allows you, set your camera to shoot in Raw and, if you are unsure, many DSLRs allow you to shoot in both Raw and jpeg so you can make the comparisons for yourself (see Settings Example 1).

Using the monochrome setting

When you are out with your camera intending to make black and white photographs, often the biggest challenge is to try to imagine what the finished photograph will look like because you see everything in colour. There is a setting

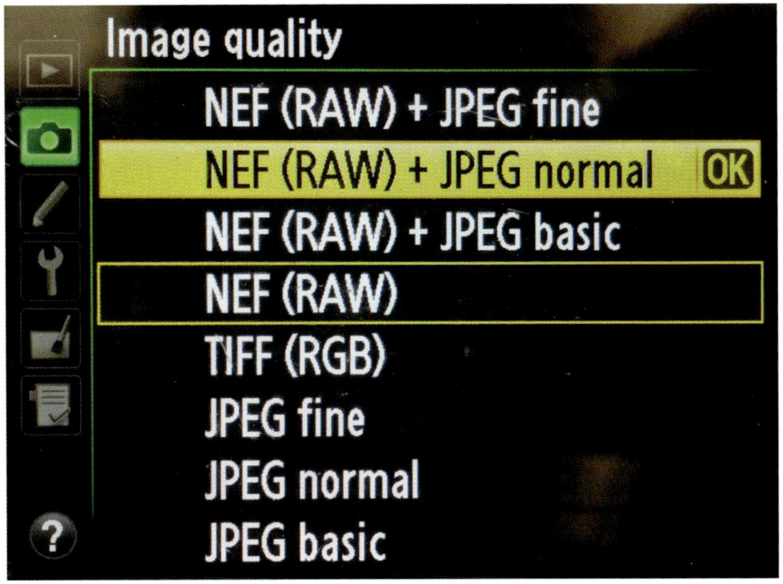

Settings Example 1.

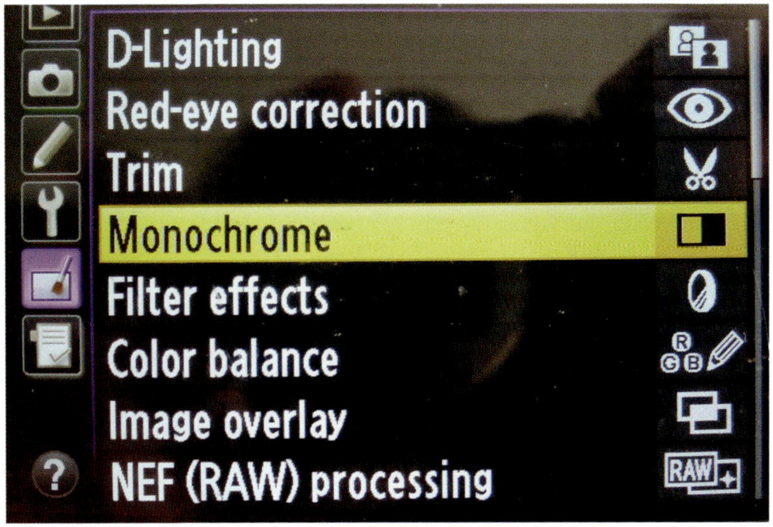

Settings Example 2.

in most cameras that enables you to change to 'monochrome' (see Settings Example 2). So, even if you have set your camera to shoot in Raw, which will collect all of the colour information in the scene, what you will be presented with is a monochrome image on the screen on the back of your camera.

It is worth mentioning here that any information that is presented to you on the screen on the back of your camera is information from a jpeg file and not from a camera Raw file. Therefore, when you set your camera to 'monochrome' what you are telling the camera to do is to process a jpeg of the information it has captured and present it to you on your camera screen in black and white. This can be a very helpful tool indeed as it gives you an idea of what things will look like in tones of grey, and your ability to 'see' in black and white will develop as you continue to use this setting. It will also give you an understanding of how shapes will appear in pictures and enable you to understand the weight and balance of shadows and highlights without the distraction of colour.

If you have set your camera to shoot in Raw only then, when you look at your image files later, they will be presented in colour only. However,

if you have set your camera to shoot in Raw and jpeg, and you have also set your camera to its monochrome setting, then when you are looking through your images you will see a colour version that is the Raw file and a monochrome version that is the jpeg. This is well worth trying and can help enormously as you begin to dip your toe into the world of black and white photography.

Other settings to use for digital black and white

When it comes to other camera settings for black and white, they can be what you would ordinarily use. Auto-focus is fine and if you want the best quality file out of your camera then use its lowest native ISO setting, which is usually 100 or 200 ISO for most modern DSLR cameras. It is worth bearing in mind, as with all settings and exposure considerations, that a lower ISO setting may give you a better quality Raw file but it will require a longer exposure time and therefore a tripod may be needed to prevent camera shake. Of course, if you are working in a more dynamic environment such as urban or street photography, then a higher ISO would be better, along with hand-holding the camera. If you set your camera to a higher ISO then the difference in the Raw file will be a slight increase in something known as 'noise', which often represents itself as a 'speckling' or coarser pixels in the shadow areas of your image. This is actually sometimes desirable and can add to the mood of photographs in a similar way that the 'grain' of the film did in days past.

7. HOW TO CONVERT TO BLACK AND WHITE

One of the most important parts of the black and white photography process is converting your image to black and white using your computer. There are many ways in which to do this but I will cover the basic methods here in order to keep things as straightforward as possible. It is very important to mention at the outset that you should avoid (in all cases except when using Adobe Camera Raw) selecting 'Greyscale' as your method of converting your image into black and white. The reason for this is that when this method is chosen you lose two thirds of your image data. This is because the image file is converted from three colour channels (red, green and blue) to a single 'greyscale' channel, and you have far less flexibility later on when you are adjusting the tones in your image. Also, I would not recommend simply selecting 'desaturate' as your method of converting to black and white. Although this method does retain the red, green and blue channels, it is rather limiting as you have missed out on the opportunity to explore the tones that adjusting colours in your image can offer.

Using Lightroom

If you are using Adobe Lightroom to view your images the first thing to do is to import your image file and then select 'develop' on the upper right of your menu bar. When you have done this you will see a long menu bar on the right side of your screen (B&W Conversion Example 1). If you then look down this menu you will see the dialogue box 'HSL/Color/B&W'. If you then click on the 'B&W' you will see your image turn black and white and you will also see a list of the different colour sliders available to you. You will see that the sliders are separated into individual colours and, to the right of each slider, there is a numeric + or – value. These values when you first click on 'B&W' are a basic representation of the colours in your image and they are a default setting (B&W Conversion Example 2). You can then explore how these individual colour sliders affect the tonality of your image as you move them. You will find that some of the sliders will change the tonality of your image far more than others. This is because there is more of that particular colour represented in your image and the further you adjust this slider the greater the effect. If you move an individual colour slider to the left, it will reduce the effect of the colour in your image, lower its tone, and the minus number will become bigger. If, however, you move your slider to the right you will see the plus number becoming greater and you will increase this tone in your image. In summary:

- 'Import' your image into Lightroom and select 'develop';
- Select 'B&W' from the 'B&W/Color/HSL' tab;
- Use colour sliders to adjust to your desired tones.

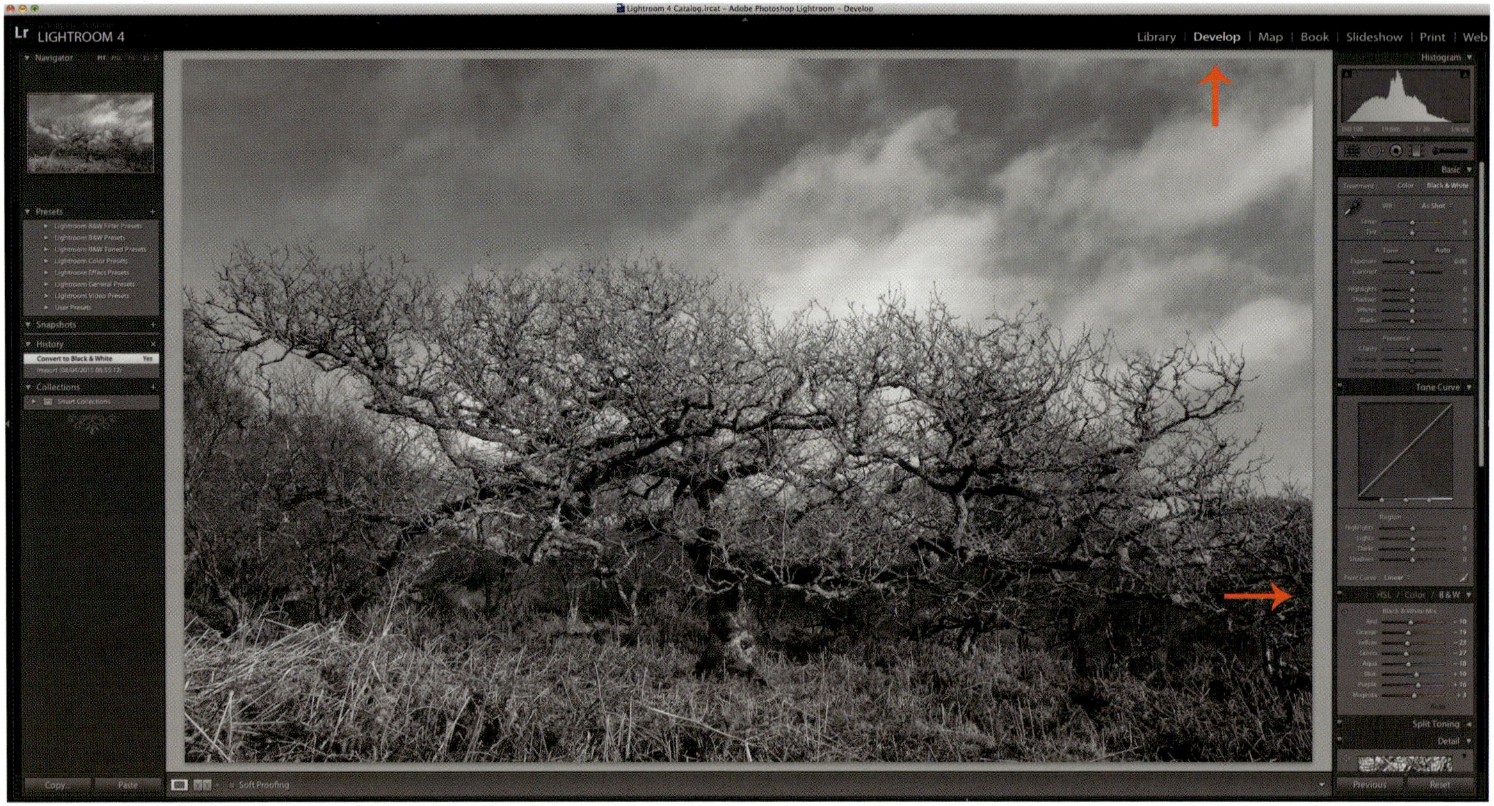

B&W Conversion Example 1.

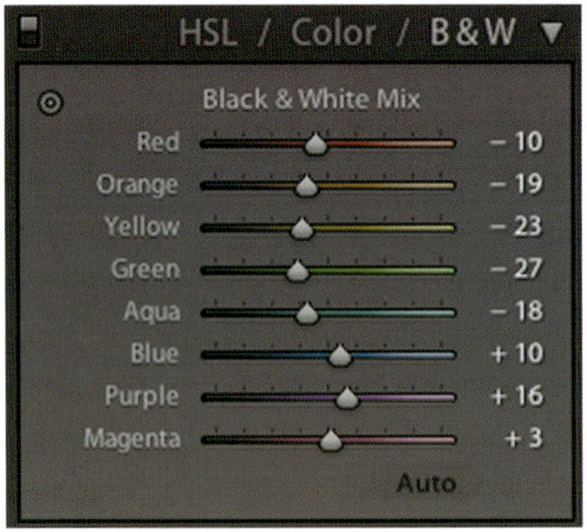

B&W Conversion Example 2.

Using Adobe Camera Raw

If you are using Adobe Camera Raw, when you first open your Raw file it will automatically open in Adobe Camera Raw. When you have done this you will see a menu bar positioned below the histogram in the upper right of your screen. Similar to Lightroom, if you then click on HSL/ Greyscale (See B&W Conversion Example 3),

and then click on the 'Convert to Greyscale' box you will see that your image will turn black and white. At this point you will see a series of sliders that are separated into individual colours, to the right of each slider there is a box with a numeric + or − value, and the tab at the top will be labelled 'Greyscale Mix'. As with Adobe Lightroom, you can then explore how these individual colour sliders affect the tonality of your image as you move them. To summarise:

- Open the image file in Adobe Camera Raw;
- Select HSL/Greyscale;
- Use the colour sliders to create your desired tones.

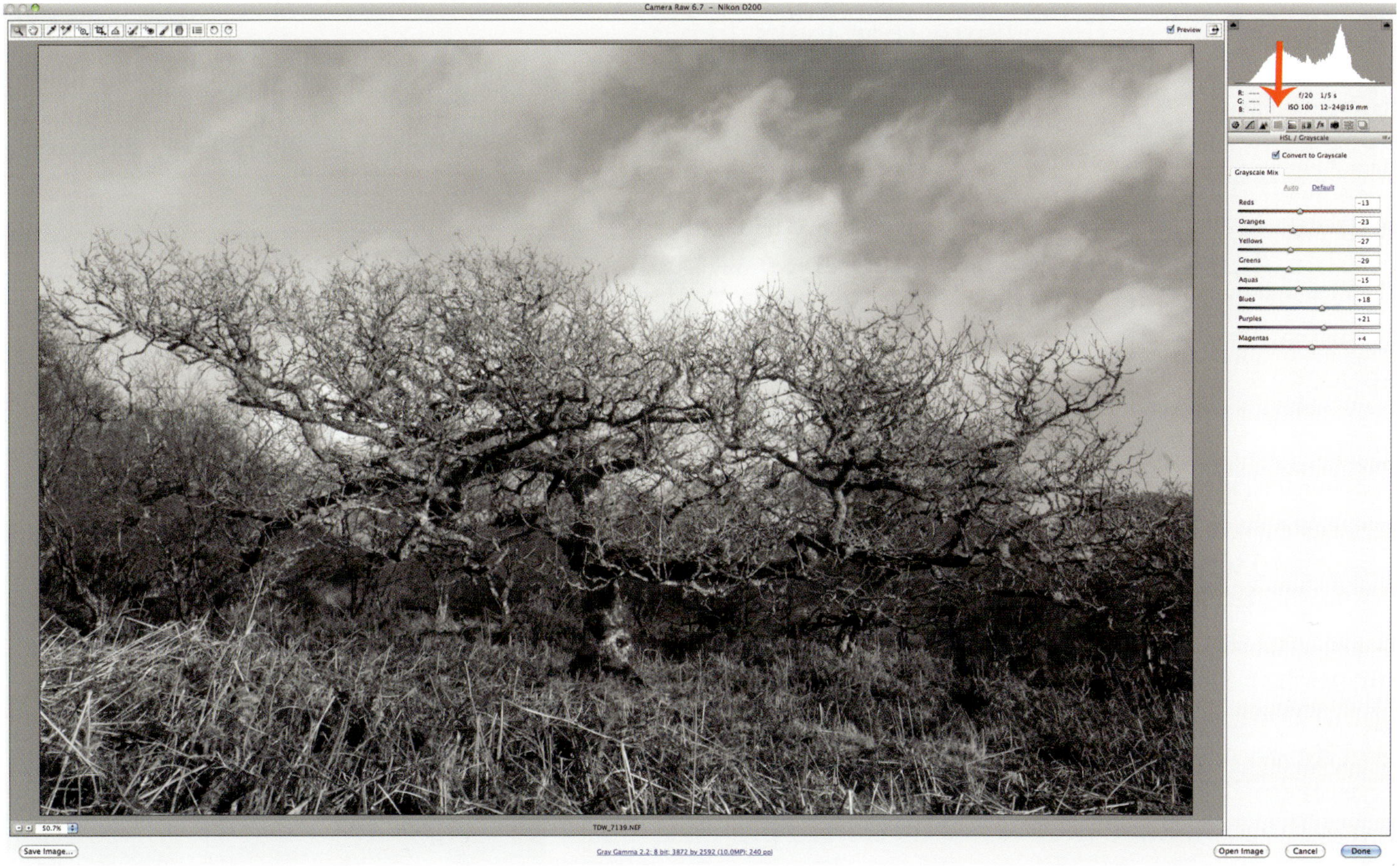

B&W Conversion Example 3.

Using Adobe Photoshop

If you are using Adobe Photoshop, then the approach is similar but can appear a little more complicated. When you have your image open in Photoshop you will also need to have your Layers palette open. If you cannot see this then go to the top menu bar and click on Window > Layers and your Layers palette will appear. When you have this pallete open you will see a small icon in the bottom of the palette that looks like a circle that is half white and half black. This is the 'create new fill or adjustment layer' icon (see B&W Conversion Example 4). When you click on this icon a long list will appear and one of the options is 'black and white'. If you then click on this, another dialogue box will appear with a list of colour sliders (as in Lightroom and Adobe Camera Raw). At the same time, a layer will appear in your Layers Palette called 'Black and White' (see B&W Conversion Example 5). Once again you can now explore how these individual colour sliders affect the tonality of your image as you move them. This method of conversion to black and white is incredibly versatile as you also have a selection of pre-sets that you can choose from which you should try. If you look at the top menu bar in the dialogue box above the colour sliders you will see a box called 'Default' with up and down pointing arrows to the right side of the box. If you click on these arrows this brings up a list. What you have here is a selection of pre-sets

B&W Conversion Example 4.

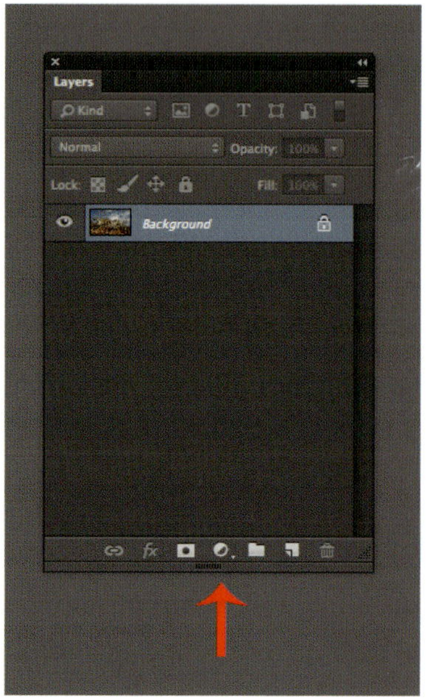

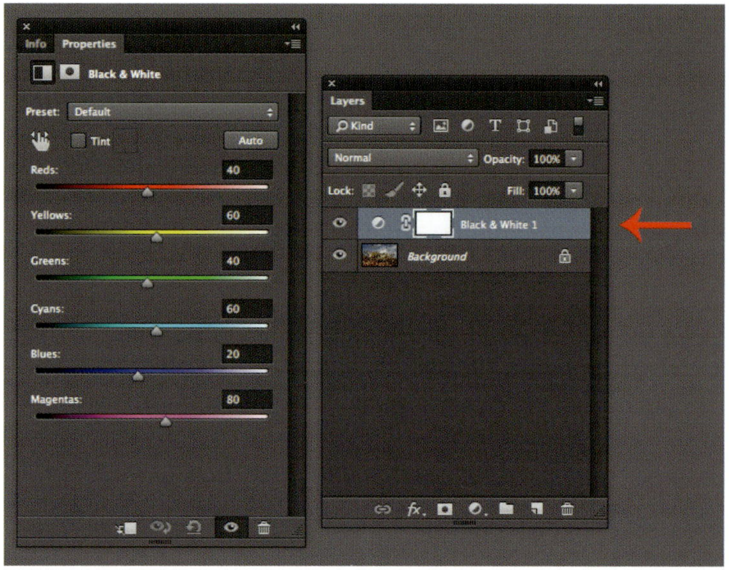

B&W Conversion Example 5.

that will digitally emulate the effect of using colour filters on a film camera loaded with black and white film (see B&W Conversion Example 6). What you will see is that each time you select one of the pre-sets, this will rearrange your sliders for you and present you with the effect of using that filter with a film camera loaded with black and white film. I would not say that they are all very accurate, but they are certainly worth exploring as a starting point. To summarise:

- Open the image file in Photoshop;
- Ensure the Layers palette is open – Window>Layers;
- Select the Black and White Adjustment Layer;
- Use the colour sliders to adjust to the desired tones in the dialogue box.

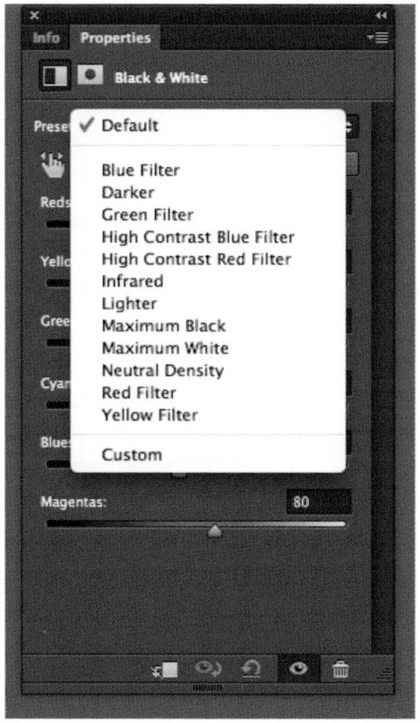

B&W Conversion Example 6.

I must say at this point that you are just beginning to 'shape' your image into a finished black and white photograph and you should not try to achieve every tonal adjustment at this stage. Also, if you 'push' and 'pull' some of the colour sliders too much you will run the risk of making your image look 'crunchy' and ugly. The thing to bear in mind is that this is just the initial conversion as these adjustments are acting globally across your whole image. In the next section of this book I will explore with you how to adjust the contrast and tonality of different parts of your image.

Using Nik Silver Efex Pro

There are other programmes that have become popular over recent years for converting images to black and white and one of the most popular is the Nik Software Silver Efex Pro. This software works slightly differently as it presents you with a vast list of options for conversion. When you click on each option you are presented with your converted image on the main screen. To access these Silver Efex Pro options you simply have to click on Filter>Silver Efex Pro and this gives you the drop-down list for your chosen option. Your image will appear and it is from here that you can explore the various conversion effects on offer and choose the one that best suits your image (see B&W Conversion Example 7).

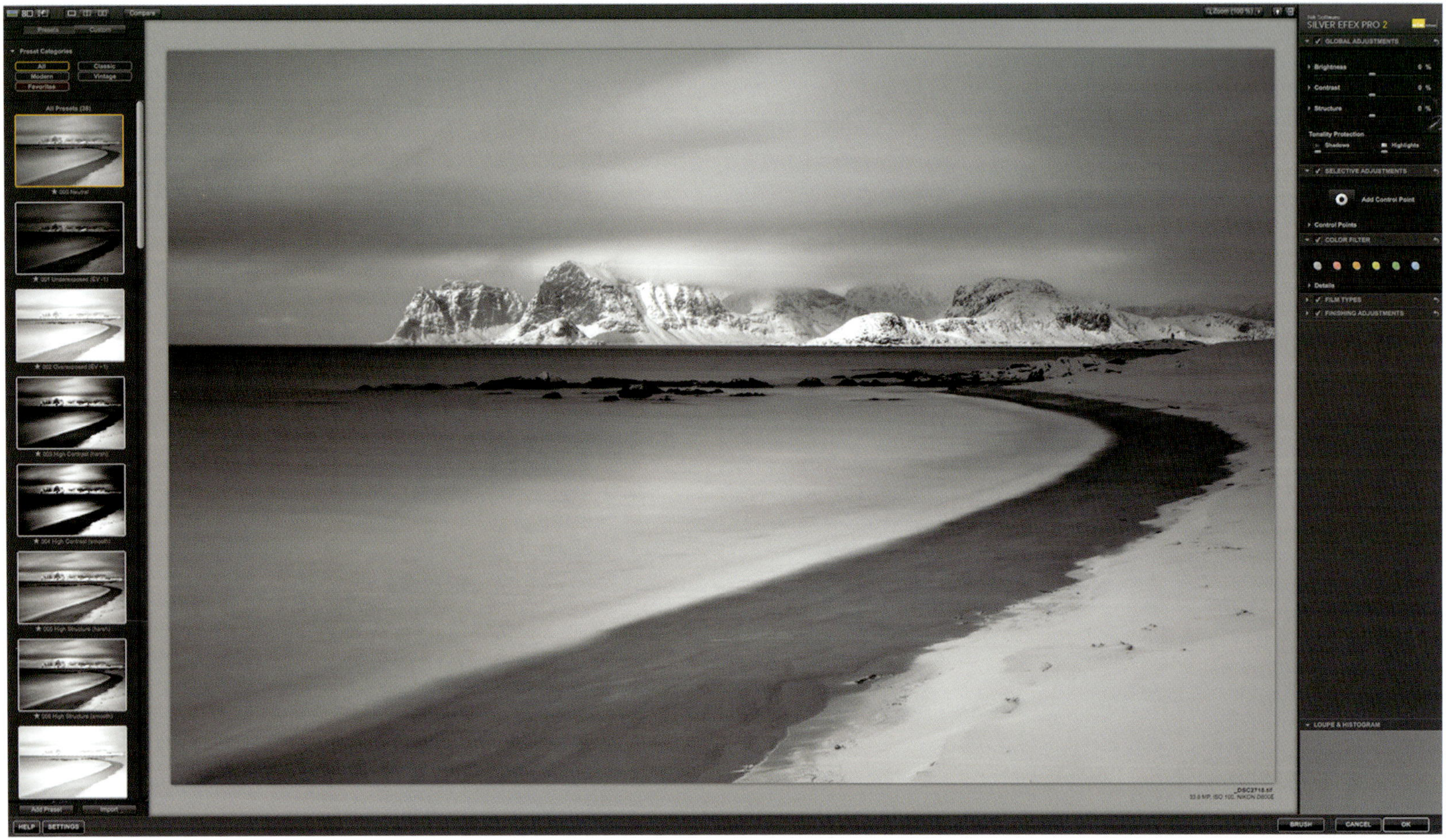

B&W Conversion Example 7.

8. CONTRAST AND TONE: SHAPING YOUR IMAGE

Even after over 30 years of making black and white photographs, I have only had a handful of photographs that have not needed localised adjustments. In the darkroom days you called these adjustments 'dodging' and 'burning', which meant you lightened and darkened separate parts of the photograph to bring out the light and tones that you saw when you were out there with your camera. You must remember that a digital camera can only do so much for you and it is up to you to bring out the drama or three-dimensionality of the photograph in the final stages. You can make this process as complicated as you like but here are a few basic ideas to follow that will enable you to explore this very exciting part of being a black and white image maker.

Adjusting contrast and tone in Adobe Lightroom

To begin with Adobe Lightroom, after you have made your conversion to black and white you will still be in the 'Develop' module. If you look at the row of tools available to you, just below the histogram in the upper right of your screen, you will see a brush icon (see Contrast and Tone Example 1). If you click on this icon, a list of sliders appears below ranging from 'Temp' to 'Density'. If you now hover your cursor over your image you will see a circle appear. What you are seeing is the brush that you can use to adjust parts of your image.

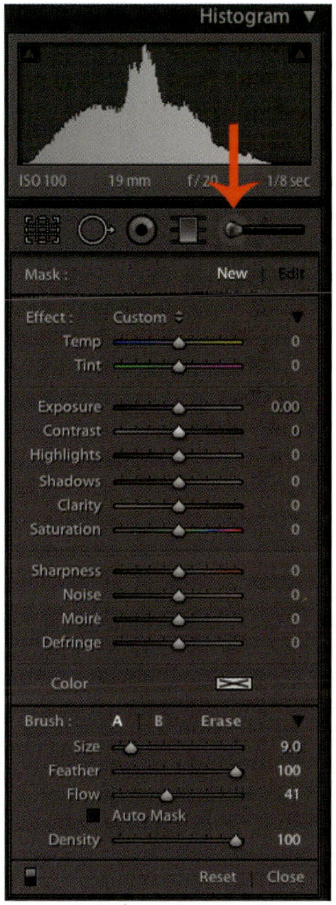

Contrast and Tone Example 1.

What you first need to do is to re-set all of the control sliders to zero. To do this, simply double click on all of them. After this you need to set your brush ready to adjust your image. At the bottom of the palette you will see a box dedicated to your brush that shows the four main sliders, which are Size, Feather, Flow and Density.

Size

The Size slider is pretty self-explanatory - if you move the slider and then place your cursor over your image, you will see your brush getting bigger or smaller depending on which way you are moving the slider.

Feather

You will see, from looking at your cursor hovering over your image, that your brush consists of two circles. This is where the Feather slider comes into play. The Feather determines how hard the edge of your brush is. The smaller the Feather setting the harder the edge of your brush, and the bigger the setting the softer the edge of your brush. The hardness of your brush is the transition between the full effect and where this effect fades away. A hard-edge brush will make a hard line on your image, a soft-edge brush will have a smooth-edged adjustment (see Feather Examples). This translates into the distance between the two circles of your brush icon, being further apart means your brush feather is large, and almost becoming one circle when you

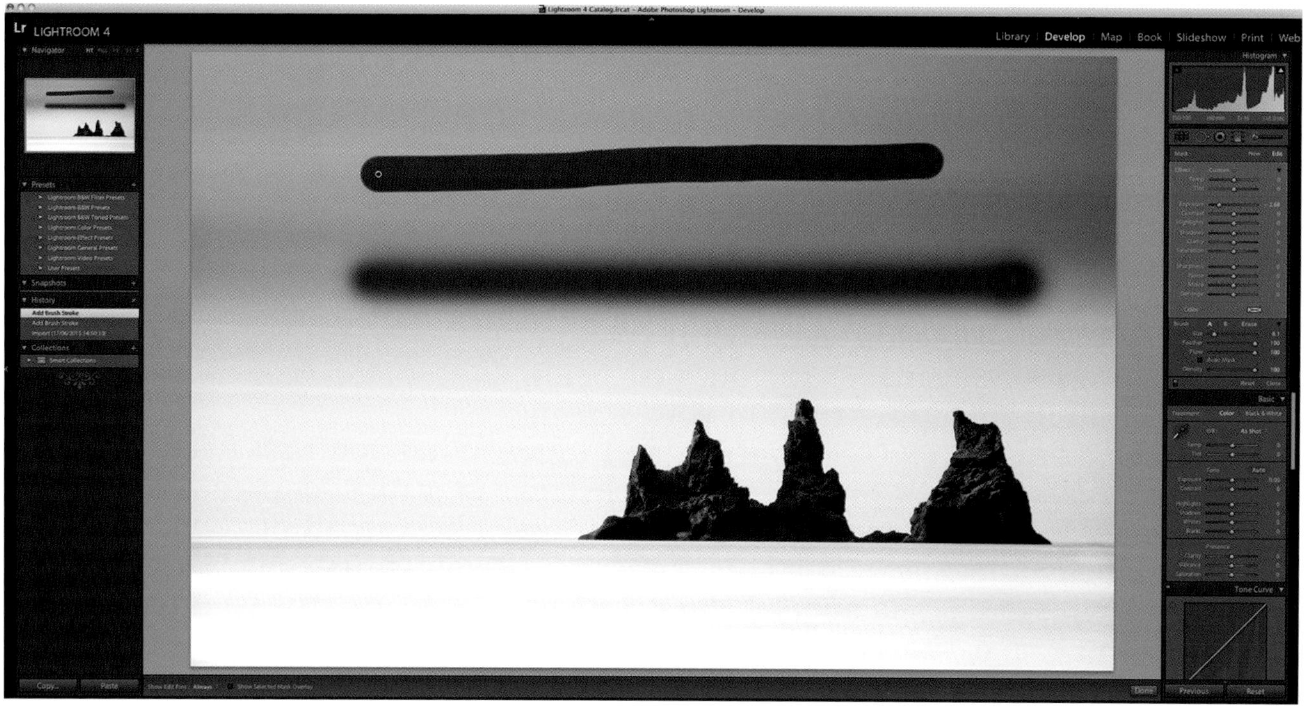

Feather Examples.

set the feather of your brush means it is very small, or hard-edged. This may take a little time to get used to but, essentially, you will adjust this throughout the work on your image to account for small areas of your image that need adjustment and also for areas where you do not want a hard edge to appear, which would make your adjustments look obvious.

Flow

The Flow slider determines how fast your brush adjustment will apply to the image. Therefore, if you set your flow value to 100 then the effect of your brush actions will be instant and will not build up gradually.

Density

The Density slider determines the maximum effect of your brush actions. Therefore, if you set this at 50 then you will only ever get half of the effect you have set all your sliders for.

I know this may sound complicated but, after a little practice, it will become intuitive. For a starter I would recommend setting your Flow at approximately 40, your Density at 100 and the Feather should be set for the size of image area on your image that you wish to adjust.

Making adjustments

Firstly, you do not have to worry about Temp or Tint as these apply to colour images and you are working in black and white. Let's begin with exposure. Imagine that you intend to darken the sky in your image. You could start by setting your exposure to -0.70 or there about. If you then move your cursor over the sky in the image and slowly brush away you will see that your sky begins to darken. After you have done this, a small circle or 'pin' will appear on your image. This is simply telling you that you have made an adjustment and Lightroom is recording this action. If you subsequently decide that your sky is not dark enough, or too dark, then all you have to do is to return to your Exposure slider and adjust it accordingly. You can move the slider after you have brushed as Lightroom remembers your brush strokes and you can adjust these strokes further.

If you look at Contrast and Tone Example 2 you will see that I have elected to darken the sky in my image of Iceland to bring out the drama, and the red arrow is pointing towards the 'pin' indicating where I first positioned my brush in the image. For this image I then returned to my exposure slider and lowered the exposure further to -1.36. If you want to see the area that you have adjusted hover your cursor over the 'pin' on your image and you will see that the area that your brush has effected has turned red (see Contrast and Tone Example 3).

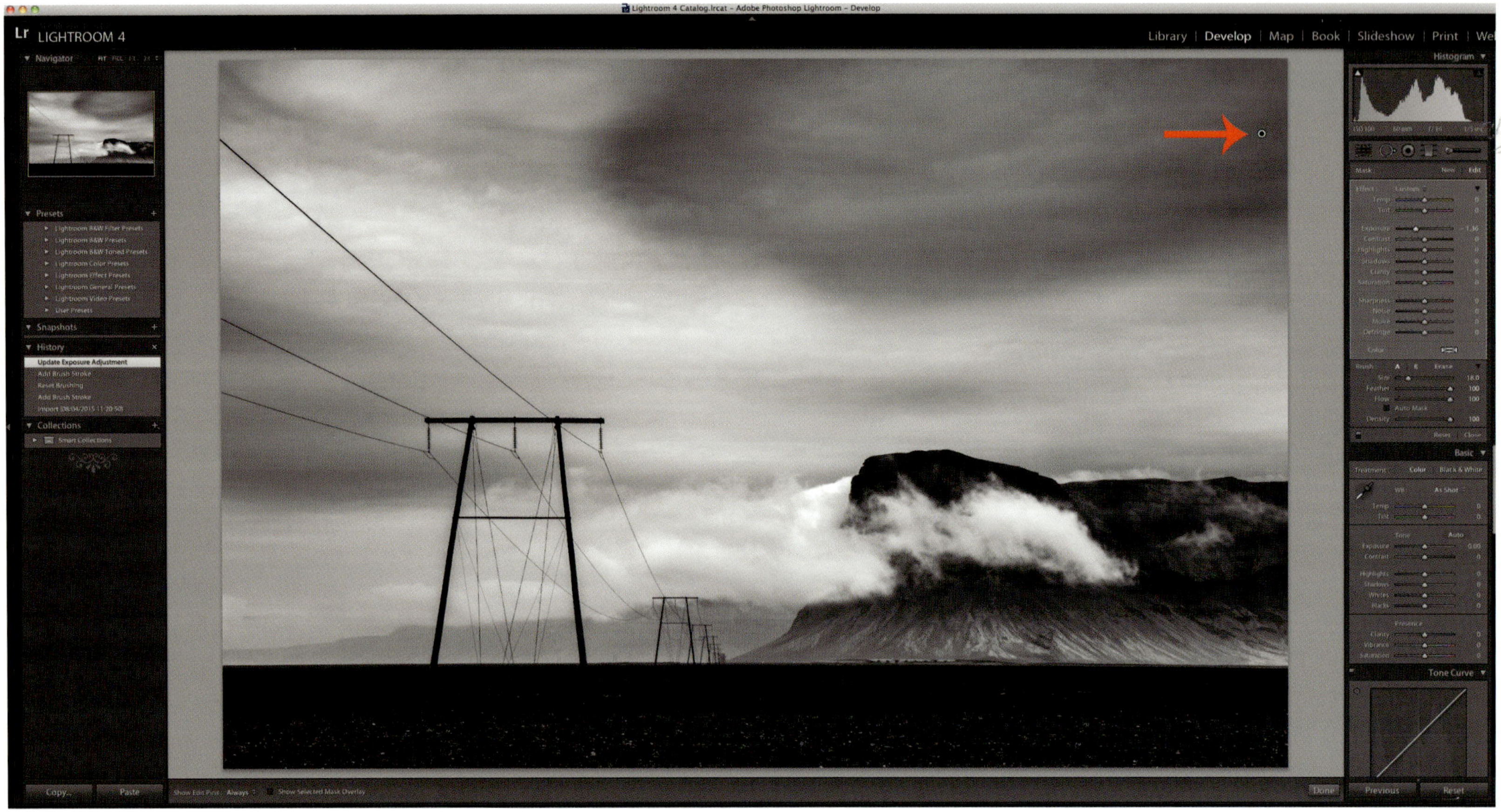

Contrast and Tone Example 2.

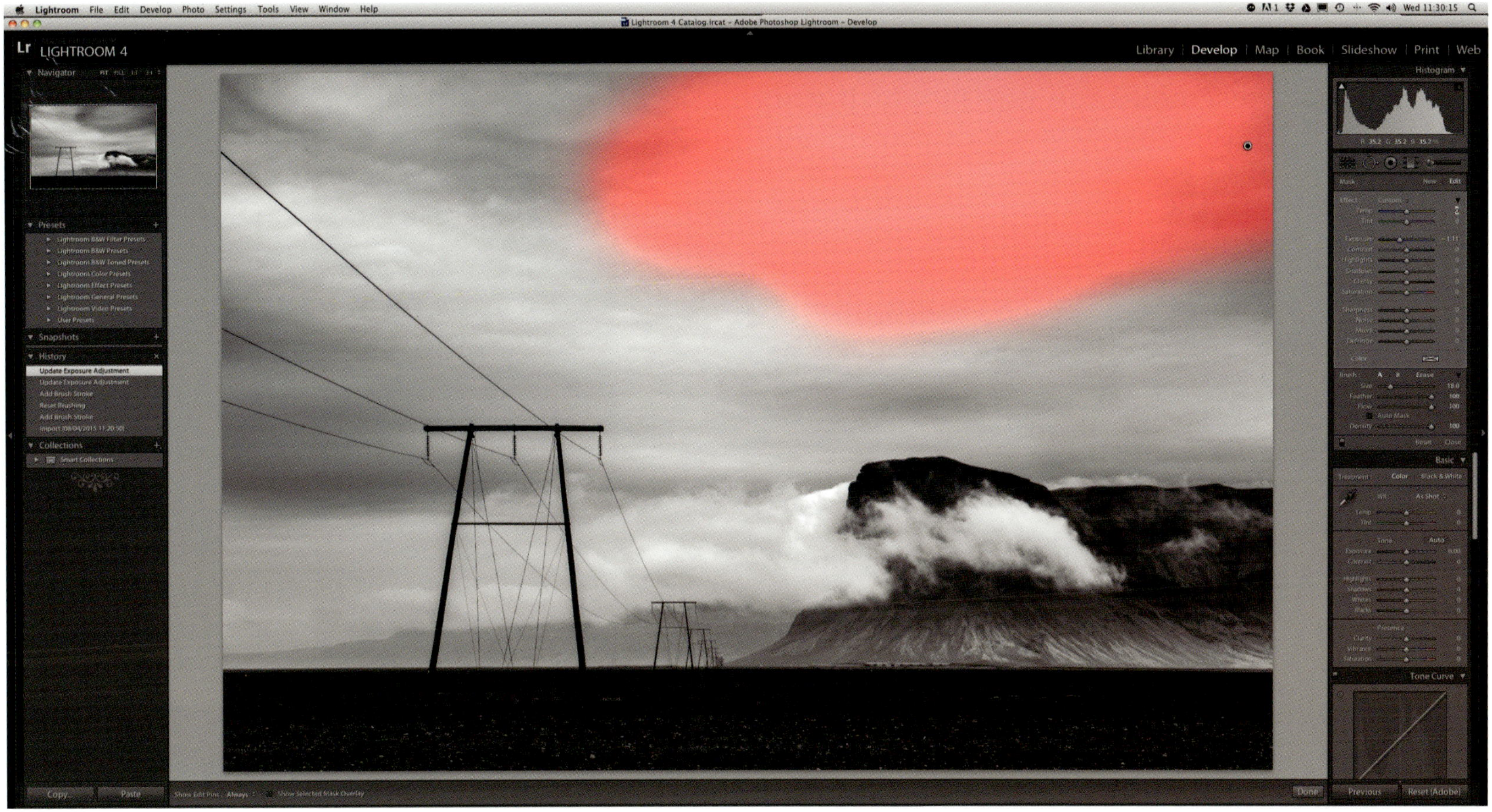

Contrast and Tone Example 3.

The above process can be followed time after time and you can gradually build up the tones in your image until it resembles the way in which you saw the scene at the time. If you want to work on a different area of your image you simply click on ‘new’ beneath the brush tool icon and begin the same process again (see Contrast and Tone Example 4).

You must remember that each time you start work on a new area of the image you have to re-set your sliders as they retain the settings from your last brush activity. Each time you use the brush tool on your image a new ‘pin’ will appear and the pin that is active will have a black centre. The previous ‘pins’ will be solid grey/white. To return to a previous ‘pin’ you simply click on it and you can further refine your image. So, to summarise:

- Select the ‘adjustment brush’;
- Reset all adjustment sliders to ‘zero’;
- Set the size of your brush for the area you wish to adjust;
- Set the ‘feather’, ‘flow’ and ‘density’ of the adjustment brush;
- Gradually brush away at the chosen area of your image;
- Select ‘new’ and reset the sliders for the next area of your image.

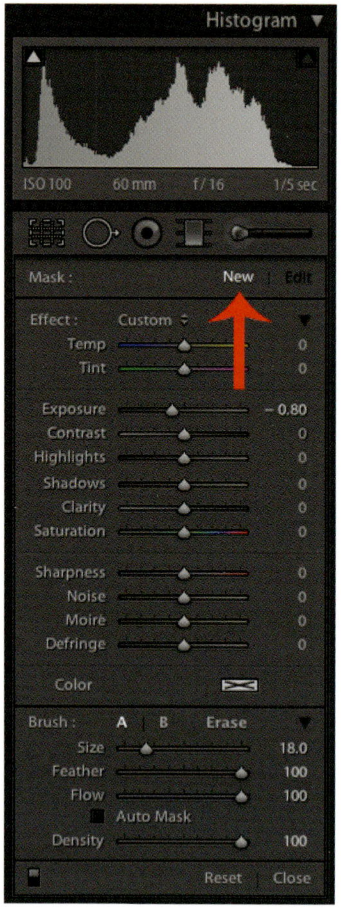

Contrast and Tone Example 4.

Adjusting contrast and tone in Adobe Photoshop

Using the Dodge and Burn Tools

One of the most straightforward methods of altering tonality in Photoshop is to use the Dodge and Burn tools. This terminology comes direct from the darkroom and 'dodge' refers to the darkroom printer 'dodging' or not allowing light to hit the photographic paper on the enlarger base board, therefore lightening that area of the finished photograph. 'Burning' is the opposite and the darkroom printer would allow light to hit the photographic paper on the enlarger base board, therefore darkening that chosen area of the print.

To use these tools you need to click on them in the Tool palette of Photoshop (see Contrast and Tone Example 5). To select between the two simply left click and hold down the click so you can choose which tool is needed. The Burn Tool is represented as a cupped hand and the Dodge Tool looks like a lollipop. After selecting your tool, you will see two options in the top menu bar of Photoshop that will be displayed as 'Range' and 'Exposure'. Here you can set the Range as Shadows, Midtones or Highlights, depending on which tonal range you would like to dodge or burn, and the Exposure can be set to whatever extent you wish to alter the chosen part of your image. If your Exposure is set to 100% then the dodging or burning will be very aggressive and happen very quickly as you brush away. I recommend using 1% or 2% so that you build up your adjustment slowly. As with all other brushes, if you right-click on the image after selecting the Dodge or Burn tool you will see a menu appear that will allow you to select the 'feather' and brush size.

This is an intuitive process and one that should be taken slowly in order to build up the tonal differences that you wish to achieve in your image.

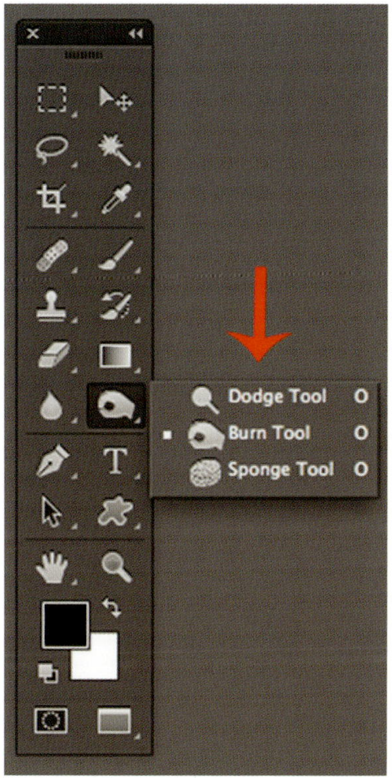

Contrast and Tone Example 5.

Using a 50% Grey Layer

Another method of gradually altering tonality in black and white photographs in Photoshop is to use a 50% Grey Layer. Although not quite as straightforward as using the Dodge and Burn tools, it is very effective and really quite simple when you get used to it. To get started, go to the top menu bar in Photoshop and select Layer>New>Layer. A dialogue box appears and you then click on the mode and change it from Normal to Soft Light (See Contrast and Tone 6). Then check the box next to 'Fill with Soft Light-neutral color (50% gray)'. At this point a grey layer will appear in your Layers palette and this is your new 50% Grey Layer (see Contrast and Tone 7).

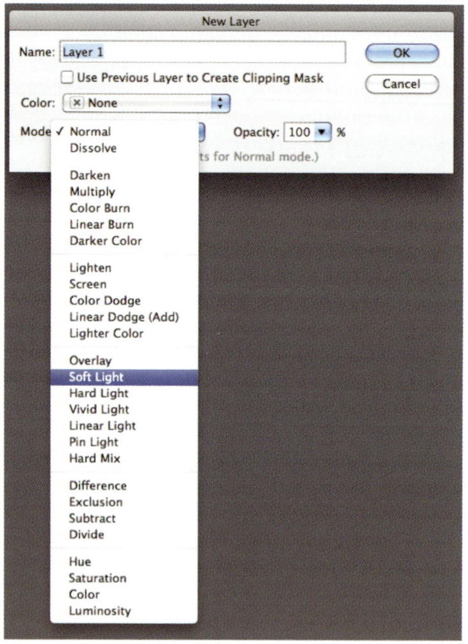

Contrast and Tone Example 6.

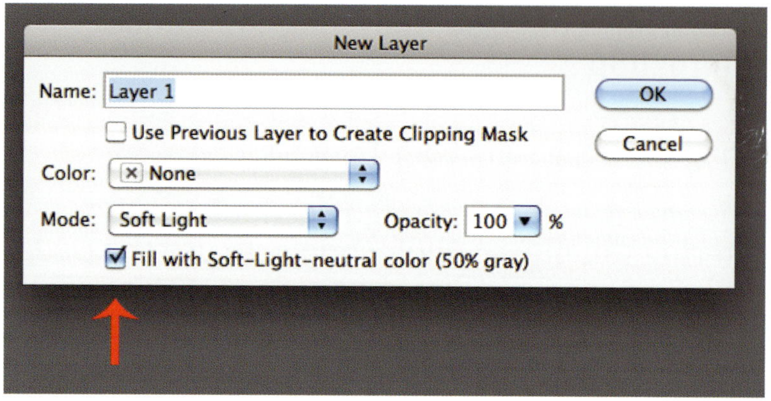

Contrast and Tone Example 7.

Next you need to select your brush tool from your Layers palette (See Contrast and Tone 8), set your foreground colour to black and your background colour to white. (See Contrast and Tone 9). If your foreground and background colours are not black and white simply hit 'X' and 'D' on your computer keyboard and they will then be set. Now, with your brush tool selected, all that you have to remember is that if you select your foreground colour as 'white', it will gradually lighten the part of your image you are brushing over, and if you select your foreground colour as 'Black' you will gradually darken your chosen area. As with any other brush I have mentioned, I would recommend setting your flow at approximately 40, your density at 100 and the feather should be set for the size of the image area you wish to adjust in your image.

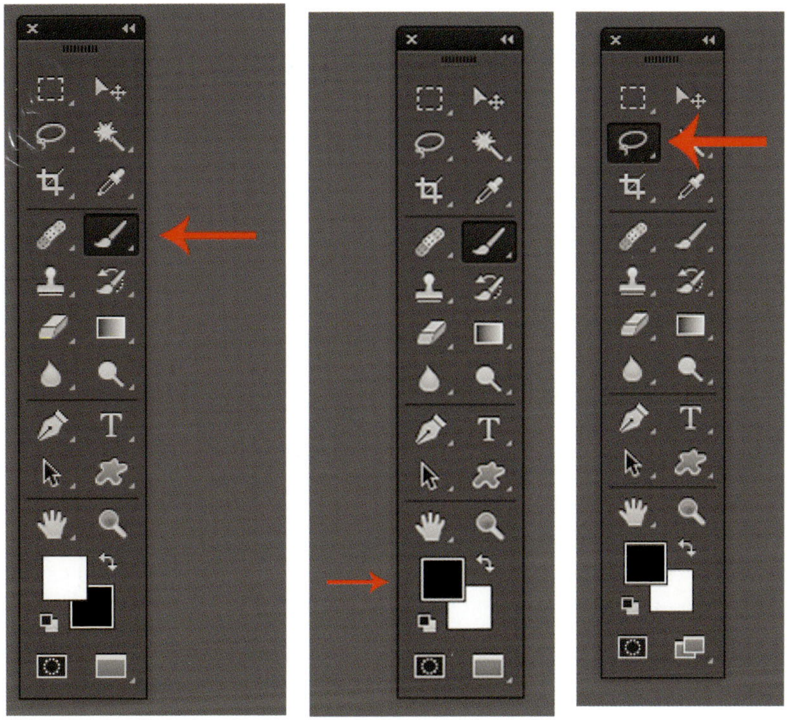

Contrast and Tone Examples 8 (left), 9 (centre) and 10 (right).

Using Selections and Curves

The method I have used for many years involves using simple Selections and Curves. I find the easiest way to make a selection of an image is with the Lasso Tool that is situated in the upper left of Photoshop's tool box (see Contrast and Tone Example 10). If you click on the lasso icon you then, as with Lightroom, need to set the feather. Also, as with Lightroom, the feather determines how hard the edge of your selection is. The smaller the feather setting the harder the edge of your selection and the bigger the feather, the softer the edge of your selection. All that you have to do is click and drag your mouse over the area that you want to adjust and the lasso tool will 'draw' the shape you require. It is worth noting that I hold down the 'alt' key at all times when making a selection using the lasso tool because, if your hand slips off the mouse, the selection will automatically complete itself with a straight line, which can be frustrating. Also, if you depress the 'alt' key, you can select beyond the edge of your image, which is critical if you want your adjustment to go to the very edge (see Contrast and Tone Example 11). In a similar way to Lightroom, if you want to see the extent of the feather that you have made you can click on the Quick Mask icon in the bottom of the Toolbox. When you do this you will see an area of red appear. This area is the part of the image that will 'not' be effected by your adjustment as it is 'masked' off, and the area you see in black and white will be the part of the image you are altering (See Contrast and Tone 12).

Now that you are ready, you can select various parts of your image with different feather settings. Then you need to understand how to do what used to be done in the darkroom – dodge and burn (lighten and darken) and increase and decrease contrast. I find the most effective and

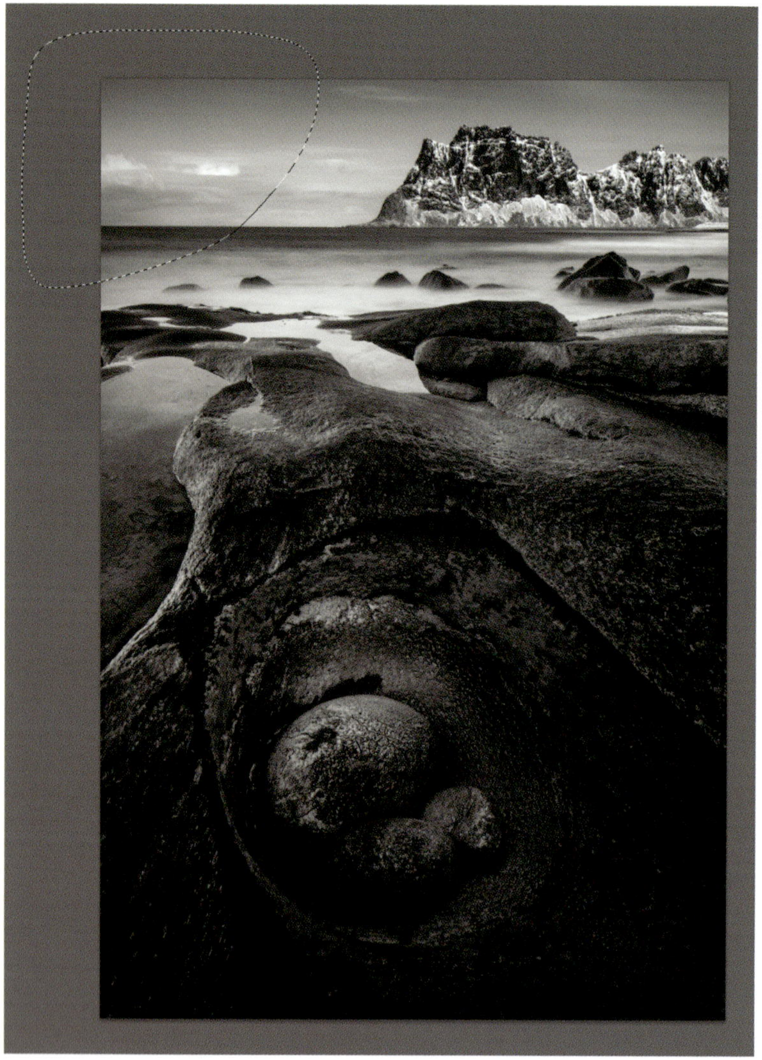

Contrast and Tone Example 11.

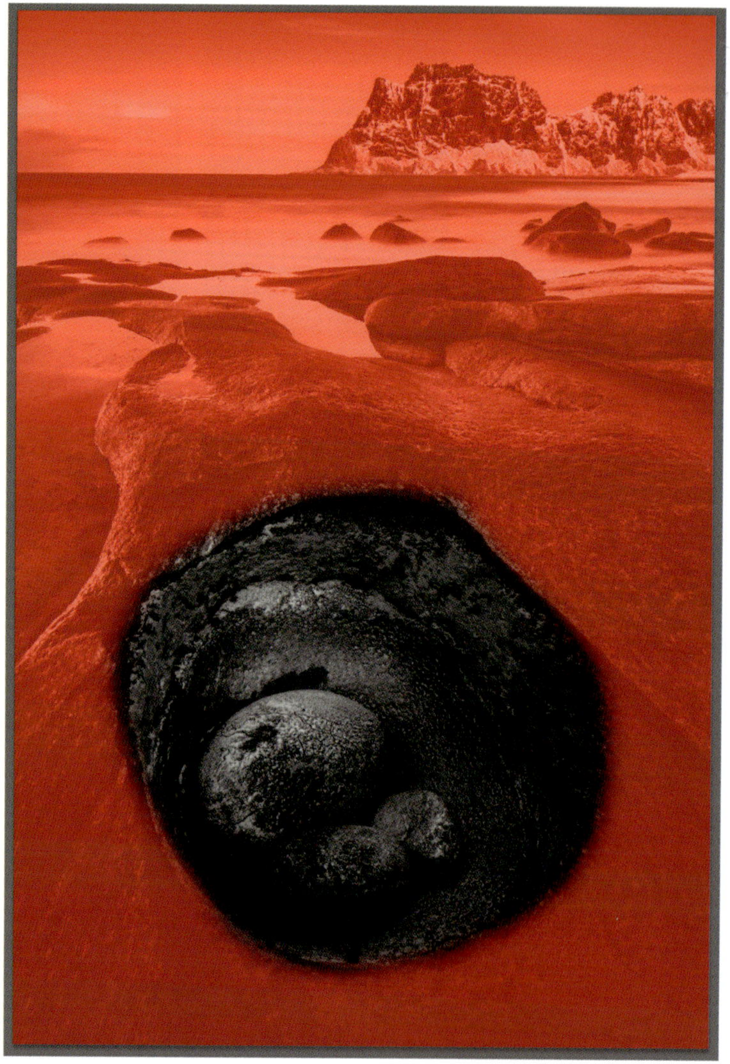

Contrast and Tone Example 12.

simple way of doing this is by using Curves. At first this may seem a little daunting, but if you follow a few simple techniques it soon becomes very intuitive. As described earlier when converting to black and white using Photoshop, you have to click on the 'Create New Fill or Adjustment Layer' icon that is a little half black and half white circle. This will then bring up a list to choose from and you will see in this list a Curves option (see Contrast and Tone Example 13). When you have clicked on this a new layer will appear in your Layers palette (see Contrast and Tone Example 14) and, at the same time, the Curves dialogue box will appear (see Contrast and Tone Example 15). The Curves dialogue box consists of two axes that gradually transform from solid black to solid white and a diagonal line. One end of the line represents white and the other represents black. If you click on any part of that line and drag it up or down you will begin to alter the tones in your image. For example, if you push the line upwards you would lighten the area of rocks I have selected in the sample image (See Contrast and Tone Example 16), if you pull the line downwards you would darken the rocks that have been selected (See Contrast and Tone Example 17), if you make an 'S' shape you would increase contrast in the rocks (See Contrast and Tone Example 18), and if you make a reverse 'S' shape you would lower the contrast in the rocks (see Contrast and Tone Example 19).

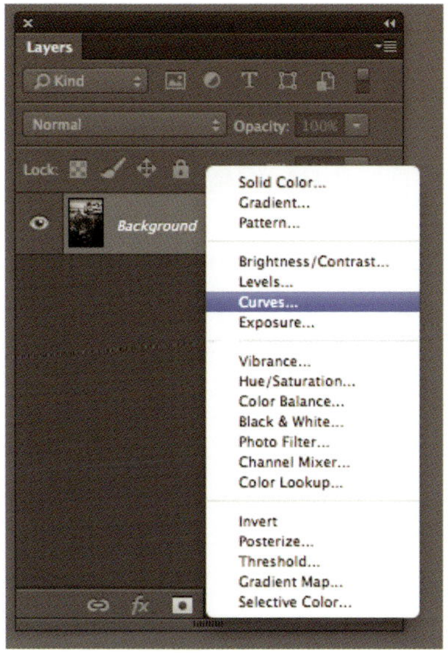

Contrast and Tone Example 13.

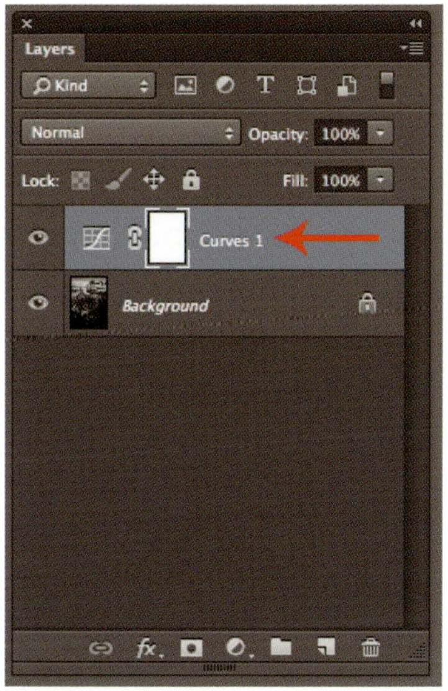

Contrast and Tone Example 14.

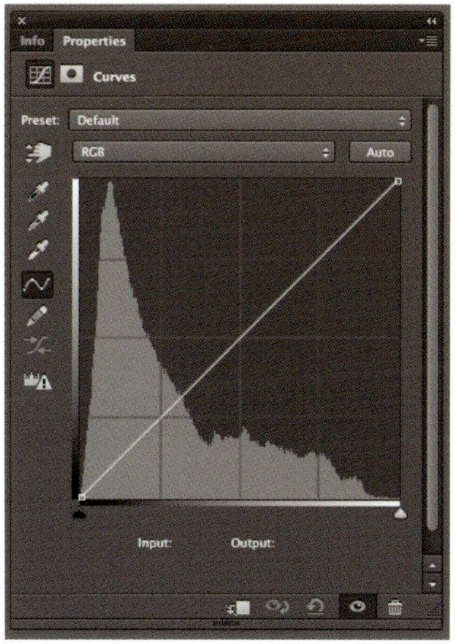

Contrast and Tone Example 15.

To summarise:

- Open your image in Photoshop;
- Select the 'Lasso' Tool;
- Set your feather for the size of the image area you are adjusting;
- Holding 'Alt' and click, drag and select the area of the image you want to adjust;
- Click on the 'Quick-mask' icon to see your selection, and then click 'off';
- Select a 'Curves' adjustment layer using the 'New Layer' icon;
- Click on the 'Curve line' to adjust the local tonality in the area selected.

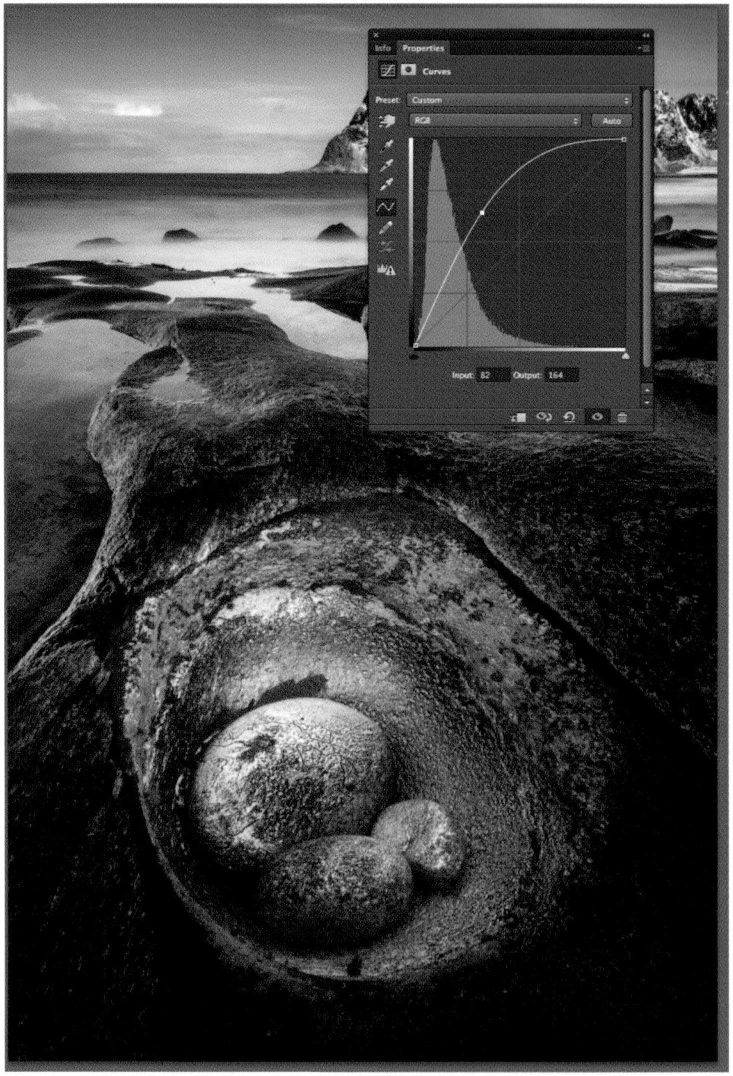

Contrast and Tone Example 16.

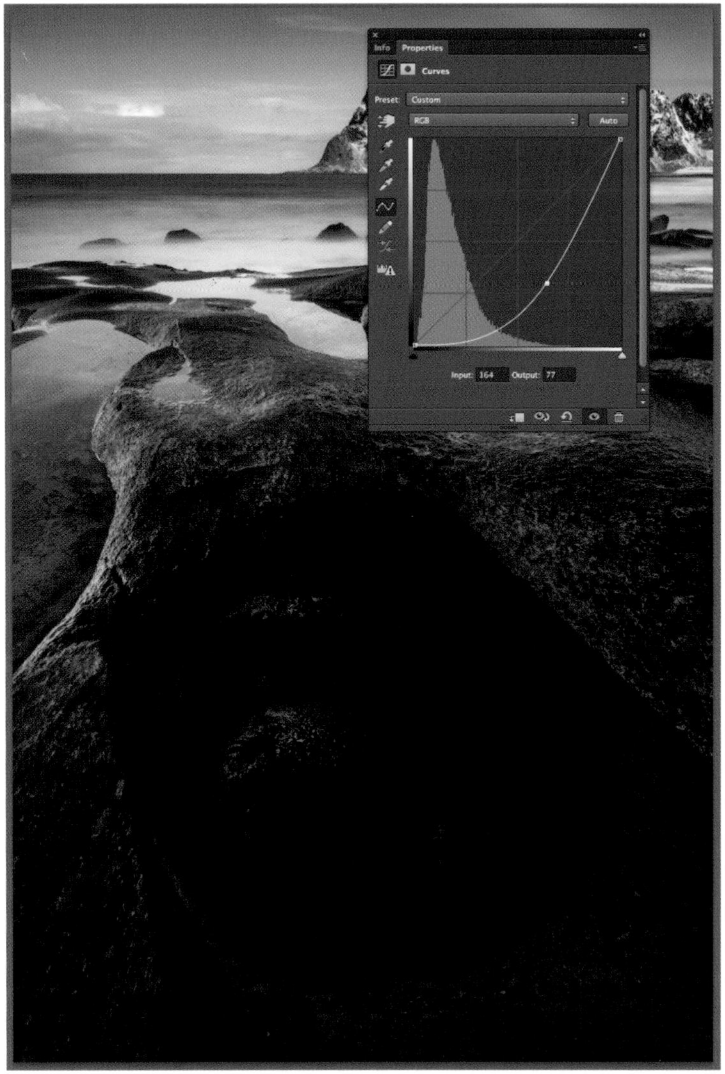

Contrast and Tone Example 17.

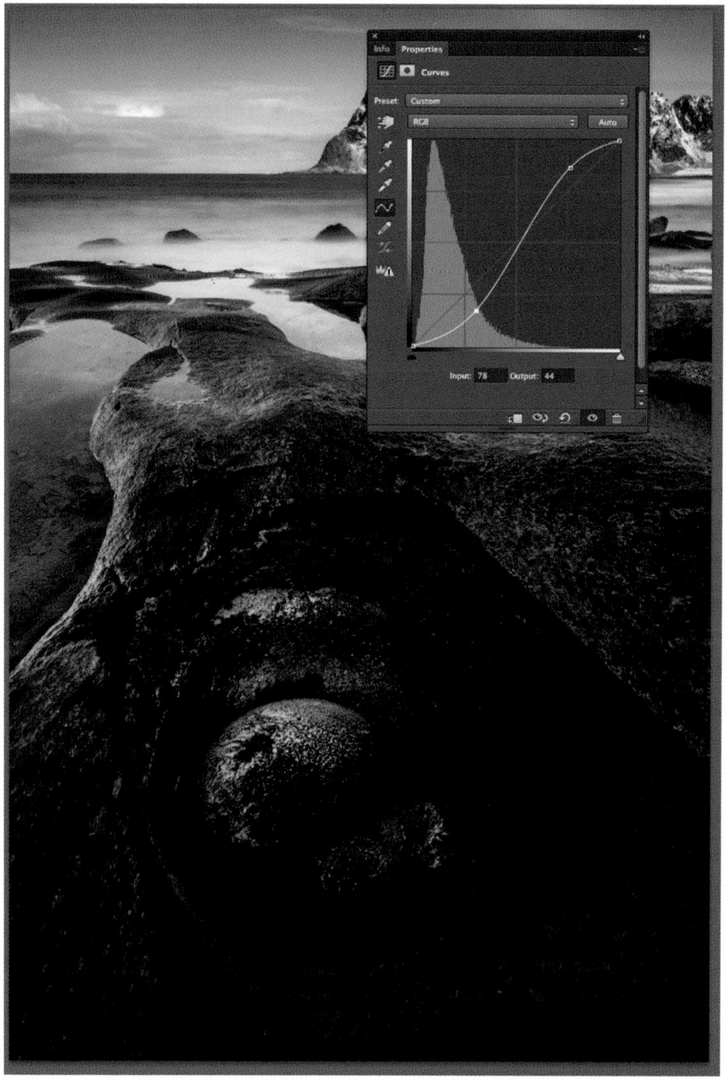

Contrast and Tone Example 18.

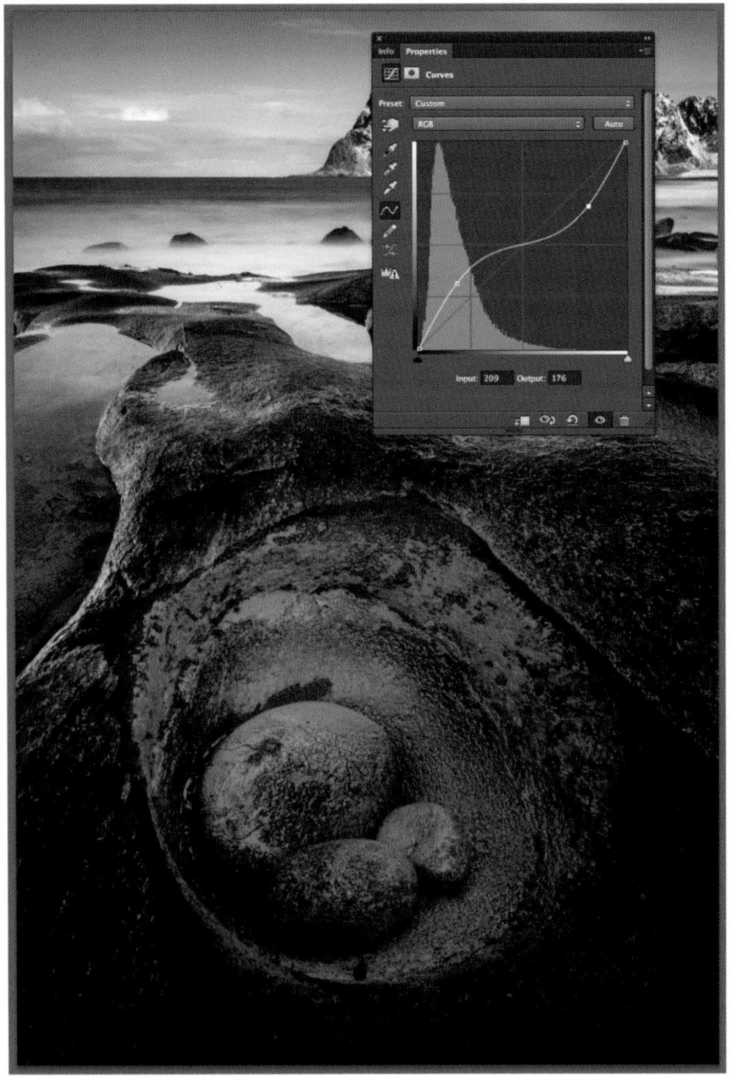

Contrast and Tone Example 19.

With these simple controls you can do all that was ever done in the darkroom and you have an amazing amount of flexibility to explore all the tones in your black and white photographs. All that remains is to try this technique out as often as you can while altering the feather of the section according to the portion of the image you are intending to alter. If this process is followed you can, with a little practice, have a finished image in which the tonal adjustments you have made are not obvious but the image has come to life as a result.

9. CONCLUSIONS

Try to consider each of the sections in this book as a beginning and a basis from which to explore the wonders of black and white photography. I must also make it clear that each individual section of the book is as important as the others. If you convert an image from colour to black and white badly, then this will affect the quality and tonality of the finished photograph. Similarly, if you use the wrong filters then this will affect your exposure and the image file you collect in your camera. Also, if you set your feather wrongly and use a brush that is too hard-edged, then this will spoil the finished photograph. What I am saying is that the accumulation of all of the chapters, used carefully, will, with time, create beautifully balanced black and white photographs that display depth, smooth tones between black and white and express what you saw and felt about the situation when you were there with your camera. Enjoy and explore the amazing world of black and white that has kept me addicted for many years.

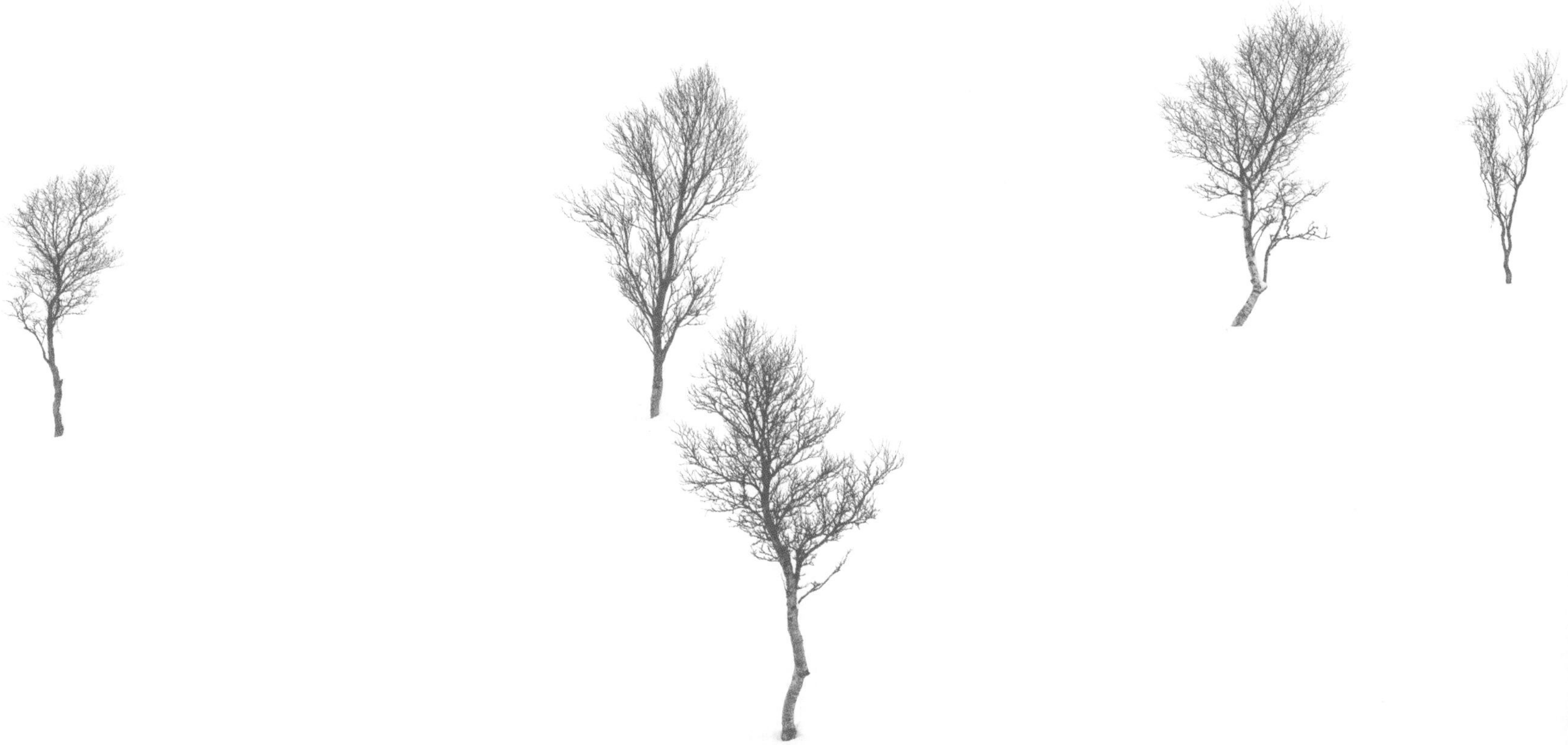

ABANDONED FARMHOUSE– THE BLACK ISLE

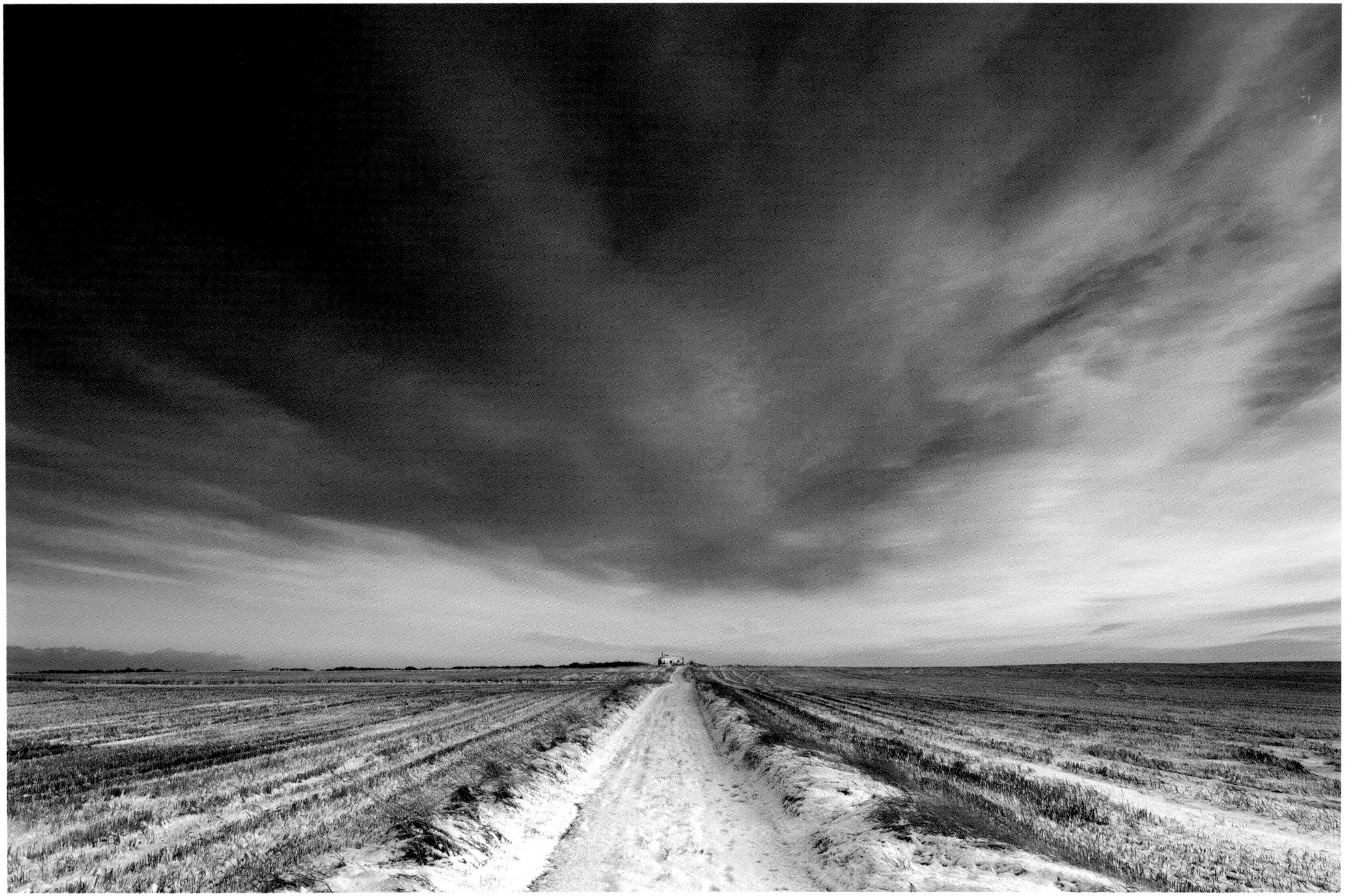

I was travelling on the Black Isle in 2010, during one of the coldest winters I have known. There was a bitter wind blowing off the coast close by and it was a very eerie place, made even more eerie by the almost frozen farmhouse at the end of the track. The dark clouds in the sky seemed to enhance the menacing feel to the place.

Nikon D700, 24mm PC-E lens, Lee Filters 0.6 Hard Grad, f13, 0.5 sec.

CLASHNESSIE BAY – SUTHERLAND

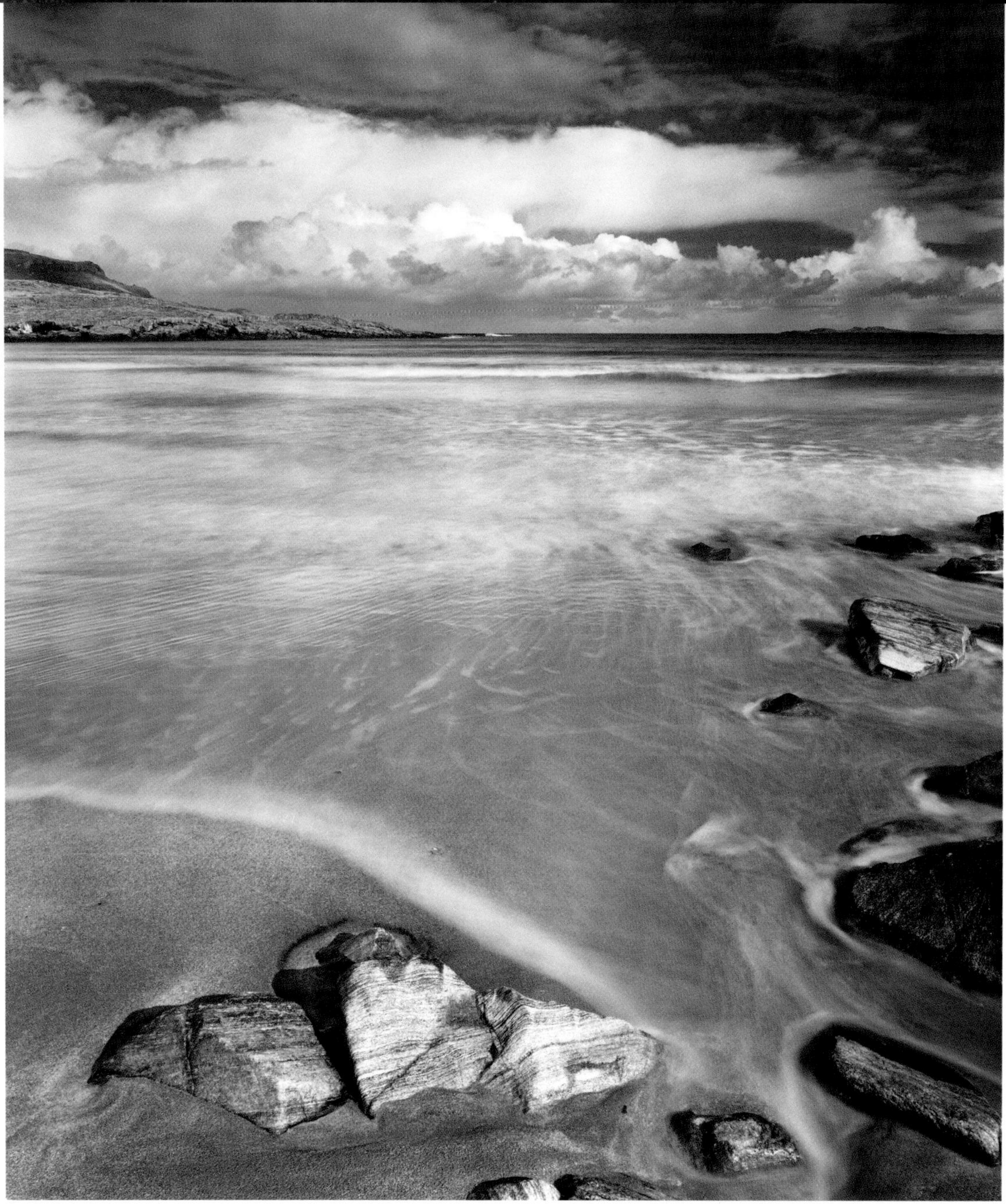

This is one of the most secluded and beautiful little beaches in the far north of the Scottish Highlands and, as with many of these places in Scotland, you can work entirely alone. There was a storm gradually building on the distant horizon and I was bathed in warm morning sunlight. I was fascinated by the waves as they receded backwards from around the foreground stones.

Walker Titan large format camera, 90mm lens, Lee Filters 0.6 Hard Grad, f22, 1 sec.

CORRIE BAY - ISLE OF ARRAN

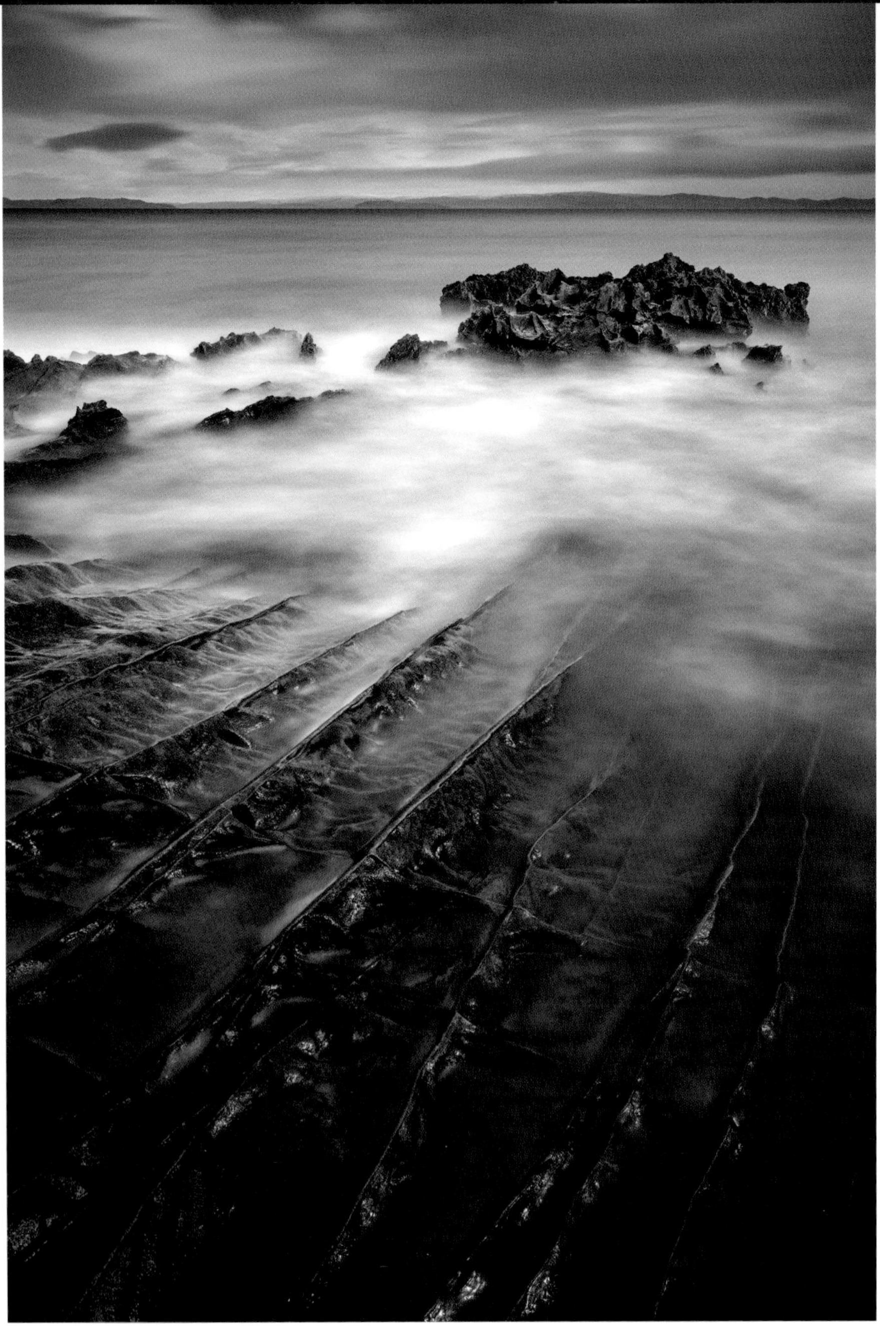

The geology of Corrie Bay is something to behold with its ridged and folded bedrocks. Every time I visit this location I find some new features to photograph. I was on my way to Kintyre and, on this occasion, the tide was perfect and its waters were washing over the small ridges at my feet, just being illuminated by weak sunlight to the south.

Nikon D800e, 24mm PC-E lens, Lee Filters 0.6 Hard Grad, Lee Filters Big Stopper, f13, 40 secs.

FALLS ASSYNT – SCOTLAND

I had seen these falls from far away on a mountain road and I made the decision one day to follow the path of the river and climb to them. The waters cascade from the high mountains surrounding the area and the rocks were so slippery that I was very concerned about falling down the ravine. The position of the camera was literally inches away from the foreground water. I made a number of exposures and then slowly made the journey down, back to my car.

Nikon D700, 24mm PC-E lens, Lee Filters 0.9 Neutral Density Filter, f13. 4 secs.

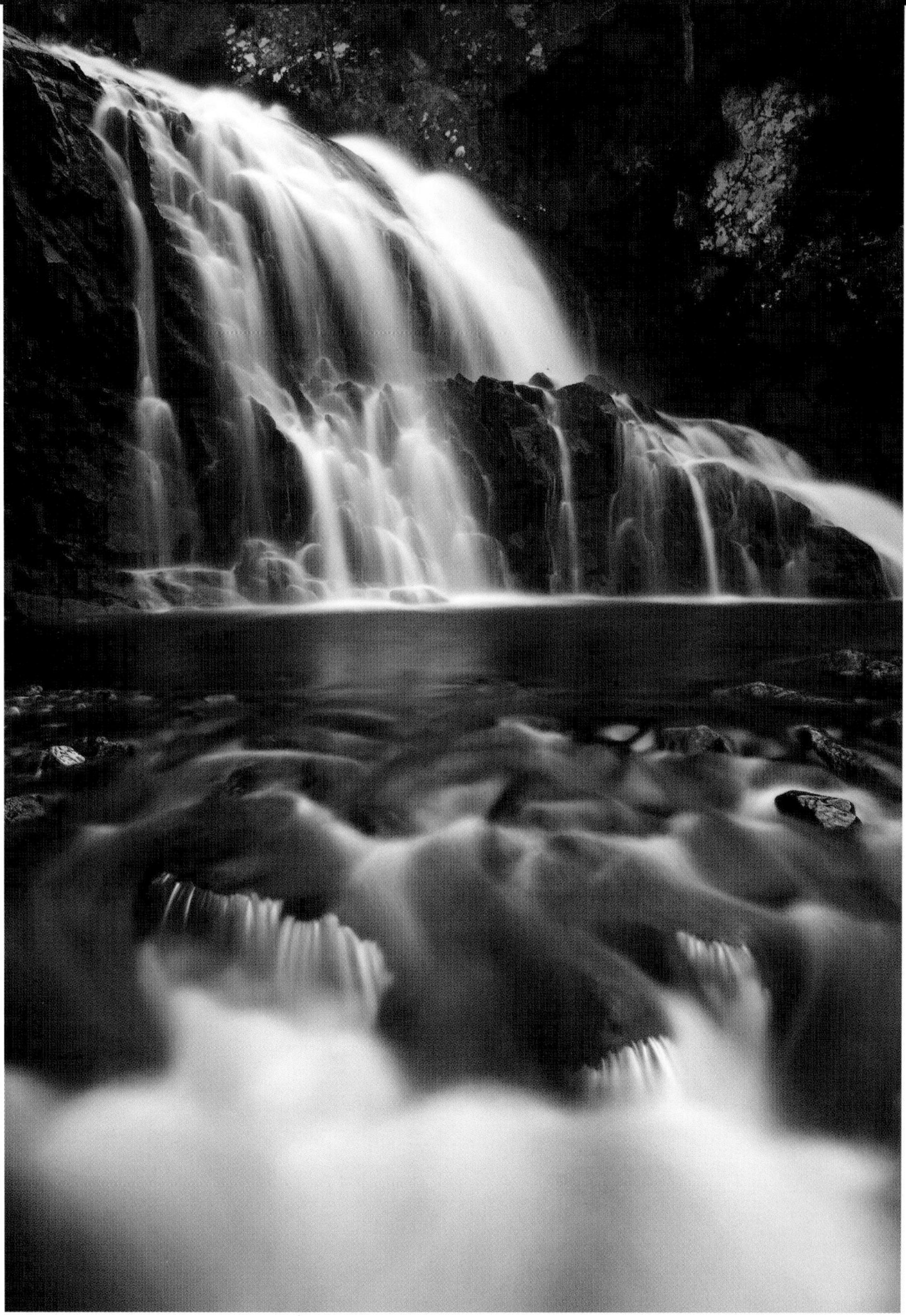

FENCE IN SNOW – ARCTIC LOFOTEN

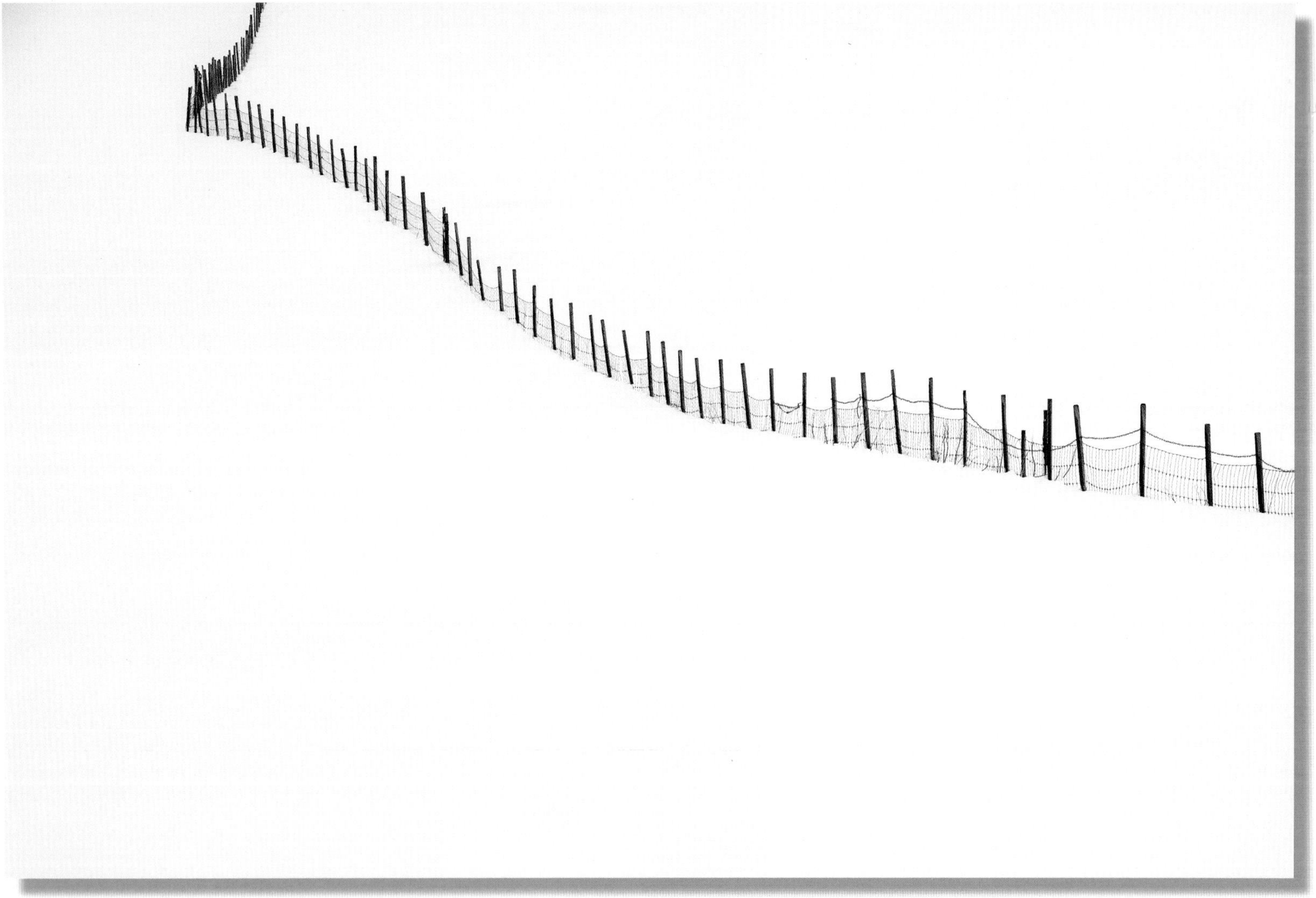

Working after heavy snowfall is a real treat and also a challenge because getting about can be tough. Everything was minimised by the snow and I was left to simply explore the shapes and rhythms of the landscape. There are no 'rules' when it comes to this type of photography and the freedom is exhilarating.

Nikon D800e, 70–200mm lens, f16, 1/60 sec.

FERNBEG – APPLECROSS PENINSULA, SCOTLAND

This area of the Scottish Highlands feels remote and is largely untouched so you can easily lose yourself in the environment. I had seen this area of rocky outcrops hugging the sea on an OS map so I parked my car and headed out for a short walk. The geological features are fascinating here and they present themselves as large platforms and sharp crags overlooking Loch Torridon. It was these sharp and graphic shapes that kept me engrossed for many hours on this day and I have been back many times since.

Nikon D800e, 24mm PC-E Lens, Lee Filters 0.6 Hard Grad, Lee Filters Little Stopper, f13, 40 secs.

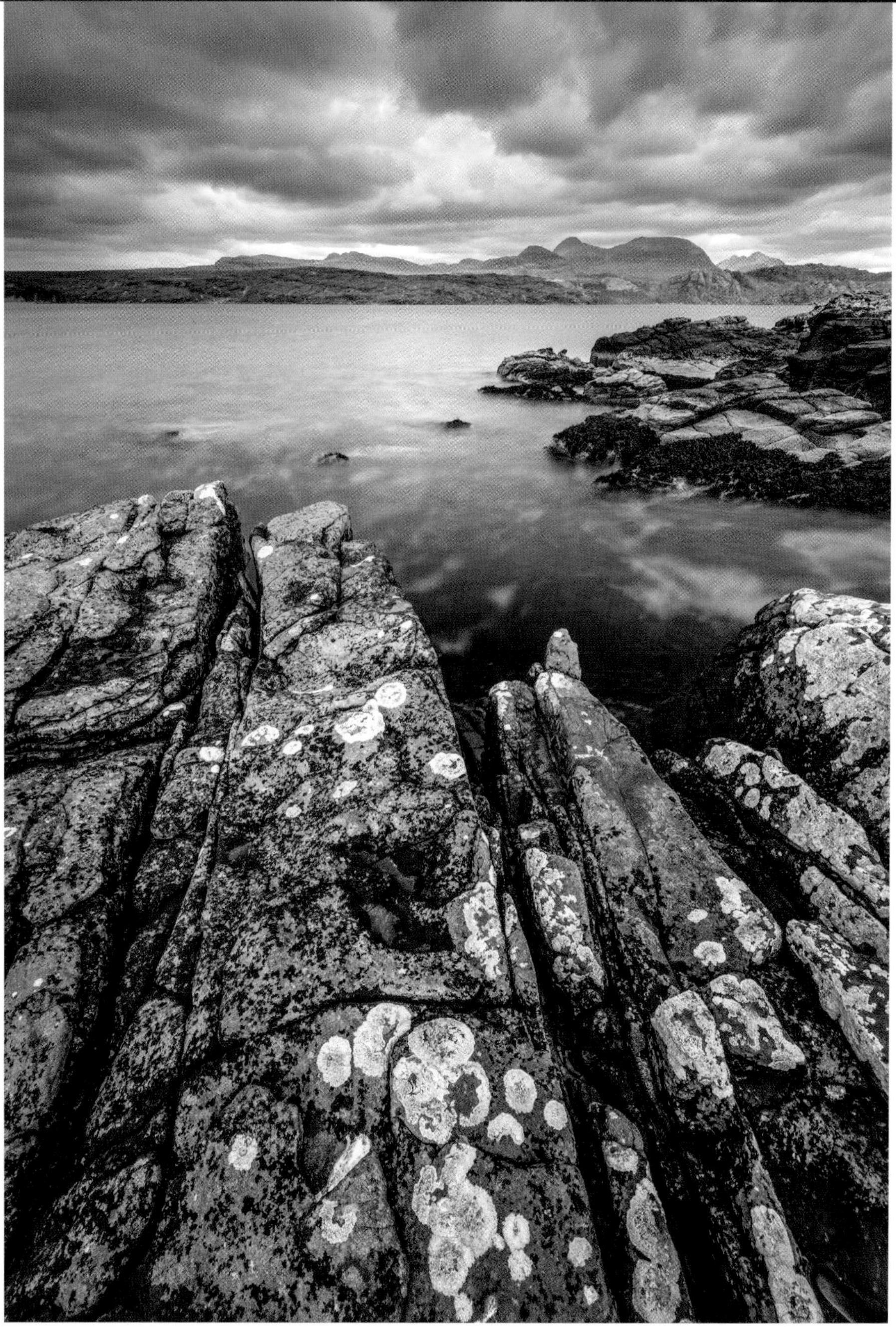

ICE PATTERNS – ARCTIC LOFOTEN

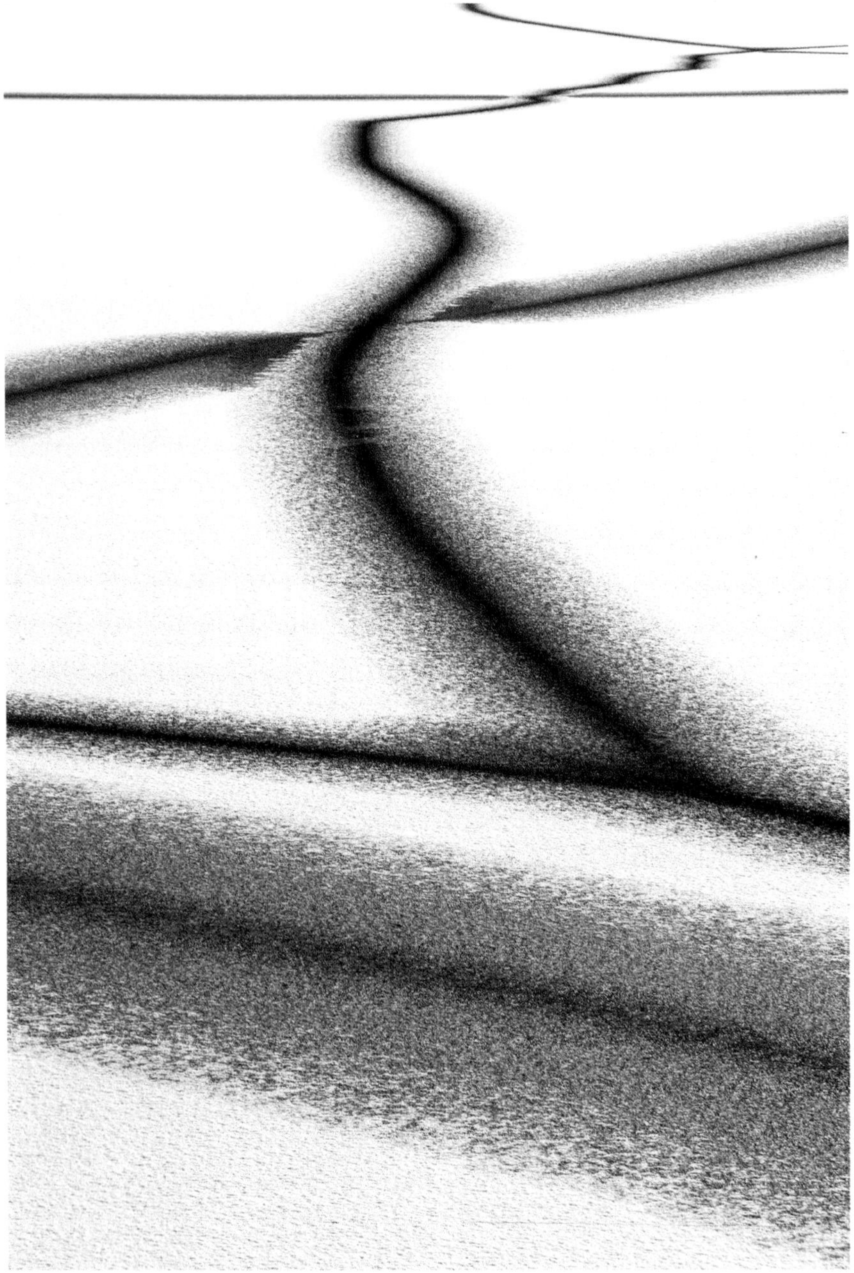

I was heading for the dramatic mountains surrounding the picturesque village of Reine when I noticed that this fresh water lake at the roadside had begun to break up due to the rising temperatures. The shapes were the epitome of what nature can offer to us as landscape photographers, and only the day before it was a solid white frozen mass. I used a long lens to deliberately 'compartmentalise' each of the intriguing curves and shapes of the cracks in the ice. On my return later that day the lake had almost completely melted and I was so glad that I had acted on intuition and stopped to capture this image.

Nikon D800e, 70-200mm lens, f18, 1/60 sec.

Looking out over the Inner Sound towards the Black Cuillin Mountains on the Isle of Skye this evening was almost meditative. The light was low as a warm sun was setting and the ebb and flow of the receding tide made for an incredibly relaxing few hours of photography. The water was gin-clear and I fitted a polariser so the pale boulders beneath the seawater could be seen in the final image.

Nikon D700, 24mm PC-E lens, Lee Filters 0.6 Hard Grad, Lee Filters Polariser, Lee Filters Big Stopper, f13, 8 minutes.

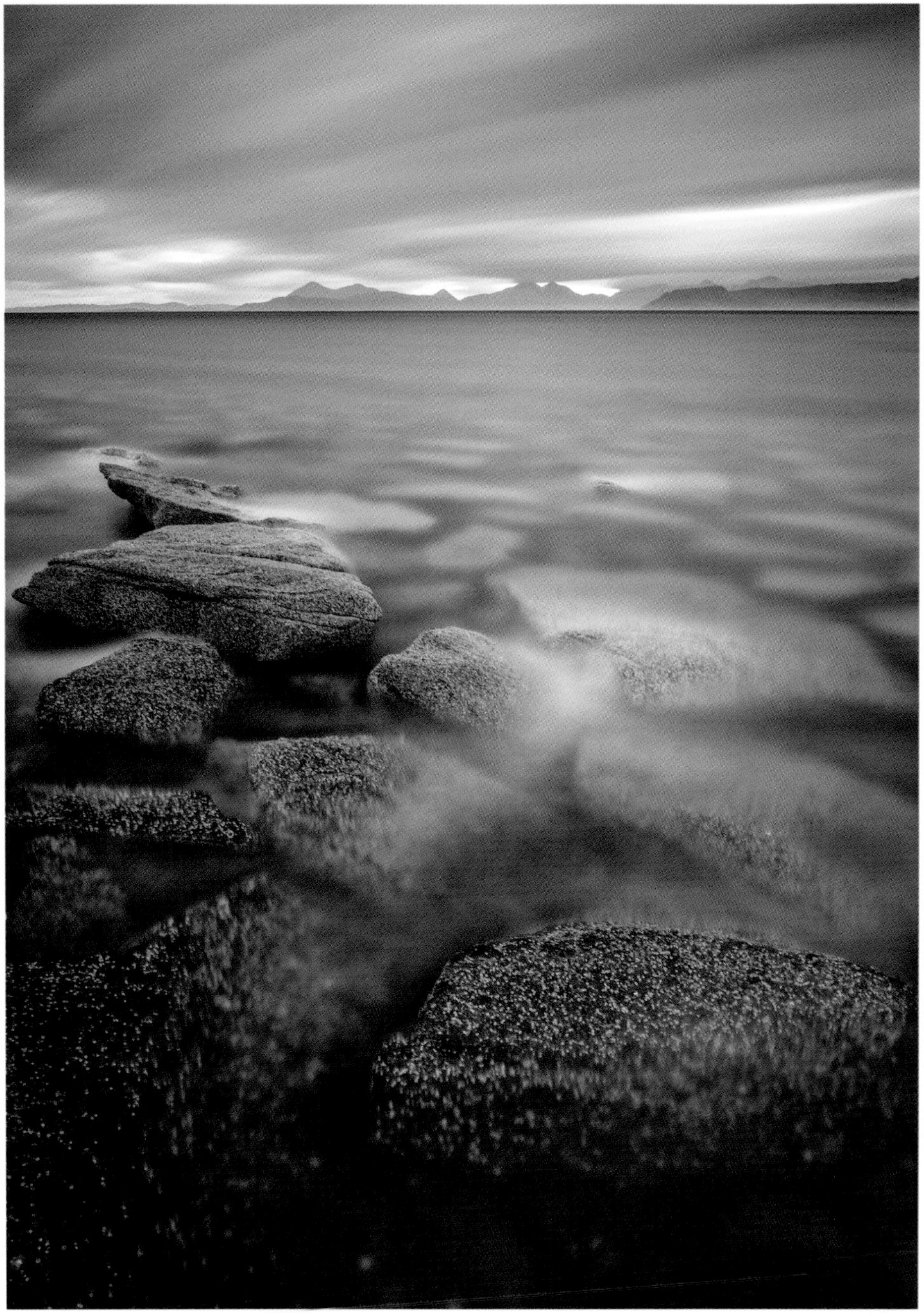

KILBRANNAN SOUND AND ARRAN

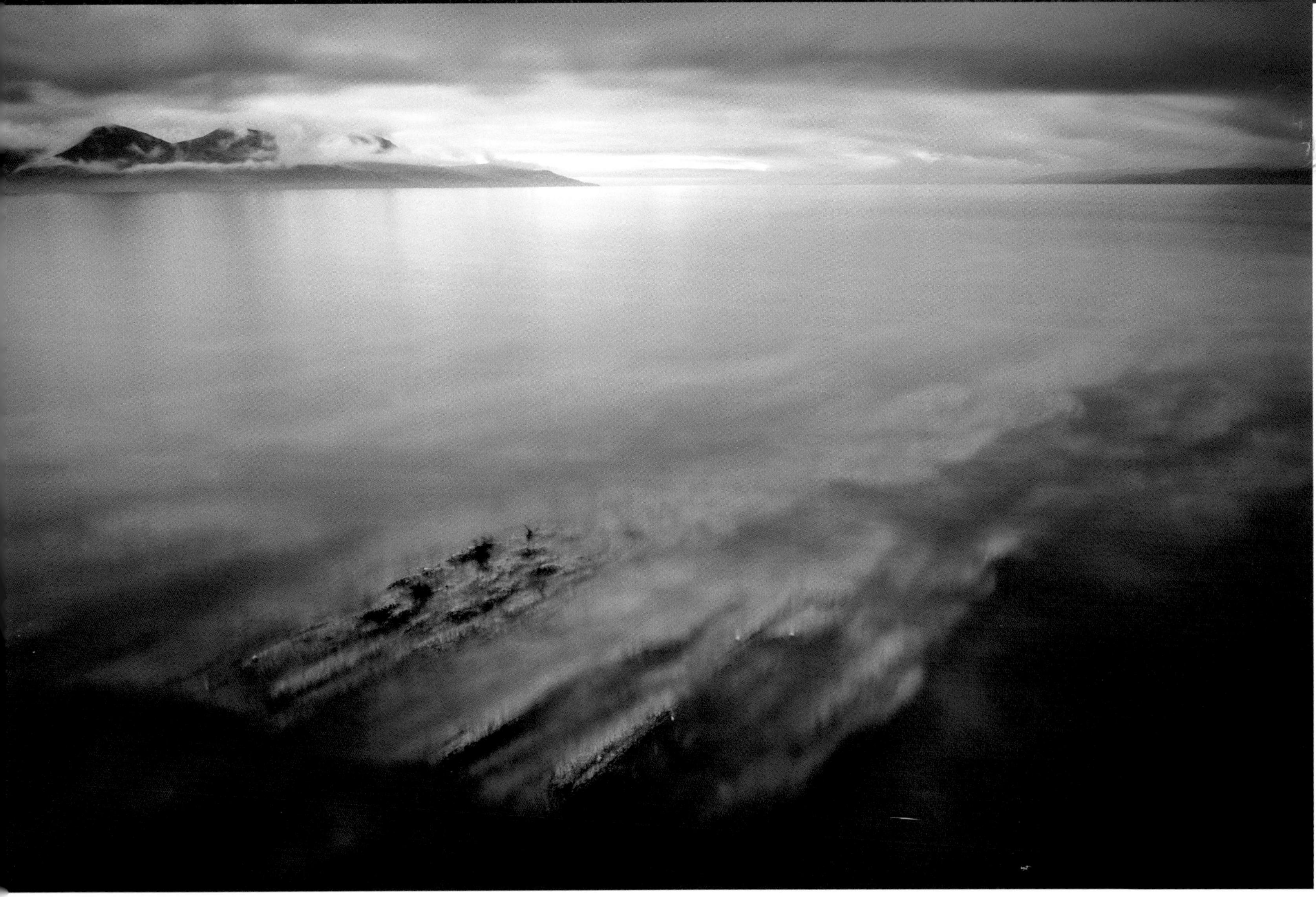

Kintyre is a place I love very much and I have been there with my camera more than 20 times over the years. As the tide slowly encroaches the peninsula the bedrocks that have been exposed all day are gradually covered until the next day. The Isle of Arran on this evening was beginning to be covered by mist and cloud, which added a certain ethereal quality to the moment.

Nikon D700, 24mm PC-E lens, Lee Filters 0.6 Hard Grad, Lee Filters Polariser, Lee Filters Big Stopper, f13, 4 minutes.

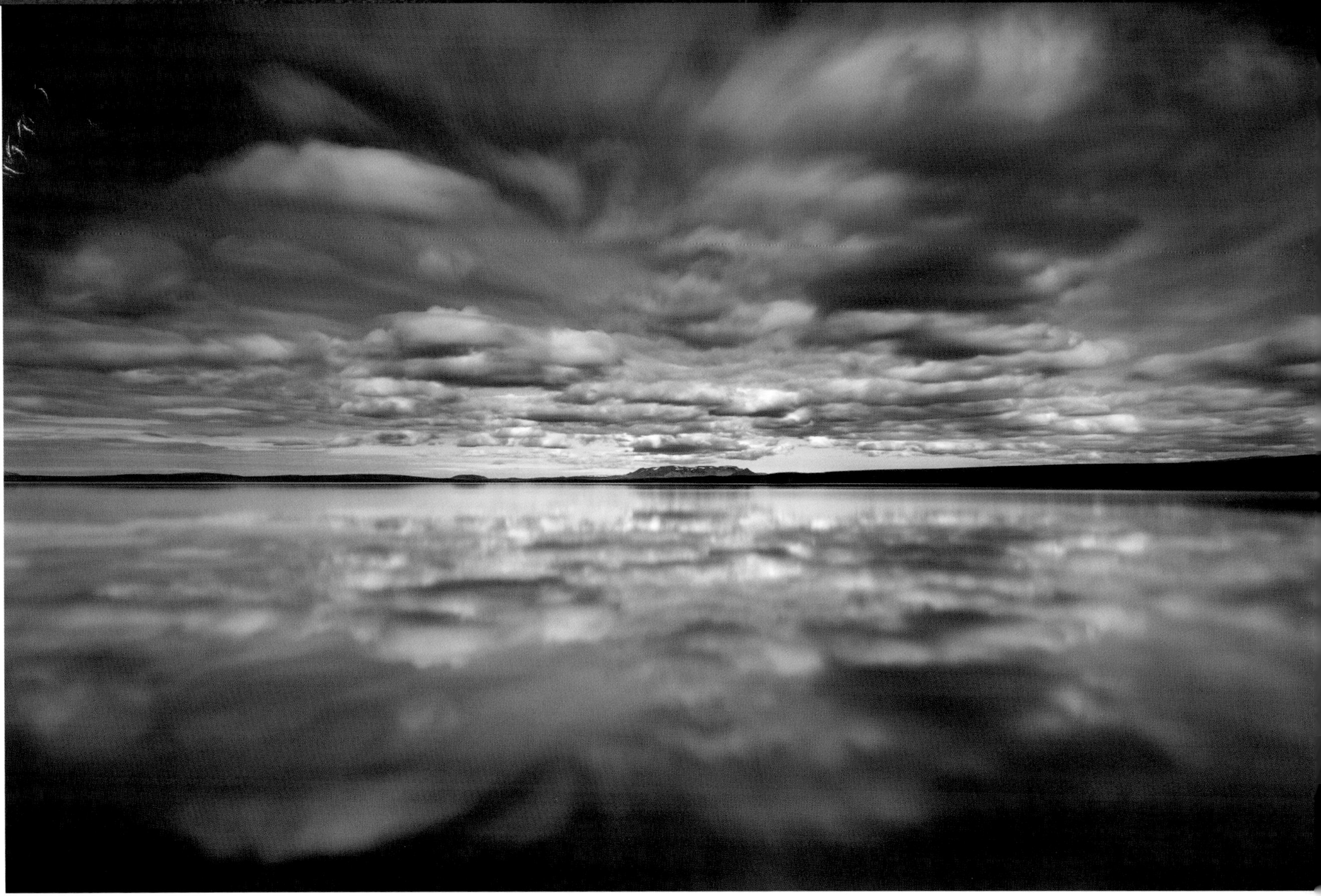

The landscape of Iceland seems to surprise me every time I go and this visit was no different. This area in the north east of the island is an almost lunar-like landscape with lakes filling the hollows left by old volcanic activity. The day was warm without the slightest breath of wind and with a smattering of cloud as I approached the mirror-like Masvatn Lake. I decided to break all the so-called rules of composition and place the horizon across the centre of the frame. As far as I am concerned, if we all stuck to 'rules' then landscape photography would soon become very formulaic indeed!
Nikon D800e, 24-70mm lens, Lee Filters 0.6 Hard Grad, Lee Filters Little Stopper, f16, 30 secs.

LOCH CLAIR – TORRIDON

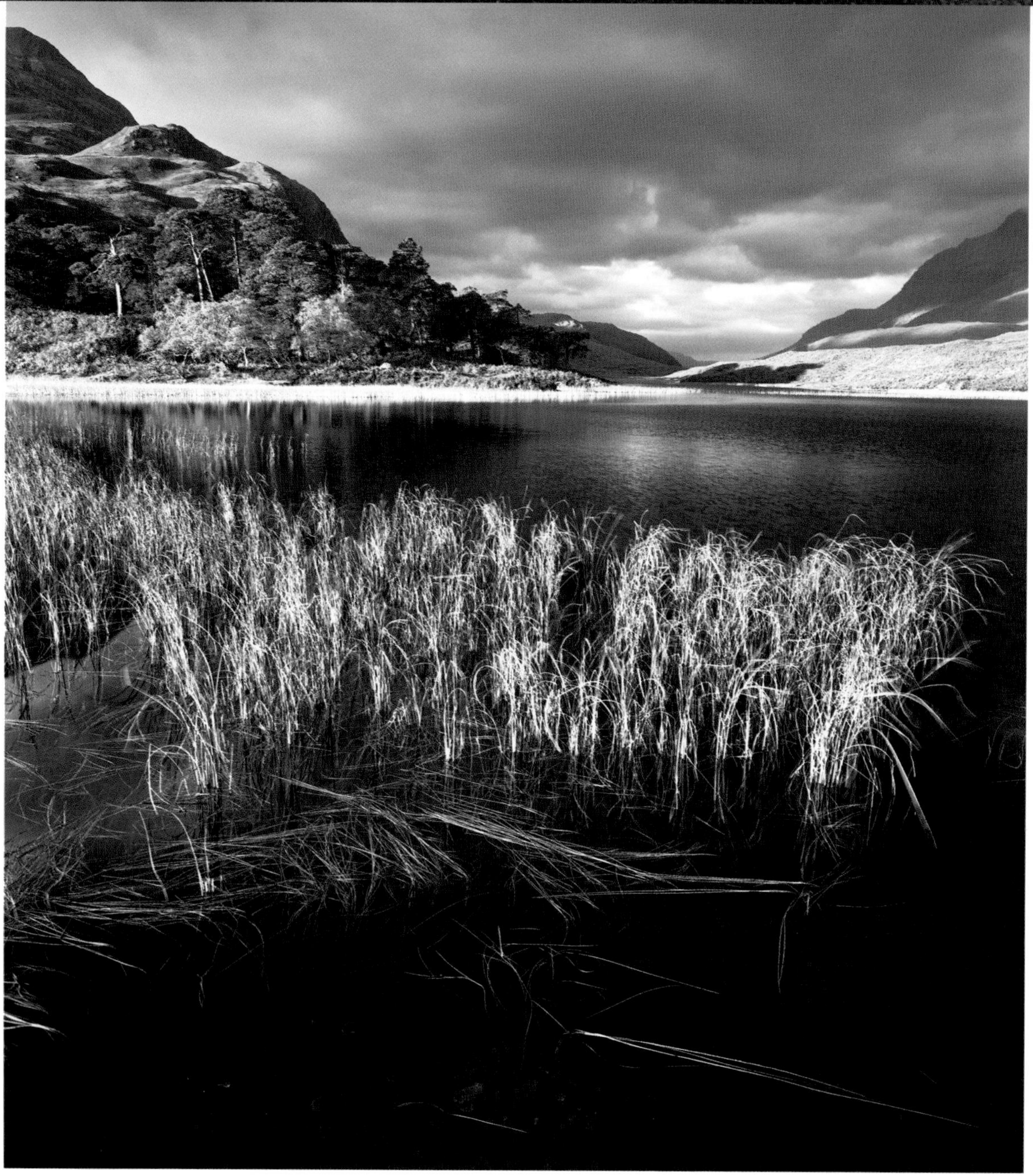

This photograph was taken while I was still using film and large format cameras. As the sun rose it shone on the far bank of Loch Clair, on the foot of Liathach and it also picked out the reed bed in the foreground of the composition. It was somewhat tricky to site the camera on its tripod in the water to enable me to get the position I wanted. For this reason alone, I wear wellington boots whenever I am out with my camera. I always say, 'The best composition is always two feet into the water, and it's often the two feet in your wellies'!

Ebony 45SU large format camera, 90mm lens, Lee Filters 0.6 Hard Grad, Lee Filters Polariser, f22, 1 sec.

LOCHAN – GLEN COE

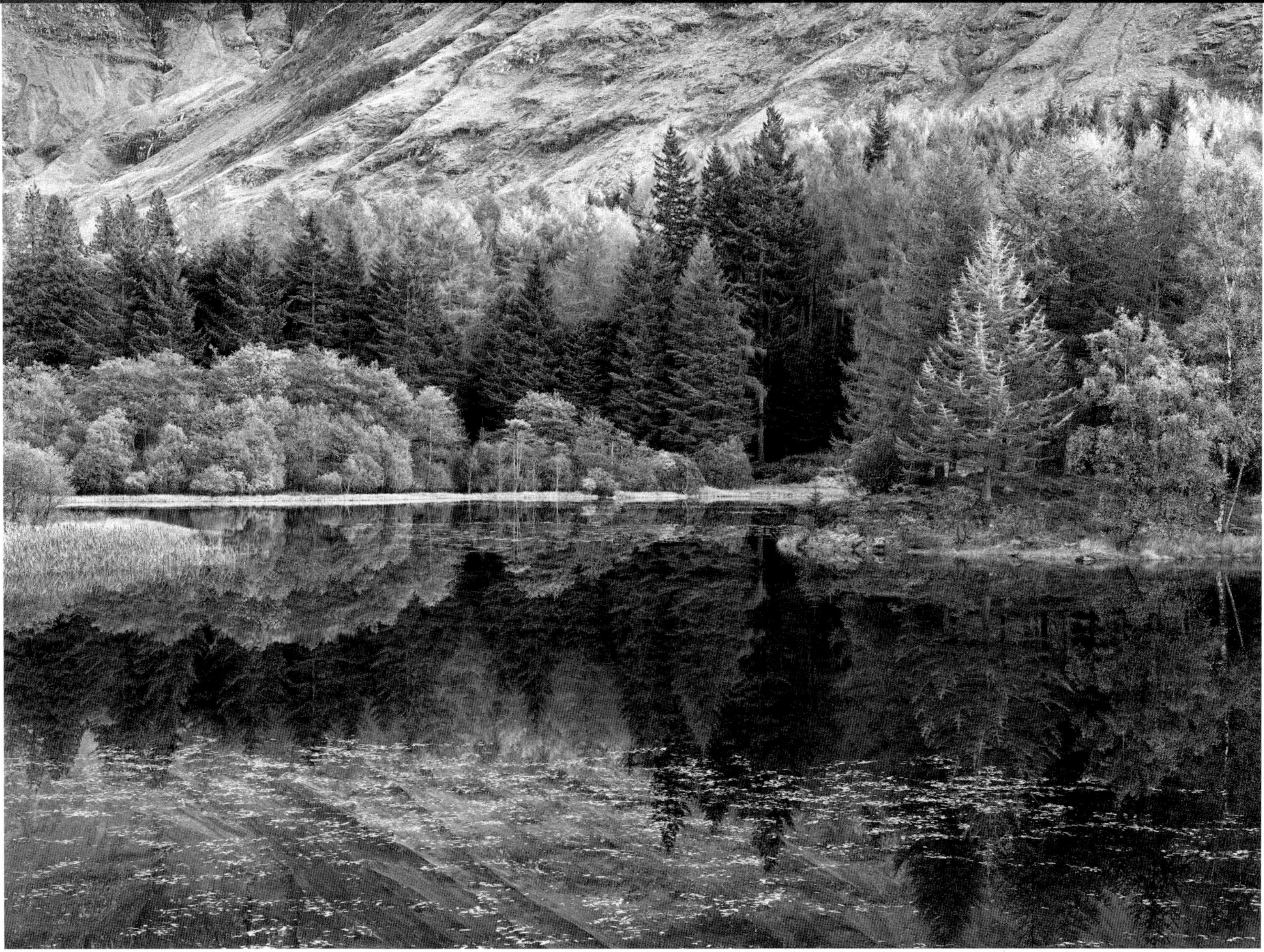

This little Lochan is almost hidden from sight and is nestled down a back road that leads to Glen Coe Village. At this time of year, I am drawn to the wonderful tones of grey that the different greens in the tree foliage will offer. This, combined with it being a very still day, made the reflections perfect for a simple and tranquil photograph with no sky needed at all. I have recently been back to this location and sadly many of the trees have now been felled.

Ebony 45SU large format camera, 150mm lens, Lee Filters Yellow Filter, f22, 1 sec.

POND STUDY – ISLE OF HARRIS

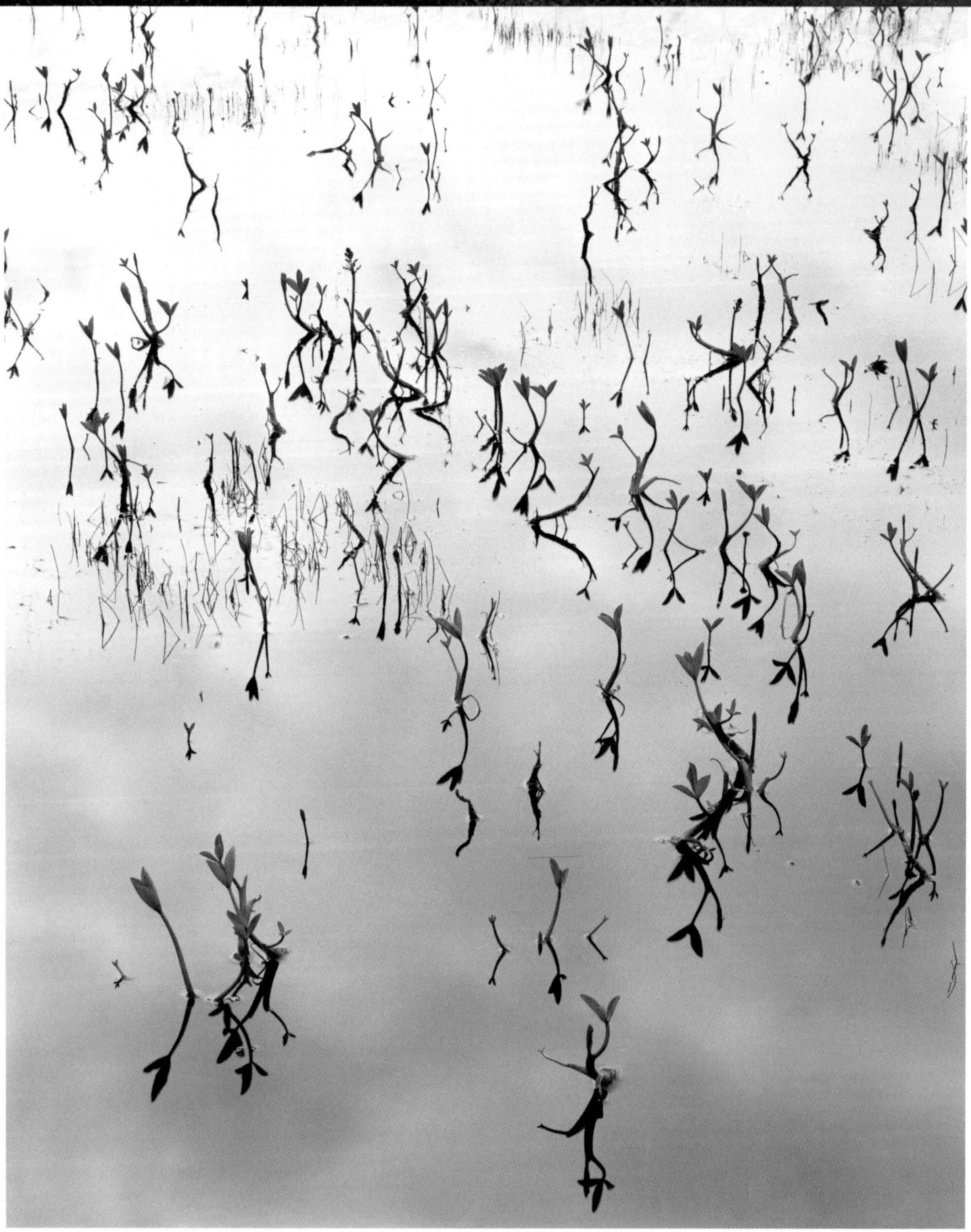

It is easy to be drawn to the wonderful, wider coastal landscapes, particularly when you are venturing around the beautiful Outer Hebrides in Scotland. In springtime these little ponds come to life with plants that grow from the mud below the surface. I was literally up to my knees in mud when I was making this photograph! The key for me was to retain the fine intricate details of the plants between gusts of wind, as well as to portray the reflected clouds above.

Ebony 45SU large format camera, 120mm lens, f22, half a sec.

RECEDING PYLONS – ICELAND

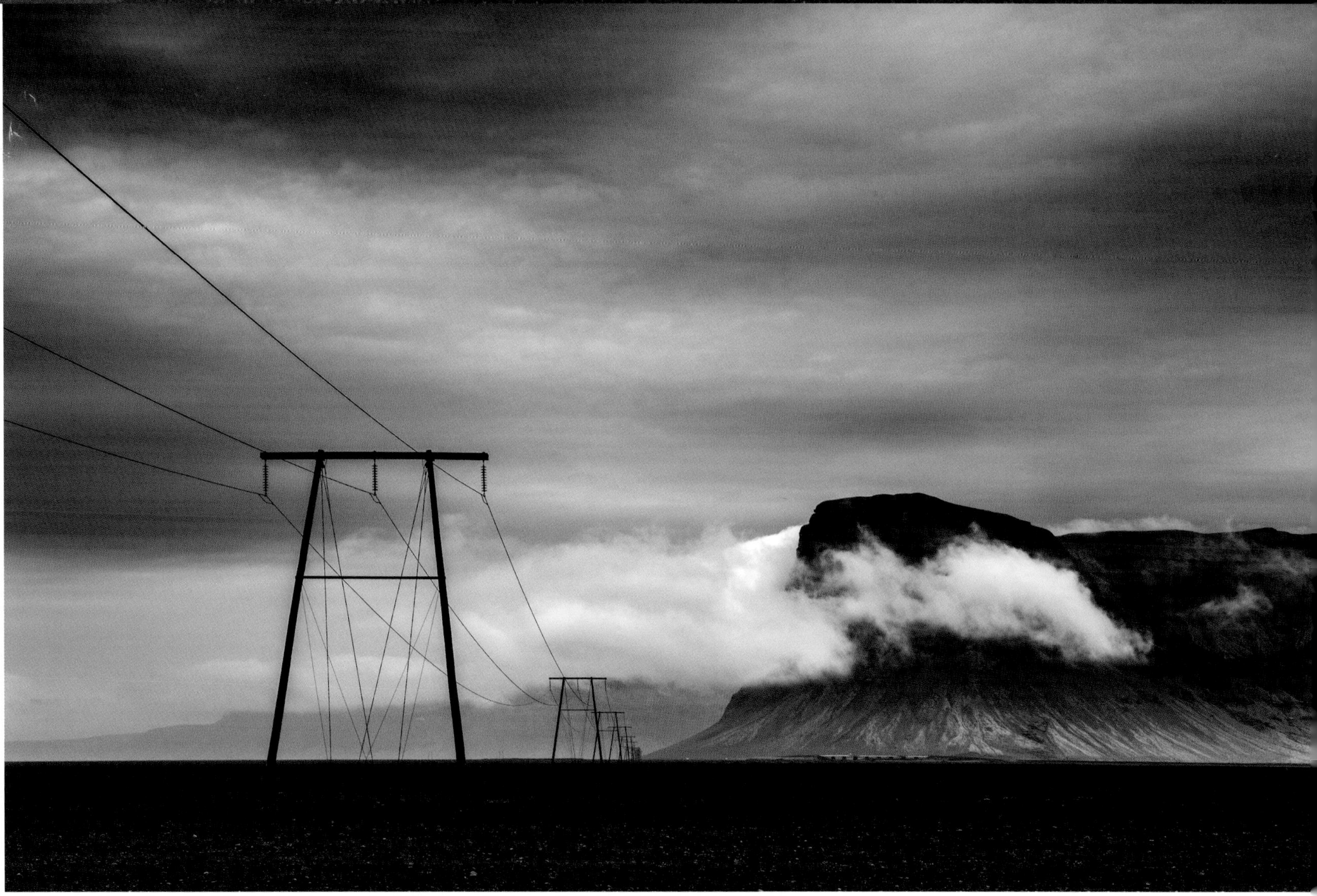

Because Iceland is a mainly very mountainous and unpopulated island, all of the man-made structures such as pylons follow the flatlands near the coast and they run in fantastic straight lines for miles. I had passed this mountain many times on my journeys through Iceland but on this occasion a cloud veiled it. I left the comforts of my car and headed out across the barren flats towards the line of pylons. I was very specific about what I wanted in the photograph – the pylons receding to the base of the mountain. As I set my camera on the tripod the clouds fortuitously broke revealing the mountaintop.

Nikon D800e, 24–70mm lens, Lee Filters 0.6 Hard Grad, f16, 2 secs.

RIVER ETIVE – GLEN ETIVE

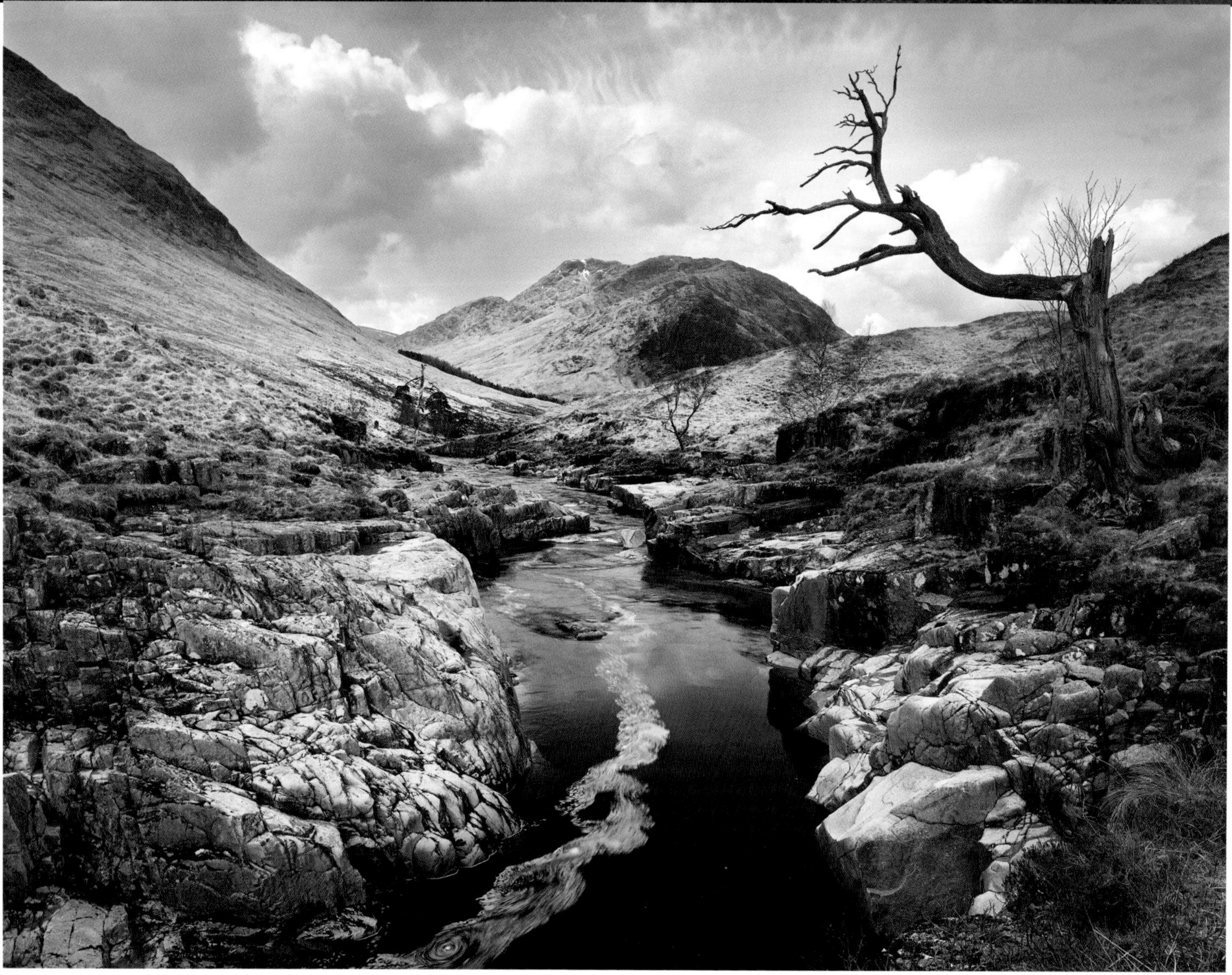

Glen Etive runs from the edge of Rannoch Moor and Glen Coe to Loch Etive and it has one of the great waterfall systems in the UK. Along its way, the River Etive cuts through pale Scottish granite and there is an array of old dead Caledonian pine trees that cling to the edge of the ravines. I had climbed down to this particular tree on many occasions but, on this particular day, there was a quietness to the place with the waters running slowly and soft light with gentle clouds in the skies above the distant mountains. The camera was perched on the very edge of a 30ft ledge to ensure the flow of water bubbles were positioned centrally in the composition.
Ebony 45SU large format camera, 90mm lens, Lee Filters 0.6 Hard Grad, f22, 1 sec.

ROCK POOL – LOFOTEN

On this cold winter's morning I ventured out to Vikbukta, which is a small community on the coast accessed only by a tunnel bored though a mountain. This coastline is subjected to the harsh arctic winters and the ferocity of the Norwegian Sea. The power of the ocean cuts hollows in the stone foreshore, in which large boulders are nestled like dinosaur eggs. I seldom use super-wide lenses but on this occasion it was imperative for me to include the dramatic shapes of the rock pool in the foreground as well as the grandeur of the distant mountain that towers over the sea. The composition leaves no empty space so I had to be careful not to include my tripod leg in the frame.

Nikon D800e, 16- 35mm lens, Lee Filters 0.6 Hard Grad, Lee Filters Little Stopper, f16, 30 secs.

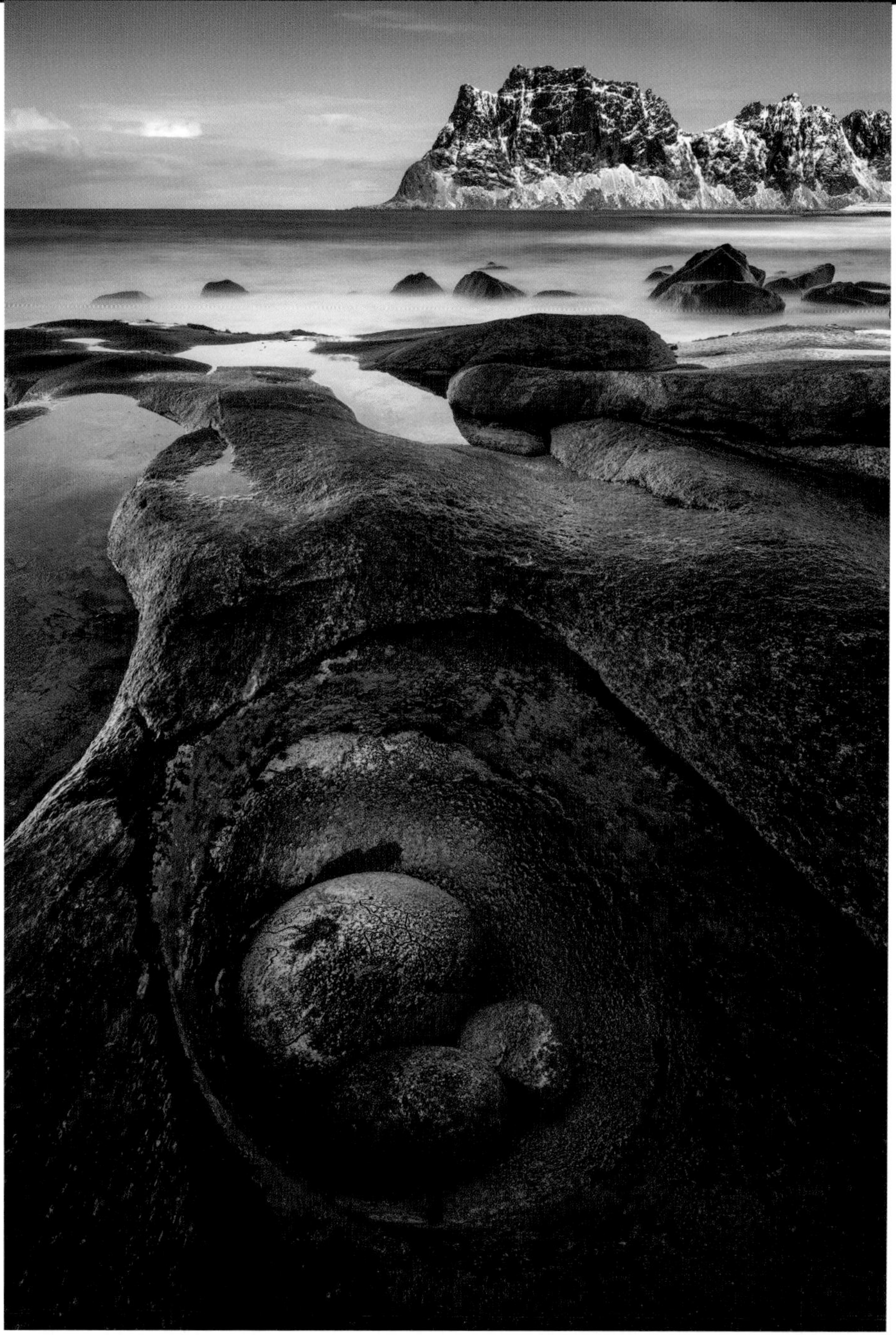

SEILEBOST – HEBRIDES

Seilebost is a breath-taking place to be with its wide open swathe of white sands and prevailing winds that never seem to calm. When the tide is completely out you can walk for hours on these untouched sands without seeing any footprints and as a landscape photographer you have a beautiful blank canvas to work with. The thing I love the most about working on coastal environments is not when the sun shines but when there is an impending storm. On this day the sky darkened, the contrast of tones between the dark clouds and white sands was made more apparent and it made me feel all the more exposed to the powers of nature.

Nikon D700, 24mm PC-E lens, Lee Filters 0.6 Hard Grad, Lee Filters Polariser, f13, 15 secs.

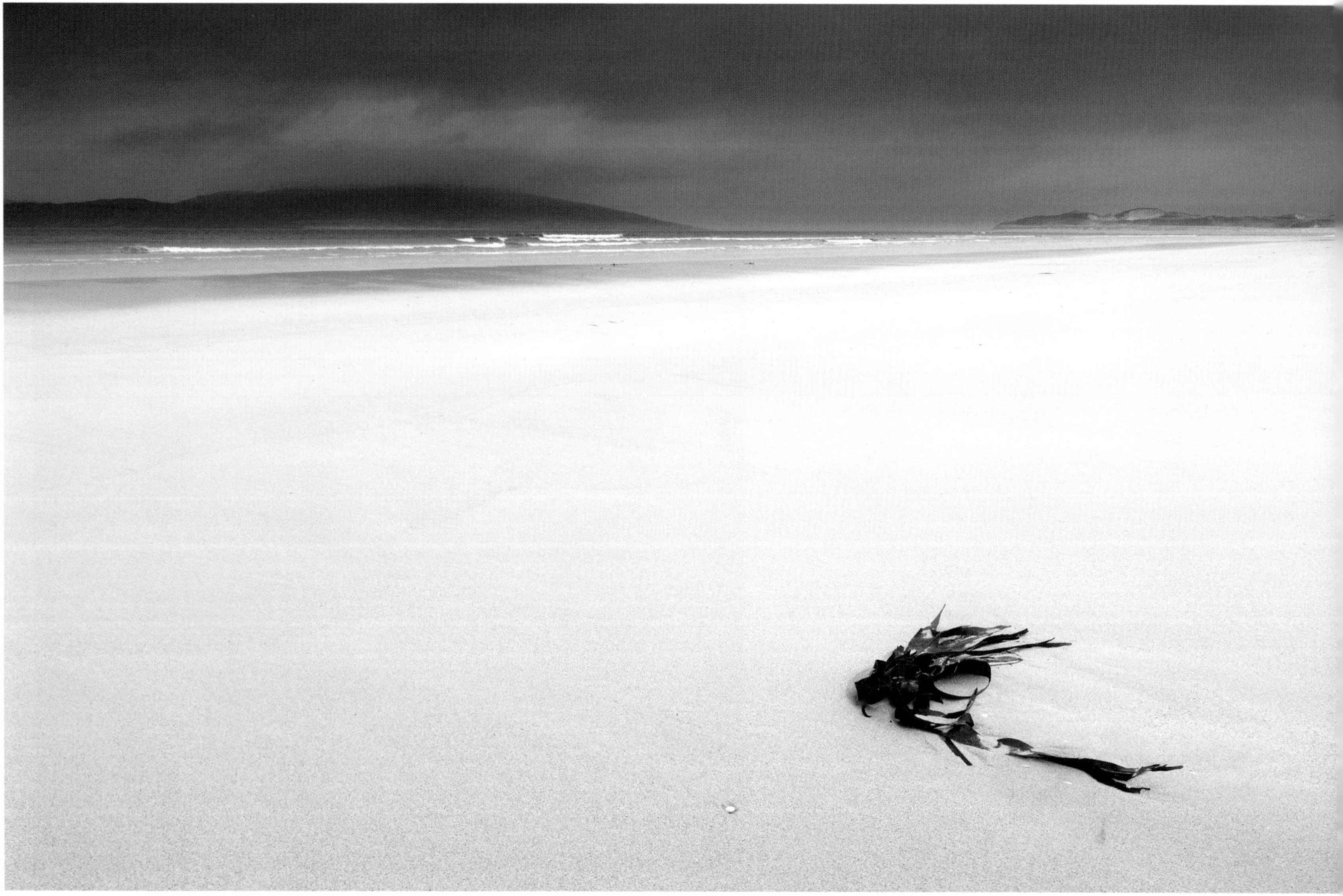

SLIOCH – WESTER ROSS

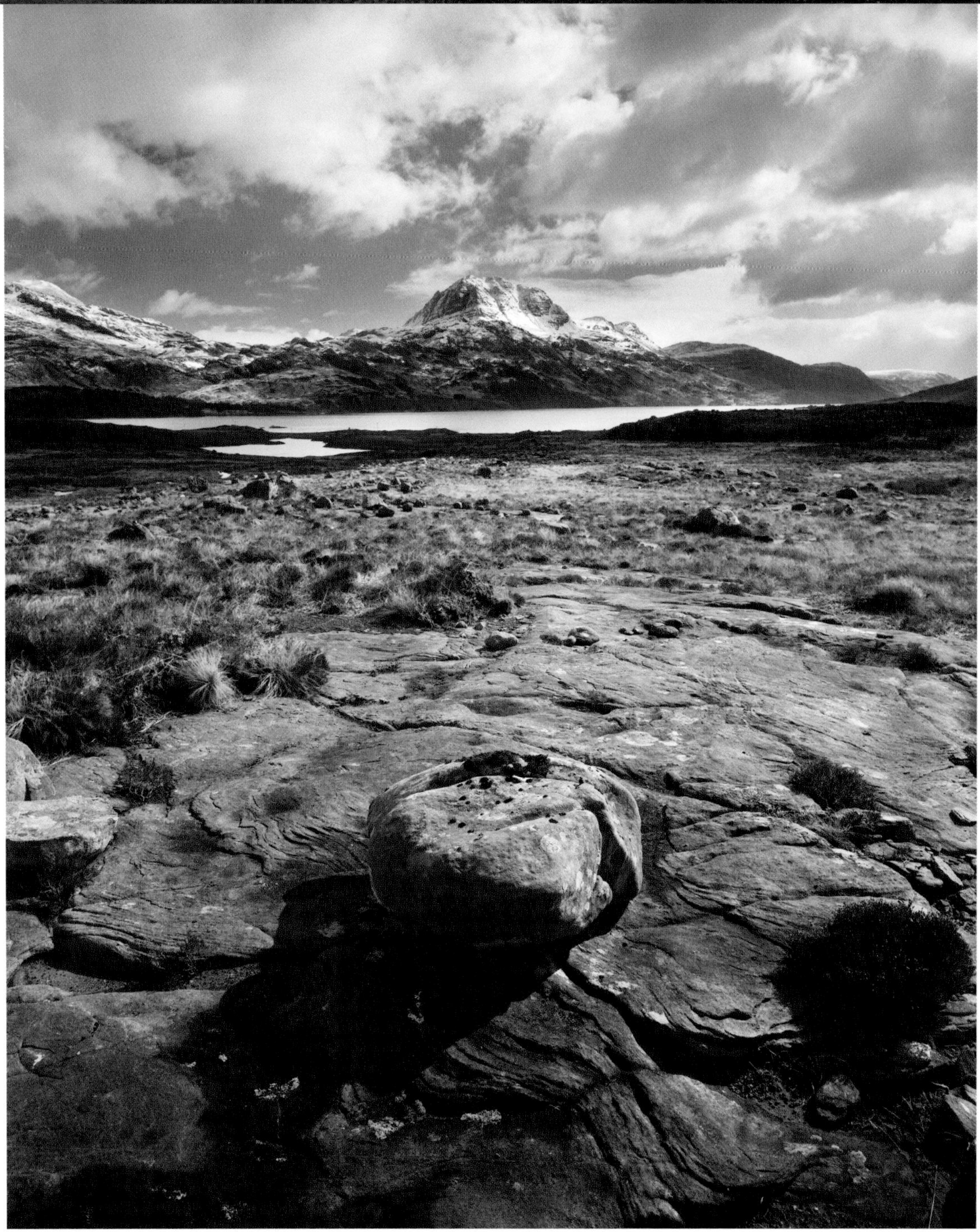

This mighty mountain stands proudly above the banks of Loch Maree, in what I would describe as my favourite part of the Scottish Highlands to be with a camera. On the south bank of Loch Maree there is a glacial boulder field in which you can find boulders perched high on rock outcrops that look as though they have been placed there by man. As you can see from this photograph, I like to use symmetry in my work and the boulder and Slioch occupy the central line of the image. I had to wait for some time before I was rewarded with a milky sunlight, which illuminated Slioch and provided a delicate shadow to the left of the boulder I had chosen for my foreground.

Ebony 45SU large format camera, 90mm lens, Lee Filters 0.6 Hard Grad, f22, 1 sec.

STORM AND WAVES

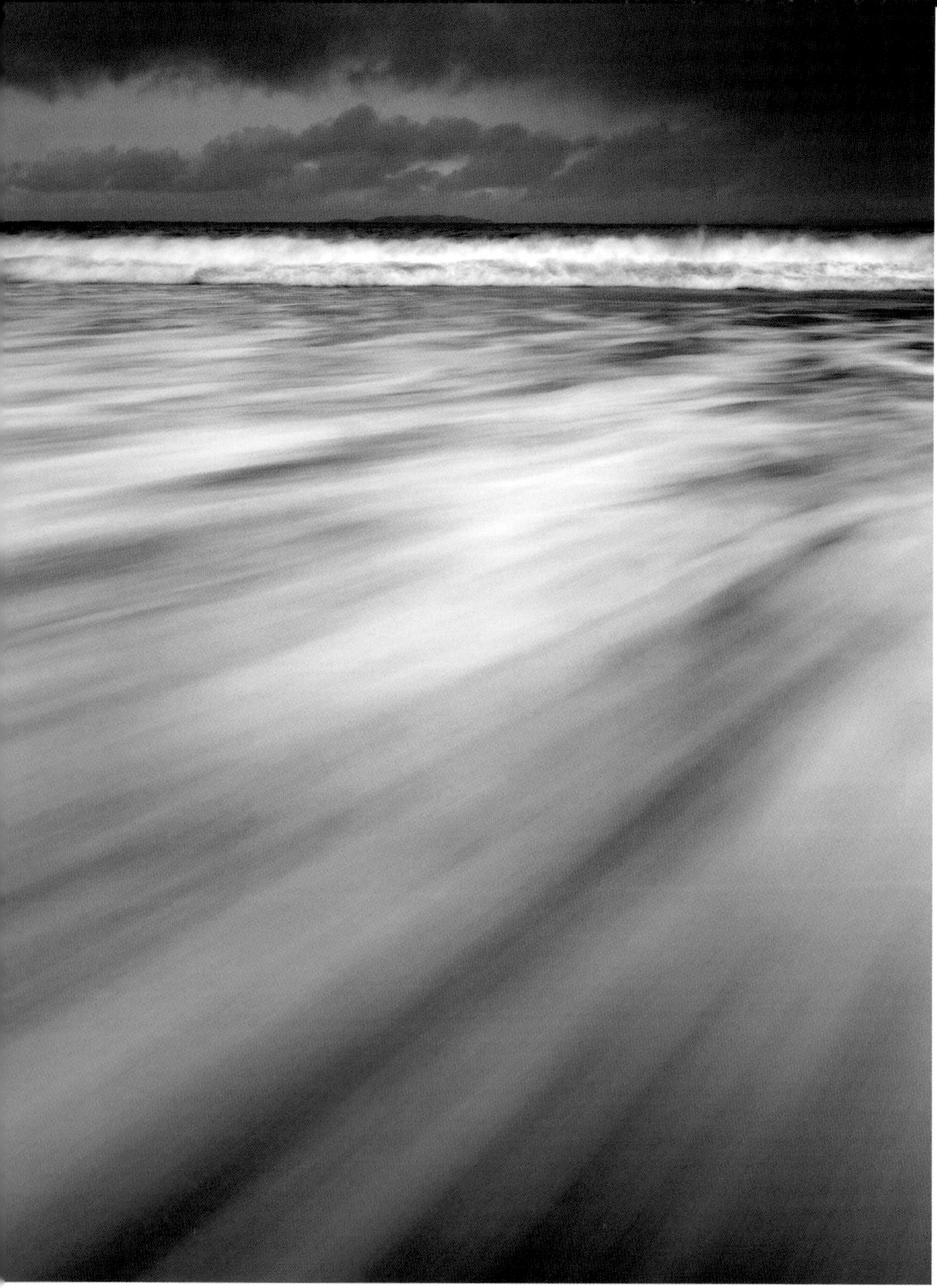

I love to stand in water and I love the feeling of its energy and strength as the waves pass by. I had set myself a challenge on this day as what I pre-visualised was the receding water and the cresting waves beneath the dark skies of the approaching storm. I walked into the sea with my tripod and set the camera dangerously low so as to maximise the water movement. At the same time I had to wait and judge the sequencing of the waves so, when I made my exposure, this feature would be clear to see. The correct exposure time was crucial as I needed the full structure of the crashing wave without it being blurred.

Nikon D800e, 24mm PC-E lens, Lee Filters 0.6 Hard Grad, Lee Filters 0.9 Neutral Density Filter, f13, half sec.

TWO TREES – ARCTIC LOFOTEN

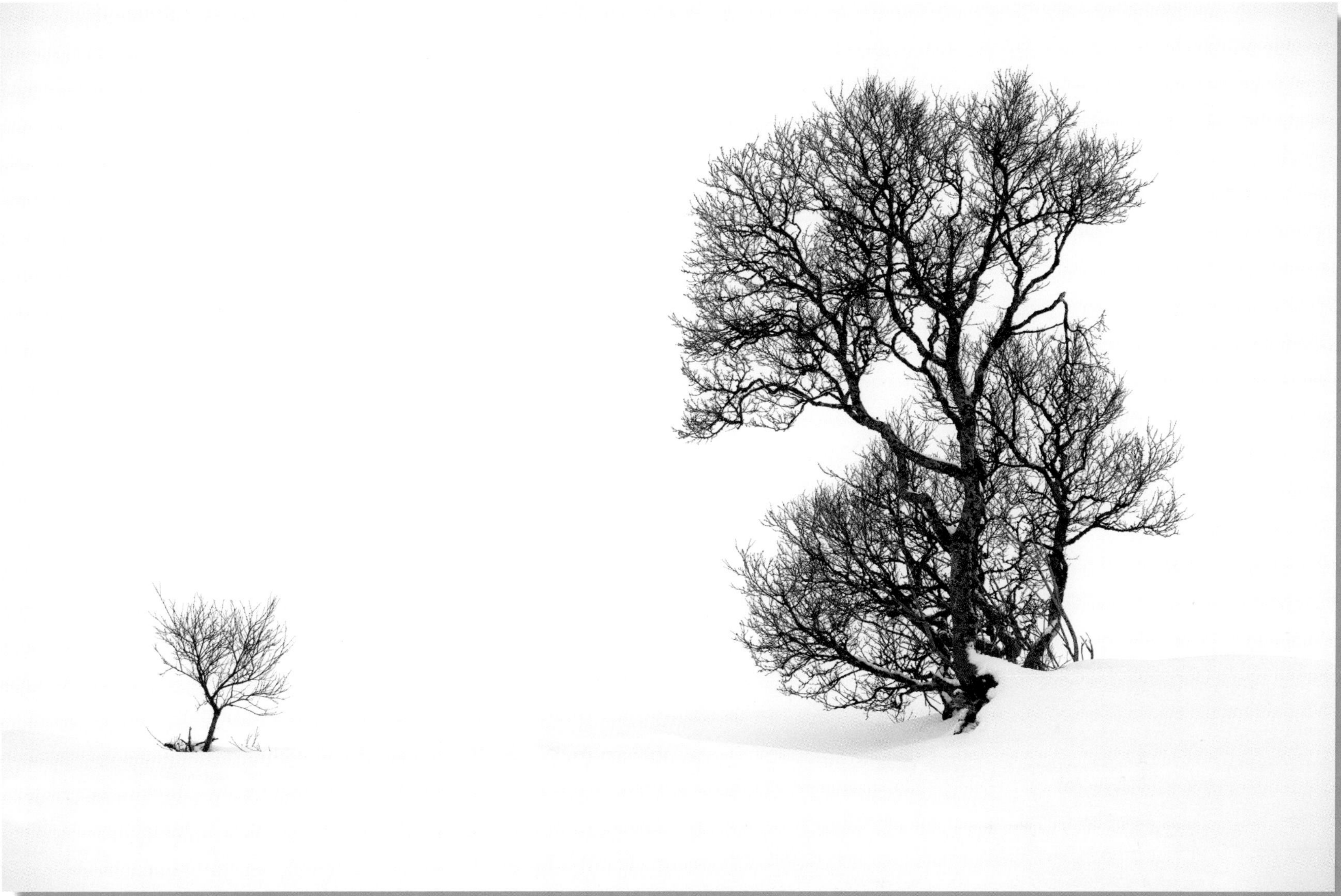

Simplicity was all I wanted to explore in these extremely cold but stunning conditions. While exploring this area I noticed there almost seemed to be a relationship between the two trees – an apparent parent and child bond. A simple photograph of what is essentially a very simple subject, in which I was careful to ensure that I had captured the important subtleties of the shadows beneath the trees.

Nikon D800e, 70–200mm lens, f18, 1/60 sec.

OLDSHOREMORE – SUTHERLAND

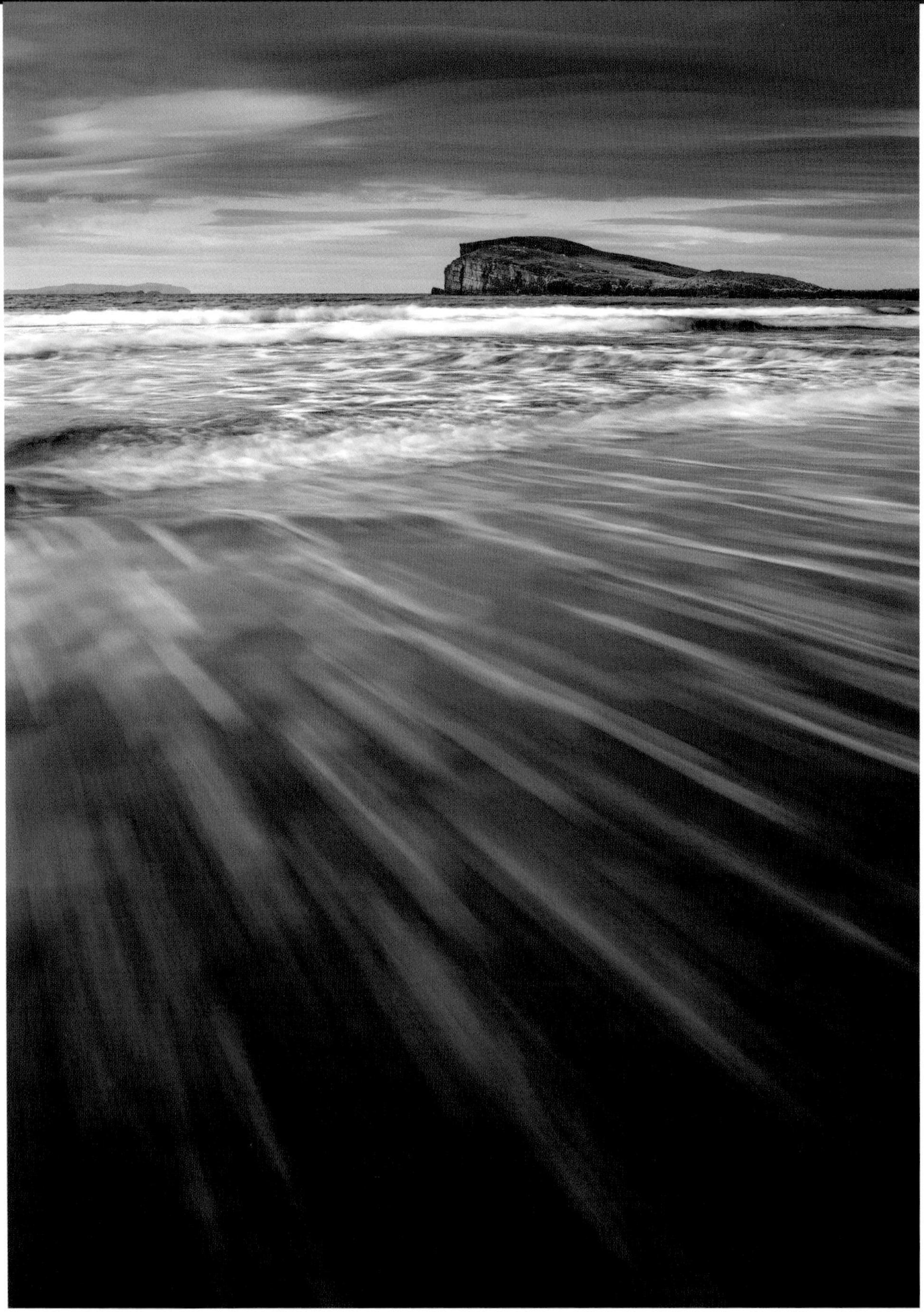

Oldshoremore is quite simply the jewel in the crown of Scotland mainland beaches with white sands and often nobody there!

Nikon D800e, 24mm PC-E lens, Lee Filters 0.6 Hard Grad & 0.9 Neutral Density Filter & Polariser, 0.5 sec., f13.

JOKULSARLON BEACH – ICELAND

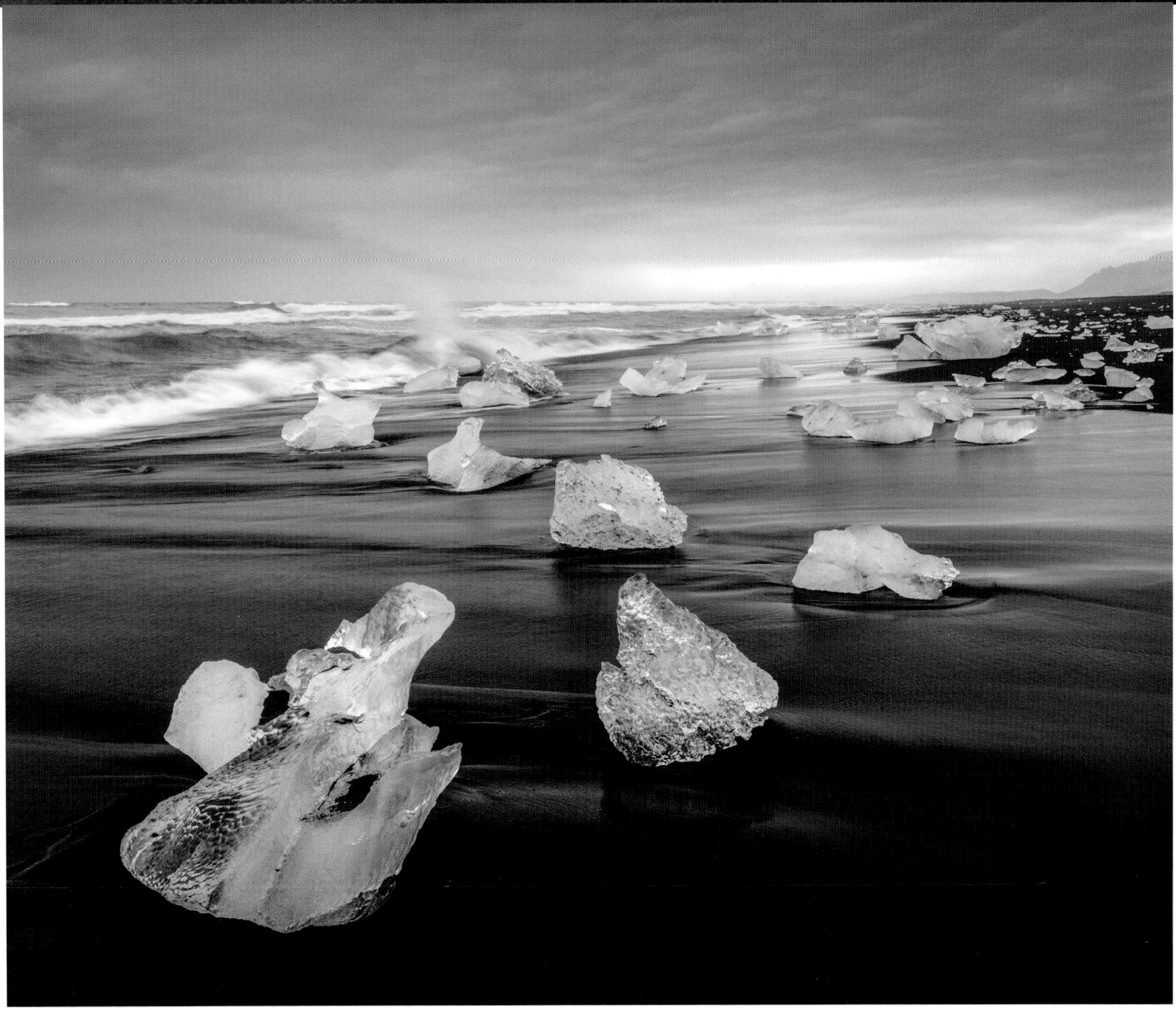

As ice is pushed into the Atlantic from Jokulsarlon Glacial Lagoon it is smashed up by the powerful waves and these jewel-like remains are laid onto the pristine black sands.

Nikon D800e, 24–70mm lens, Lee Filters 0.6 Hard Grad & Polariser, 15th sec, f16.

FLAKSTAD MOUNTAINS – LOFOTEN, ARCTIC NORWAY

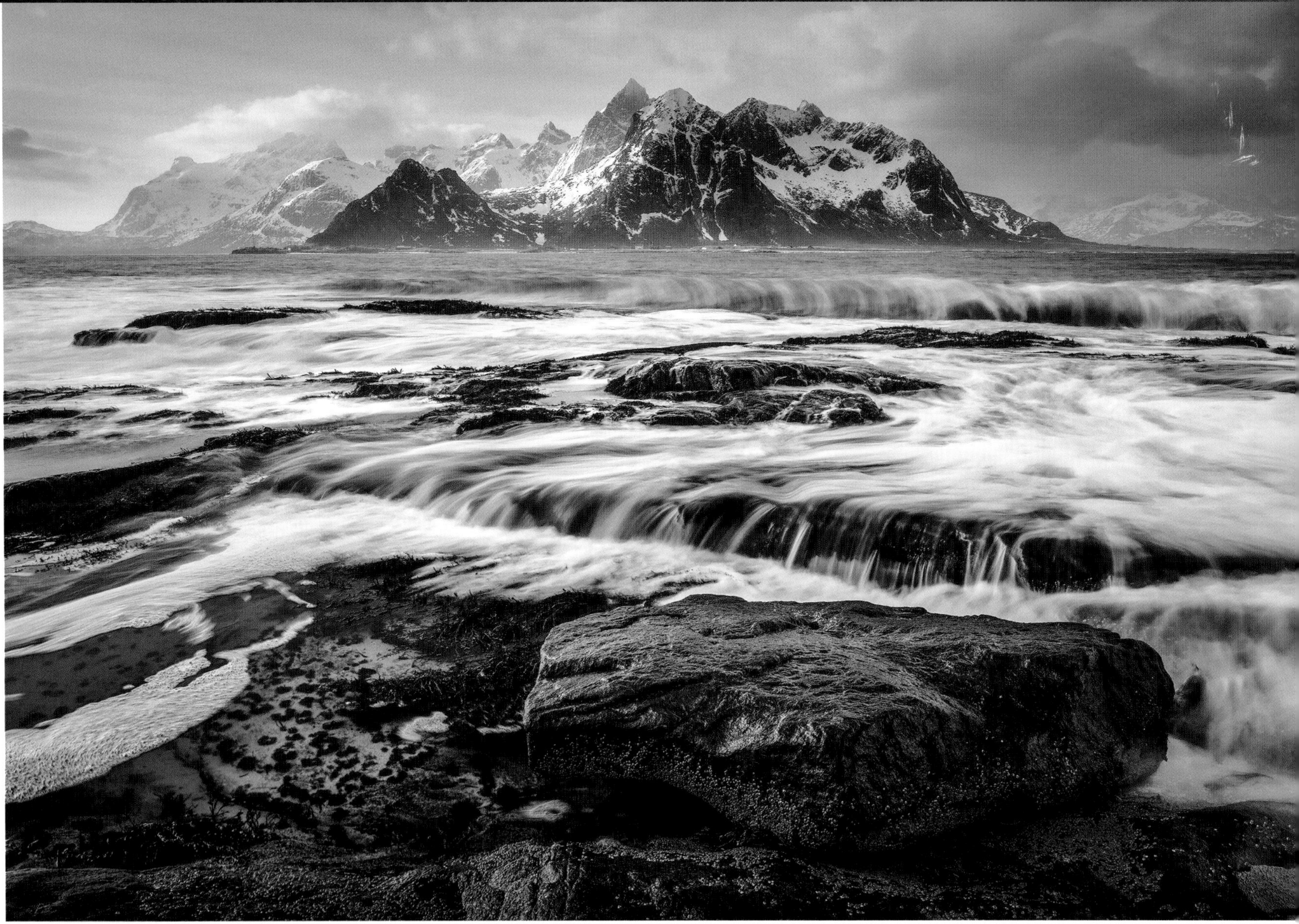

The tide returns as the distant storm clears and begins to lap over the rocky shore. Moments later the entire platform was beneath the fjord.

Nikon D800e, 42mm PC-E lens, Lee Filters 0.6 Hard Grad & Polariser, 0.5 sec., f13.

EL CAPITAN & MERCED RIVER – YOSEMITE VALLEY

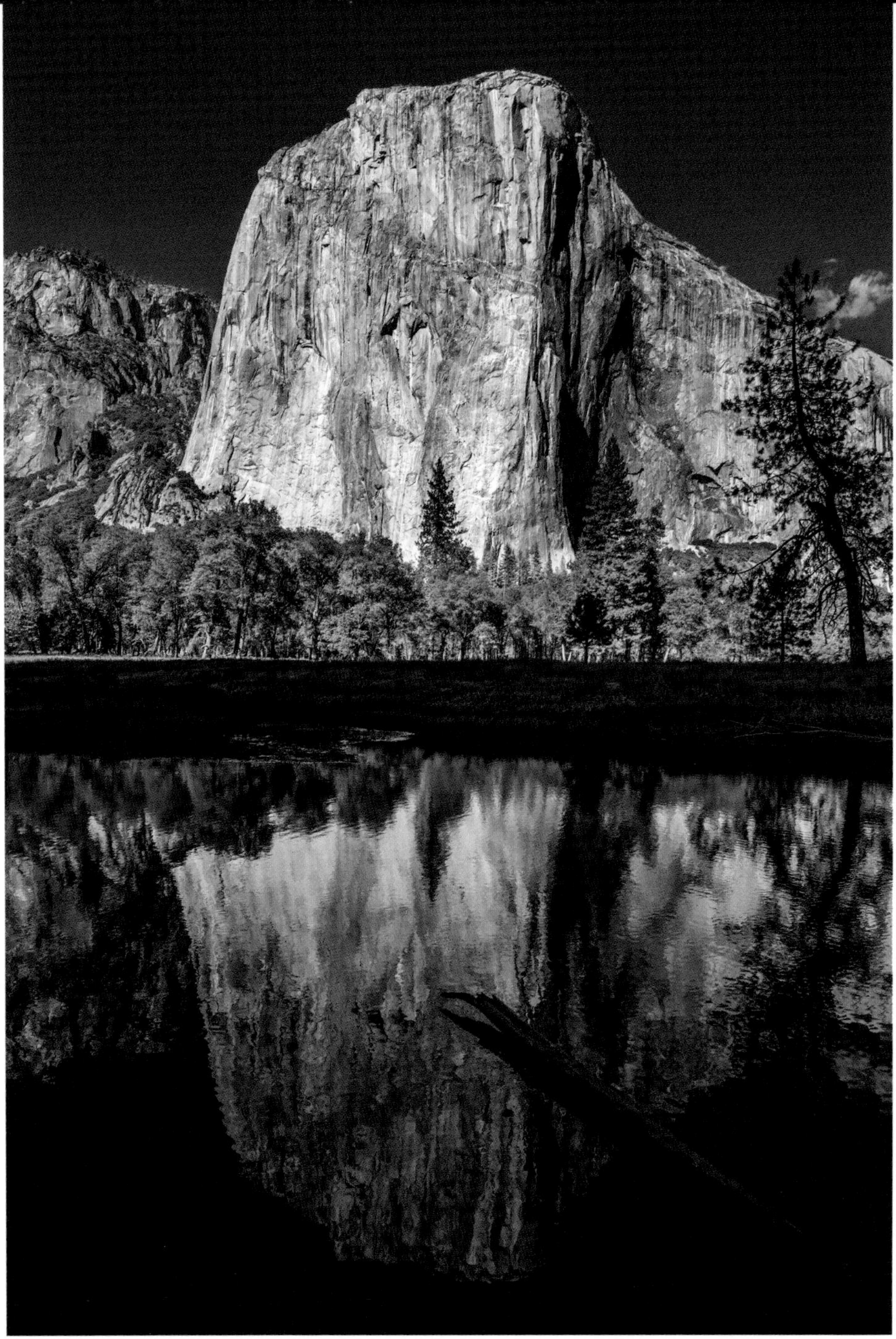

Yosemite Valley was deathly still and silent without a cloud in the sky and it was a treat to see the 3,000-foot monolith of El Capitan towering above me as well as reflected in the waters at my feet.

D800e Nikon, 16–35 mm lens, 40th sec., f14.

APPROACHING STORM – YOSEMITE VALLEY, CALIFORNIA

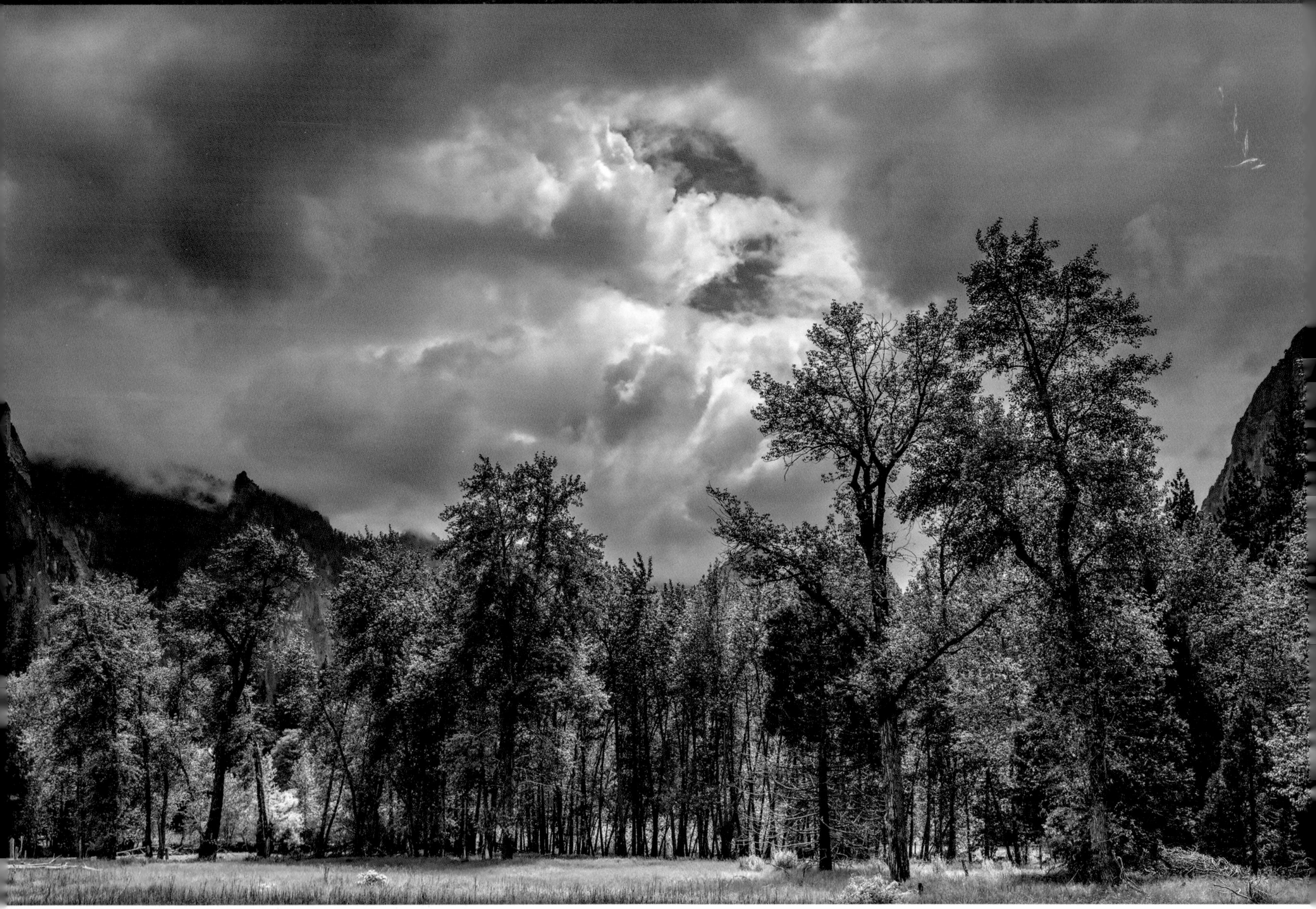

I had to work very swiftly as the light was breath-taking but the weather rapidly closed in and, soon after, a downpour took place. *Nikon D800e, 70-20mm lens, Lee Filters 0.6 Soft Grad, 50th sec., f16.*

TUOLUMNE MEADOWS – YOSEMITE NATIONAL PARK

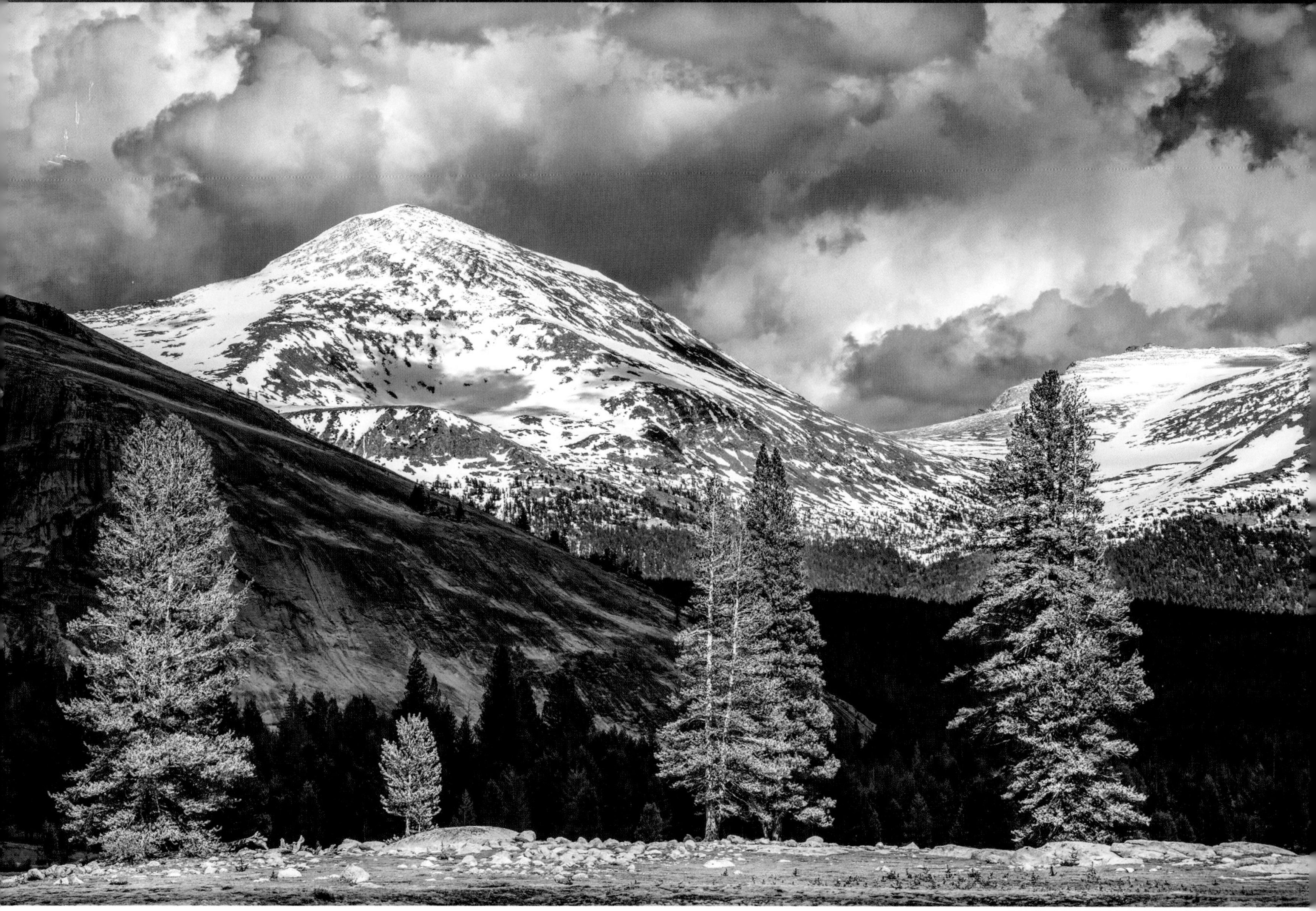

At almost 8,000 feet above sea level the weather conditions at Tuolumne Meadows can change quickly and the cloud on this late afternoon made for a spectacular theatre of transient light.

Nikon D800e, 70–20mm lens, Lee Filters 0.6 Soft Grad, 40th sec., f16.

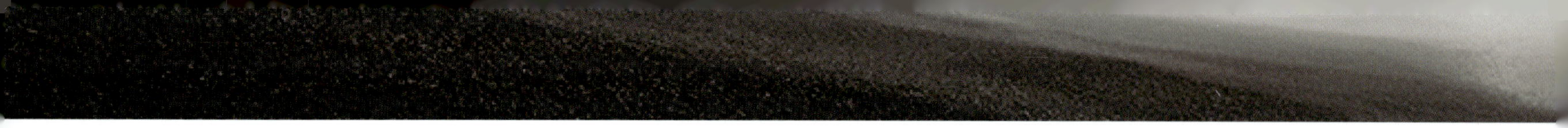

RHE Media Photography Titles

Series Editor: Tony Worobiec

Photographing Landscape and Weather by Tony Worobiec
Using Free Image Manipulation Software by Peter Cope

MASTERCLASS TITLES:
Developing a Photographic Style by David Penprase
Exploring Black and White Photography by Paul Gallagher

For more information about our PhotoActive and PhotoWise series please visit our Photography website at **www.RHEMediaPhotography.co.uk**

RUSSIAN COOKING

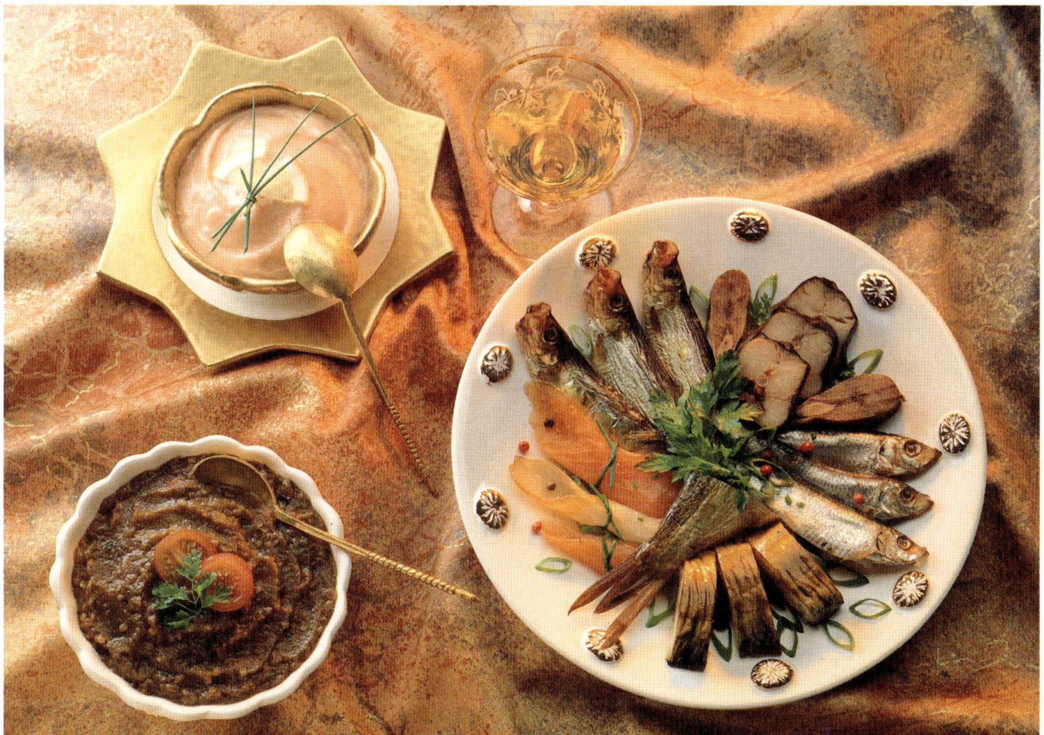

HAMLYN

Acknowledgments

The publishers thank the following people, companies and organizations for their contributions to this book and for their help in producing it:

Prascovie Brun and Anne Le Prat (text); Bernard Mandin (photography); Guy Bouchet/ Conran Octopus (photos, pages 5 and 7); Marie-Hélène Clauzon (food preparation); M. Leonid Semionovitch at the Régal; Siècle; Orfèvrerie Christofle; Bernardaud; Jacques Molin; Philippe Deshaulières; Porcelaine de Limoges; Union Limousine; and the restaurant A la ville de Petrograd, Paris 8e.

First English edition published 1990 by
The Hamlyn Publishing Group Limited
a division of the Octopus Publishing Group
Michelin House
81 Fulham Road
London SW3 6RB

ISBN 0 600 56543 2

ISBN 0 600 57013 4 (unjacketed)

First French edition published 1990
by Librairie Gründ, Paris

Produced by Mandarin Offset
Printed and bound in Hong Kong

Note: all recipes, unless otherwise stated, provide servings for six people.

Contents

RUSSIAN COOKING

Russia, that vast land straddling the continents of Europe and Asia, has always been a land of excesses. The seas which surround it to the north and touch its southern shores, and the rivers which flow across it provide an abundance and variety of fish. The huge forests covering great expanses of the country have for centuries yielded not only game but also herbs and edible plants, especially mushrooms, which people still love to gather and cook. The plains of the Ukraine are devoted to grain crops, the Caucasus to orchards, while the prairies, stretching as far as the eye can see, are ideal grazing land. In short, Russia is a bountiful country and what we call Russian cuisine, although it varies widely from region to region, is bountiful too, not only in its culinary style but also in the generous and welcoming spirit in which it is served. A Russian meal can be modest in cost, but it always creates a festive atmosphere. It is this pleasure in cooking for your friends' enjoyment that we want to share with you.

Right: a wooden church, dating from the 16th century, in the Novgorod region south of Leningrad.

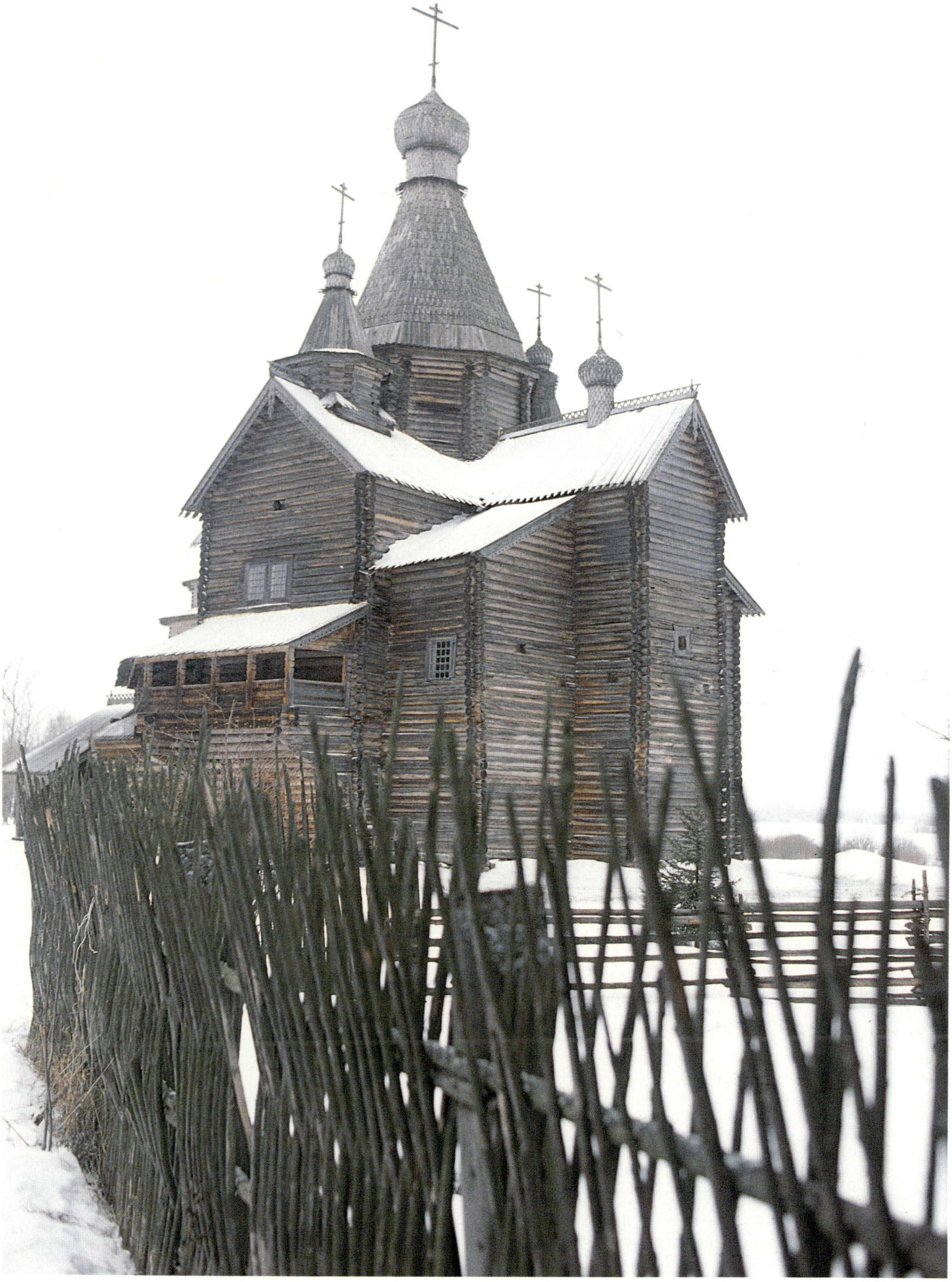

There is no single national cuisine in Russia. The land stretches almost halfway round the world; its northern shores are deep in the Arctic circle and in the south its borders reach the latitudes of Rome, Athens, and Istanbul. It is home to a huge range of culinary styles and it is this complexity that has created a rich, colourful and multifaceted cuisine.

Many influences have left their mark over the centuries: from Scandinavia came soured cream and smoked meats and fish; the Orient contributed aubergines, mutton and grapes, Eastern Europe supplied sauerkraut and later, at the court of Peter the Great, French chefs introduced fine china, embroidered tablecloths and the caviar of the Caspian sea which we inevitably associate with Russia. The combination of sweet and sour flavours and the idea of accompanying meats with fruits owes its origins to intermarriage with German families.

With typical Slav hospitality, each region has absorbed external influences while retaining its traditional specialities, so cereal-based Ukrainian dishes, like the Christmas *kasha* (buckwheat groats), or mushrooms, exist side by side with food that reflects the Mediterranean and Middle Eastern cookery of Greece and Turkey in such dishes as *shashlik* or aubergine caviar.

The Feast of Feasts

Even more than Christmas, Easter is the occasion for celebration in large, happy gatherings. At this time, every house is open to family and friends, and everyone must partake of the buffet. The Easter table, covered with a white cloth, is decorated with painted eggs and flowers. Cold meats are served, lamb or roast suckling pig, sometimes chicken or game, with, of course, the traditional cakes, *pashka* and *kulich*, each proudly displayed and made using recipes handed down by each successive generation.

The painted hard-boiled eggs belong to a very ancient tradition. As Easter approaches, dyes can be found in all the Russian cake shops, but natural colours from spinach, shallots, and beetroot may also be used. Red, symbol of the festival, is the most popular colour.

At the beginning of the meal everyone chooses an egg and, holding it tight, knocks it against his neighbour's egg. The one who keeps his egg intact the longest is the winner. The eggs are then eaten as a starter accompanied by vodka.

Custom also dictates that at Easter young girls are given one or several decorated eggs, sometimes made of semiprecious stones, that they wear on a chain around their neck until Ascension Day.

Blini

A legacy from pagan times when they symbolised the spring sun, blini are traditionally made at *Maslenitsa* (Shrovetide, the week before Lent). They are pancakes made from a yeast dough, served with melted butter, *crème fraîche*, smoked fish, taramasalata, salmon eggs or even caviar, and vodka. It is customary to eat as many as the appetite will permit and then to have a light *borshchok* followed by fruit salad or a sorbet, a dessert famed for its digestive properties.

Yeast dough is used in the preparation of many dishes. It appears to have been introduced during trading with the Scythians and the Greeks, and became so widely used that folk tales made it into a plump and mischievous little character called Kolobok.

Zakuski

Zakuski may be one of Russia's contributions to Western civilisation – many of the canapés and 'nibbles' that have become standard fare at cocktail parties seem to echo Russian recipes. Typical of Russian hospitality, *zakuski* are traditionally served to unexpected guests while the mistress of the house busies herself in the kitchen: and it is a tradition that is still very much alive. Made quickly, they are served either as appetisers (in which case they are simple canapés and *pirozhki*) or as a starter. The vegetable *zakuski* – cucumber, gherkins, mushrooms, radishes – are served first, followed by the fish and meat zakuski: the important thing is that they should be plentiful and varied. They are accompanied with iced vodka which is drunk in one gulp after proposing a toast.

Tea

The samovar, as famous as the nests of dolls, is usually associated with tea, although that is not its main function.

The word comes from *samo*, meaning "self" and *varit*, "to boil". It is a sort of potbellied kettle with a central funnel, which sits on a grate for hot cinders. The water inside the body of the samovar heats up on contact with the funnel and the boiling water may be drawn from it by means of a tap at the base. The samovar industry brought renown to the town of Tula in particular, which boasted about 50 factories in the 19th century, when the samovar was a traditional wedding present.

Made of precious or base metal, they come in all shapes and sizes, some even designed with a special compartment for cooking hard-boiled eggs. The samovar brings together family, friends and visitors. Its soft whistle accompanies the conversations born of the warm atmosphere it creates.

Tea, introduced by the Mongols, has been grown in Georgia since the 19th century. In those days, the Russians attributed all sorts of virtues to the beverage, including that of keeping them awake in church.

Tea is served in cups or in glasses with metal rims, with honey, milk or jam. It is traditional to place a lump of sugar on the tongue through which the strong, fragrant beverage may be delicately sucked.

Preservation and cooking of food

In a country as vast as Russia, obtaining food supplies is often uncertain, and Russian women learned early to use the cold to preserve foodstuffs, freezing whatever they needed. Over the centuries they have perfected other means of preservation: pickling, marinating, drying, smoking and salting foods, especially cabbage, fish and mushrooms.

Other than grilling and frying food, most dishes used to be cooked on the *pech*, a huge stove which served equally for cooking and for heating the house. Meats would simmer for hours and dough rise gently in earthenware pots before being baked.

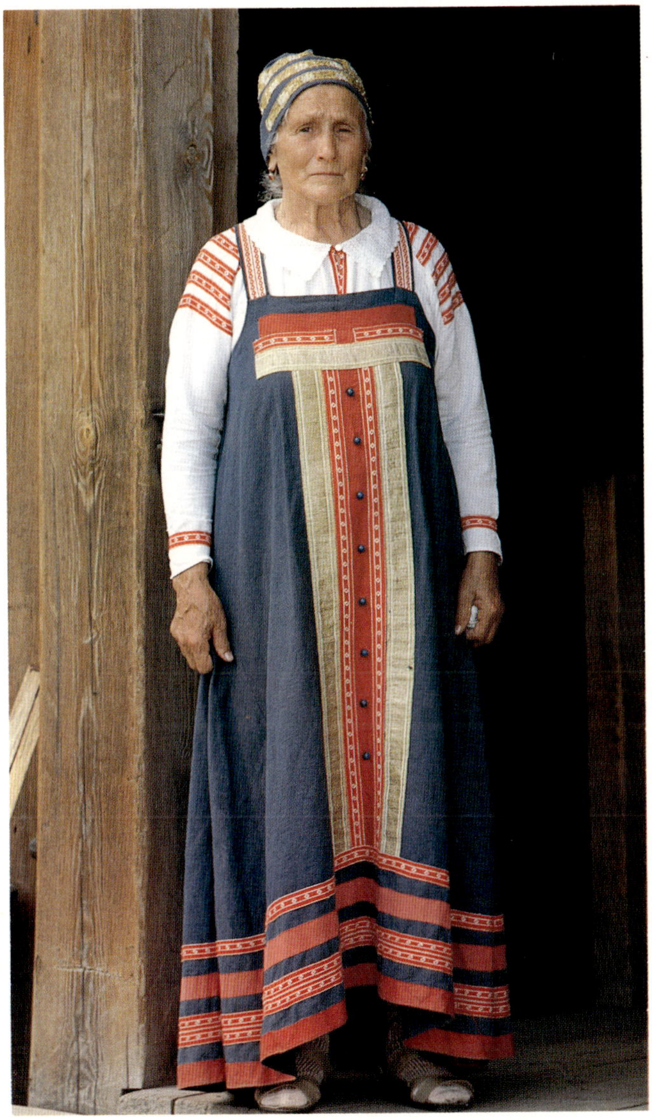

This woman in traditional costume is standing in front of one of the wooden houses of the village of Log, built before the abolition of serfdom in 1861. The house is today part of the open-air museum of Suzdal, north-east of Moscow.

Drinks

Russian vodka, famous throughout the world, is a very popular drink. It is made from grain and usually bottled at between 39 and 45 per cent of alcohol. Some of the cheaper vodkas are distilled from potatoes or even beetroot. Vodka literally means "little water".

White vodka is almost tasteless, and is often flavoured with herbs and spices: the yellow *Zubrovka*, "with buffalo grass" derives its flavour and its name from a plant found in the pastures of the *zubr*, a sort of buffalo. Red *Pertzovka* has chillies in it and *Gorilka* is flavoured with pepper. Other flavourings and additives include seeds such as aniseed and caraway, herbs, nuts, fruit stones, and berries. You can flavour vodka yourself with blackcurrant or similar edible plant by steeping it in white vodka. The bottle must be left in the dark, and as the alcohol is drunk ice cold, the freezer is the ideal place to store it.

Equally appreciated is *kvas*, a thirst-quenching fermented drink made from cereals and stale bread. *Kvas* is sweetish, mild, yeasty in taste, and is usually served without being chilled, like English draught beers. It is also used in cooking as a basis for soups and for marinating meat and fish.

Brandy too, is popular and is consumed as readily before the meal as after it with coffee and fruit. Brandy is produced mainly in Armenia, Georgia and Azerbaijan and Moldavia. The strongest brandies sold under the labels *Dvin* and *Erevan* may be as strong as 50 to 57% alcohol.

Finally, although less famous, Russian wines are not devoid of interest. Russia was producing wine three thousand years ago; Homer himself celebrated its bouquet. Some varieties of vine were introduced by the French, but the grapes they bear taste quite different from the original stock.

Georgia is the most ancient and the largest wine growing region. The wines are sometimes made following an original process (*kakhetinskoe vino*): whole grapes ferment in huge clay pitchers which are placed in big holes dug out of the ground.

The Crimea on the other hand, is known for sparkling wines of unparalleled clarity, called "Crimean champagne", and for the quality of all its wines. Vineyards also contribute to the prosperity of the Don Valley of Moldavia and Armenia.

Special Ingredients

Almonds (mendal): originating from Asia, they are used whole or crushed to flavour desserts.

Aubergine (baklazhan): this vegetable, which came from India, is used in the popular aubergine caviar.

Beetroot (sviokla): mainly used to colour and flavour **borschschi**, but may also be eaten in a salad with other vegetables. It is also used to sweeten and colour grated horseradish.

Buckwheat (greshnevaia kasha): a cereal from the Orient, buckwheat was introduced into Russia during trading with Byzantium. The Russian people have always loved it, and many sayings evoke "our mother, kasha". It may be eaten alone or as an accompaniment to dishes with a sauce. It can be found in most specialist grocers and health food shops. Before use it is a good idea to pick over the grains to remove chaff or the occasional small stone.

Cabbage (kapusta): introduced into Russian cookery by the neighbouring countries, the cabbage has gradually become one of the basic foods. It is used abundantly in the north and in the centre of Russia, where they make traditional cabbage soup (**shchi**), as well as in Siberia and in the Urals. This vegetable is believed to possess many medicinal properties.

Caviar (ikra): salted sturgeon roe, famous for its refined taste. There are three qualities of granulated caviar, according to origin: **Beluga**, produced by the larger fish, has large dark eggs and is the most expensive. The smaller grained **Osietra** is tastier and many people prefer it. Lastly, and most widely available is **Sevruga**, which is produced by very fertile small sturgeon. Crushed caviar is obtained at the end of the fishing season from the ripest eggs. It is saltier than other forms but still delicious. Caviar is eaten alone, or on toast or blini, and is served cold but not iced. Salmon roe, sometimes called "red caviar" is less of a delicacy but still greatly appreciated. It is served in the same way as black caviar.

Chives (zelinoyiluk): originally from China, chives are snipped with scissors and used fresh to bring out the flavour of a dish. They may be replaced by spring onion stems.

Cream: see **Smetana**

Cream Cheese: see **Tvorog**

Dill (ukrop): a herb similar to fennel. Very pungent, it is used in Russian and Scandinavian cookery to flavour vegetables, meats and fish. It grows easily in gardens and window boxes, but can also be bought dried. It retains all its flavour when frozen. To freeze, use scissors to snip unwashed fresh dill very finely into a small container. Seal it and freeze. To use the chopped dill, scrape off the required amount with a fork. Do not touch the dill with your fingers; it will thaw at once if you do. Put the container back in the freezer immediately.

Fish: Russian cuisine includes many fish dishes. Salmon, trout and halibut, which make excellent

1. Cabbage 2.Pumpkin 3. Yellow vodka 4. Red vodka 5. White vodka. 6 Samovar 7. Tea 8. Dark rye bread 9. Loaves with poppy seeds 10. Pirozbki 11. Eggs 12. Smoked sprate 13. Onion 14. Garlic 15. Onions 16. Potatoes 17. Black radish 18. Carrots 19. Aubergine 20. Dill 21. Honey fungus (armillaria mellea) 22. Birch bark 23. Cep 24. Cream 25. Blini 26. Salmon 27. Vobla (smoked fish) 28. Salt herrings 29. Bay 30. Caviar 31. Salmon eggs 32. Eels 33. Gherkins 34. Beetroot 35. Grated horseradish 36. Buckwheat 37. Smyrna raisins 38. Redcurrants 39. Boletus mushrooms.

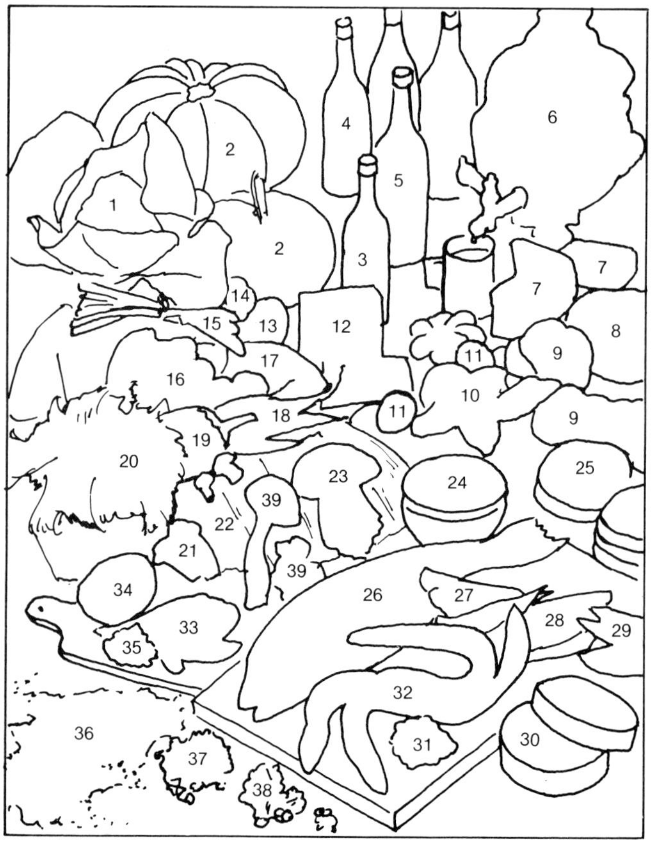

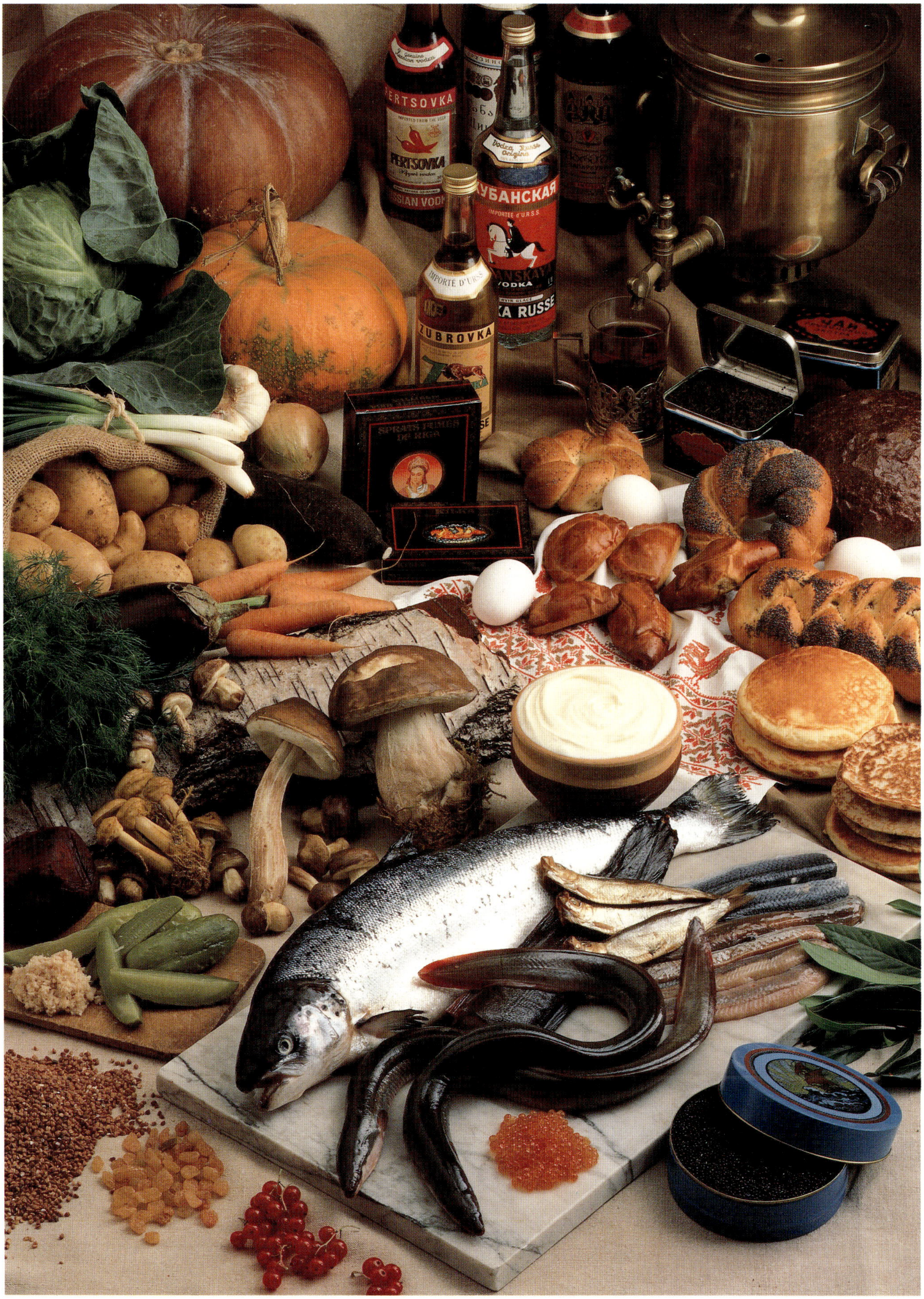
PERTSOVKA
PERTSOVKA
ZUBROVKA

zakuski, may be found in most supermarkets. Trout and Scotch salmon are ideal for this purpose. Their delicious roe can be used to make pretty canapés.

Gherkin (ogurets): this is a variety of tiny cucumber. Gherkins are generally used as an appetiser, **zakuska**, but they can also be included in dishes and soups such as chicken liver soup.

Horseradish (khren): originally from Eastern Europe where it grows wild, horseradish is served alone as a condiment or is used in sauces. Only the root, which is very rich in vitamin C, is edible. Grated horseradish can be found in supermarkets in jars, sometimes mixed with beetroot. To prepare it yourself, choose a thick root and grate it finely into a bowl. Mix with half an apple, peeled and grated, add 3 tablespoons of vinegar and put the mixture into a jar. Seal and store in the refrigerator for up to 2 weeks.

Kasha: very popular, **kasha** is made from buckwheat groats, crushed or in the form of semolina. It is part of every festive meal as it symbolises happiness and wealth.

Kvas: a fermented drink made from rye bread, sugar and yeast, sometimes flavoured with mint. Very thirst-quenching, **kvas** is also used in cooking, when dry cider may be substituted. It is the main ingredient of iced soup.

Mushrooms (griby): Fresh, dried or marinated, mushrooms are very much in evidence in Russian cuisine. Mushroom gathering is a favourite pastime. Ceps, boletus mushrooms, the lactarius species, chanterelles and honey-coloured armillaria mushrooms enrich sauces and gratins with their delicate flavours.

Onion (luk): originally from northern Asia, the onion was introduced into Russia by the Greeks. In the southern regions, mild varieties are eaten raw. It is used in most dishes with sauces, as well as in dishes of chopped meats and vegetables.

Poppy (mak): poppy seeds give a pleasant flavour to certain cakes, served with tea, such as **baranki**. Readily available in delicatessens and large supermarkets.

Raisins: it is the white sultanas from Smyrna that are most often used in cakes.

Rice (ris): from Byzantium, rice first appeared in Russia in the 17th century. It is often served with **shashlik**.

Smetana: soured cream is frequently used not only in Russian cuisine but throughout Eastern Europe. Made by fermentation, **smetana** does not keep for long. Double cream mixed with yoghurt may be used as a substitute, or cream flavoured with a trickle of lemon juice. In the successive stages milk goes through before becoming butter, **Smetana** comes fifth – after the **kephir** (a fermented drink which is very popular in the Middle East and in Southern Russia), **riazhenka**, **prostokvasha** and **slivki**.

Tvorog: many Russian desserts have a milk base. **Tvorog** is a full-cream cheese, strained and pressed until it is dry. It can be found all year round in Russian shops, but especially at Easter as it is the main ingredient of **pashka**.

Viziga: Sturgeon, it may be said, is a fish with no waste, for even the **viziga**, the cartilage around the spinal cord, is used dried. **Viziga** flavours the stuffing of **piroshki** and **kulibiaka**. It can be found in Russian shops; before use, soak it in cold water for 3 to 4 hours.

M/e/n/u/s

Breakfast

Salted Ewe's Milk Cheese
Buttered White Bread
Cream Cheese
Salami on Bread
Fried Eggs
Tea

Lunch

Herring Zakuski
Green Shchi with Nettles
Baked Stuffed Carp
Cream with Fruit Juice

Dinner

Fish Soup
Breaded Cockerel
Mixed Vegetables
Vatrushka

Cold Buffet

Selection of Zakuski
Beef Croquettes
Kulibiaca
Vegetable Salad
Fresh Fruit

Christmas Dinner

Fish Zakuski
Goose Stuffed with Apple
Christmas Kasha
Dried Fruit and Nuts
Prianiki

Easter Dinner

Coloured Eggs
Selection of Zakuski
Borschch
Roast Suckling Pig
Kasha
Pashka
Kulich

Summer Lunch

Selection of Zakuski
Cold Borschch
Mutton Shashlik
Cream Cheese with Fruit

Winter Supper

Zakuski or Hot Borschch
Siberian Ravioli
or Kiev Cutlets
Vatrushka

Zakuski

These starters, which are meant to whet the appetite, vary enormously. Vegetable zakuski are served before smoked or marinated fish and meat pâtés. They can be in the form of canapés or bite-sized pieces. In the past zakuski were served in an ante-chamber to the dining room as a separate buffet, and then as now a full-scale, formal zakuski course consisted of a large and greatly varied selection not unlike a Swedish smörgåsbord. Vodka, which traditionally accompanies zakuski, is served chilled in small glasses which are raised in a toast to an individual or to the success of a project.

Aubergine Caviar

Baklazhanaia ikra

1 kg (2 lb) aubergines
1 kg (2 lb) onions, roughly chopped
4 tablespoons oil
1 kg (2 lb) tomatoes, finely chopped
salt and pepper
1 bay leaf
1 tablespoon sugar
1 tablespoon vinegar

Arrange the whole aubergines on a rack over a baking tin. Bake in preheated oven 160°C (325°F), Gas Mark 3 for about 30 minutes, until soft, then leave to cool.

Heat the oil in a frying pan, add the onions, and fry until soft. Add the tomatoes, with plenty of salt and pepper. Add the bay leaf and cook over a gentle heat for about 45 minutes until the juice has evaporated.

Cut the aubergines in half and scoop out the flesh with a spoon. Coarsely chop it with a knife and add to the tomatoes and onion mixture. Stir gently, then continue cooking until the mixture is dry and any remaining juice has evaporated, stirring frequently to prevent the mixture catching on the base of the pan. Remove the bay leaf, reserving it for later use.

Then put the whole mixture through a vegetable mill, using the coarse grating plate. An electric blender should not be used.

Stir the sugar and vinegar into the mixture with the reserved bay leaf. Pour the mixture into a gratin dish with the reserved bay leaf and bake in a preheated hot oven, 230°C (450°F), Gas Mark 7 for 15 to 20 minutes or until the mixture has thickened. Leave to cool then refrigerate. Serve chilled.

Note: Aubergine caviar may be frozen but do not fill containers to the brim as it expands upon freezing.

Mushroom Caviar

Ikra iz gribov

1 kg (2 lb) fresh mixed mushrooms
3 onions, finely chopped
3 tablespoons oil
1 teaspoon vinegar
salt and pepper
a few chives, finely chopped
a few dill leaves, finely chopped
1 egg, hard-boiled

Remove the mushroom stalks and set them aside for stock. Rinse the caps under cold running water, then drain them.

Bring a saucepan of water to the boil, add the mushroom caps and blanch them for 1 minute. Drain on absorbent kitchen paper, then chop finely.

Heat the oil in a saucepan, sauté the onions and the mushrooms. Cover the pan and simmer for 15 minutes. Stir in the vinegar with salt and pepper to taste.

Transfer the mixture to a bowl and sprinkle with the chives, dill and mashed hard-boiled egg. Mix lightly. Refrigerate for 3 to 4 hours before serving.

Black Radish with Cream

Chornaia redka v smetanie

1 black radish, peeled
2 tablespoons double cream
salt

Coarsely grate radish into a bowl. Add the cream and mix well. Sprinkle with salt to taste and serve at once.

Note: It is not necessary to add pepper because the radish is hot.

Fish, Aubergine Caviar and Taramasalata (page 18) Zakuski.

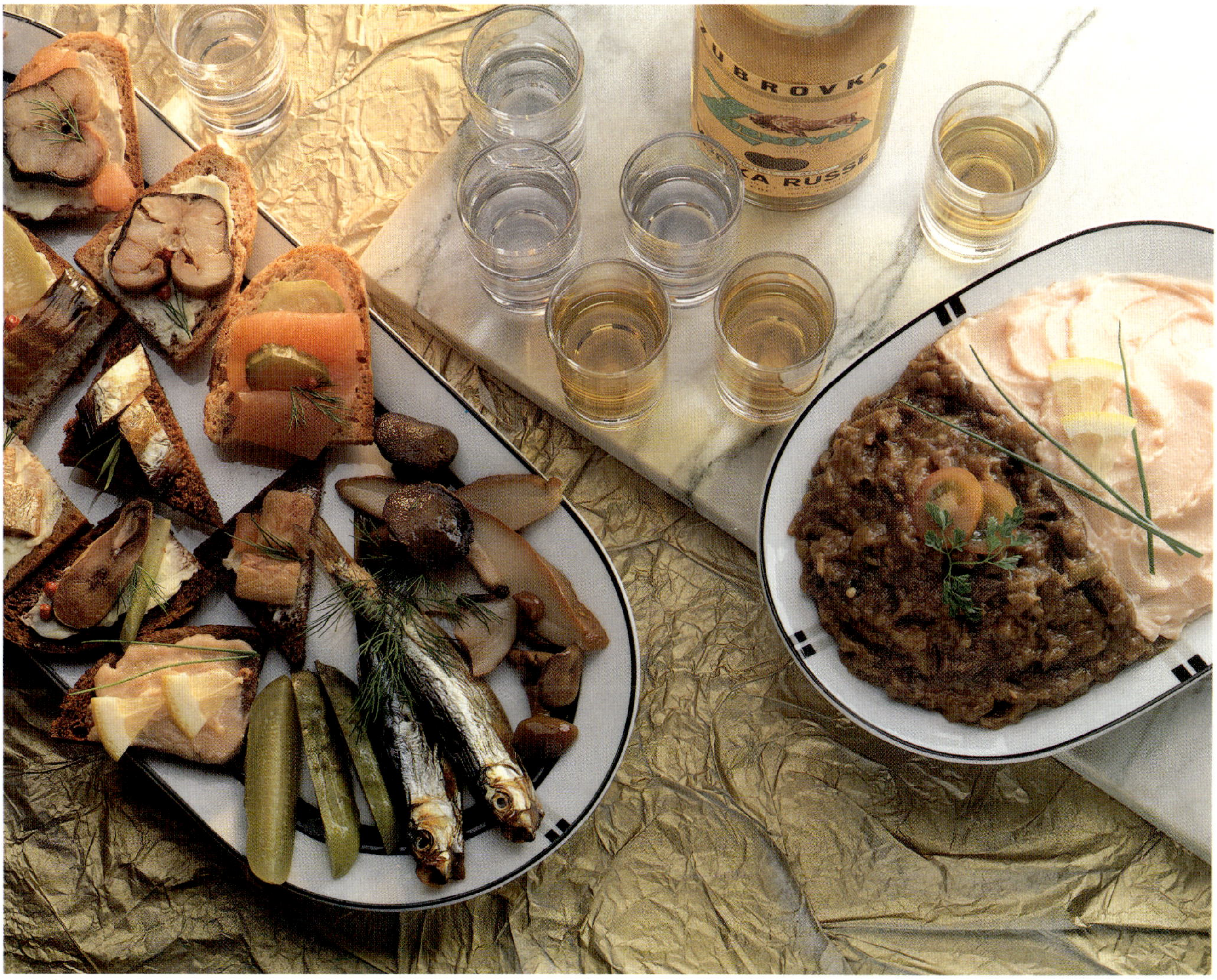

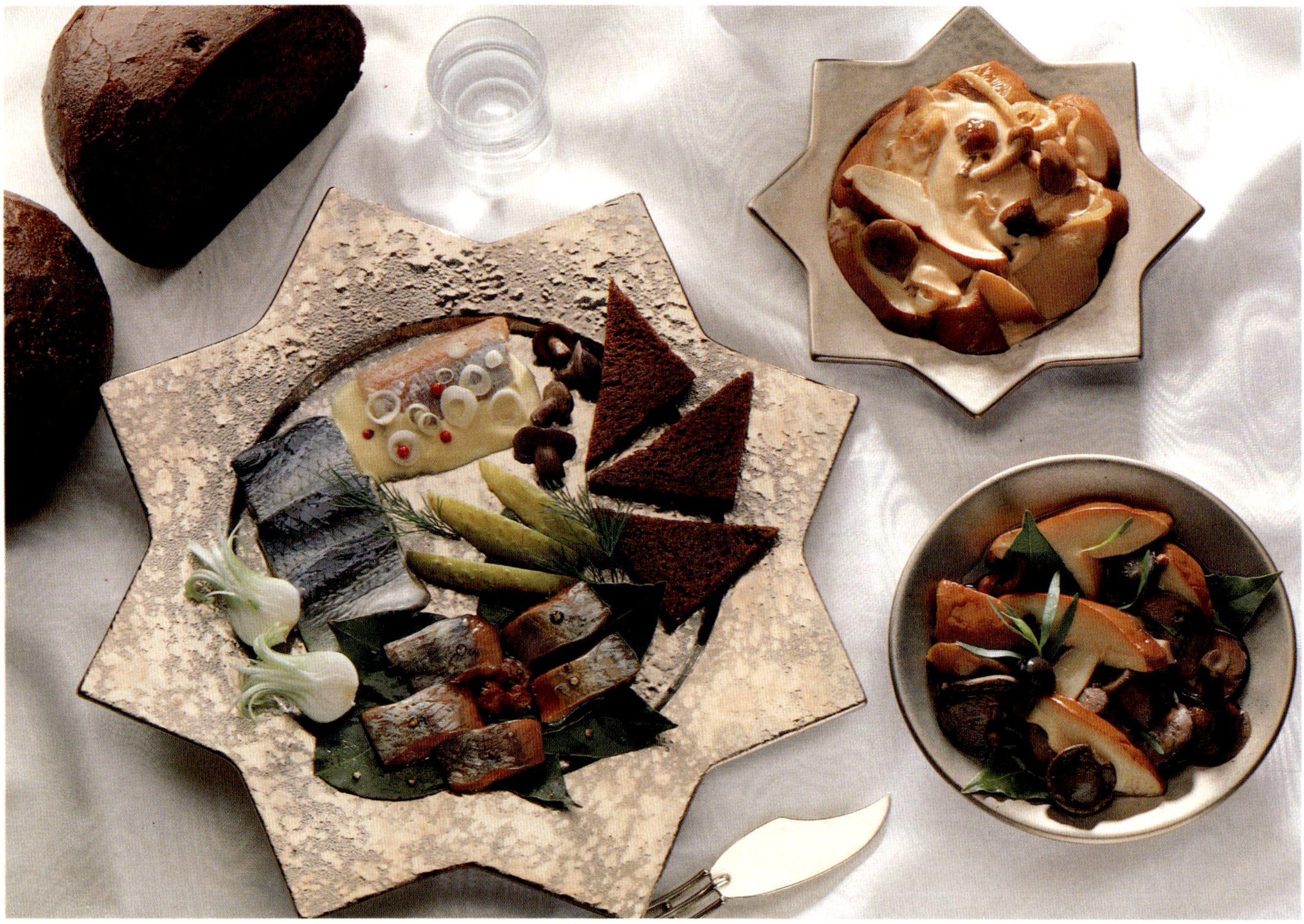

Russian Salt Herring, Herring in Mustard Sauce, Creamed Ceps, Marinated Ceps.

Creamed Ceps

Belyie v smetanie

500 g (1 lb) firm young ceps
25 g (1 oz) butter
1 small onion, finely sliced
about 600 ml (1 pint) crème fraîche
salt and pepper

Remove the mushroom stalks from the caps and set them aside for stock. Rinse the caps under cold running water. Drain them well. Cut the mushroom caps into slivers and put them into a frying pan with the butter and onion. Sauté over a high heat for 2 to 3 minutes. Add the cream, removing the pan from the heat the minute the cream begins to boil. Add salt and pepper to taste and serve at once.

Marinated Ceps

Marinovannyie belyie griby

1 kg (2 lb) small firm ceps or boletus mushrooms
1 teaspoon salt

Marinade:
600 ml (1 pint) water
300 ml (½ pint) wine vinegar
1 tablespoon coarse salt
2½ teaspoons sugar
2 tablespoons peppercorns
2 cloves garlic, cut in half
2 bay leaves
3 cloves
1 sprig tarragon

Remove the mushroom stalks from the caps and set them aside for stock. Rinse the ceps quickly under cold running water. Bring a saucepan of water to the boil with the salt. Add the mushroom caps.

Bring to the boil three times, each time removing the pan from the heat for a few seconds, then carefully drain the mushrooms in a sieve.

Combine all the ingredients for the marinade in a saucepan. Bring to the boil over moderate heat.

Boil for 10 minutes then leave to cool.

Arrange the mushroom caps uppermost in a jar, pour over the marinade and seal.

Note: The ceps may be eaten a week later and will keep for up to 1 year in a sealed jar. Keep in the refrigerator after opening.

Herring in Mustard Sauce

Selodka v gorchichnom soussie

2 Russian or Dutch plump salt herring
300 ml (1/2 pint) milk
1 tablespoon English mustard
1 tablespoon sunflower oil
1/2 teaspoon sugar
1 onion, cut in rings

Using a sharp knife, remove the heads of the herrings. Skin them, then remove the fillets. Put these in a dish, pour over 250 ml/8 fl oz milk and soak overnight to remove the excess salt.

The next day, drain the fish. Cut into pieces, each about 2 cm (3/4 inch) in length.

Arrange the pieces of fish on a serving platter. Garnish with the onion.

In a jug combine the mustard, oil and sugar. Stir in the remaining milk, mix well and pour over the fish and onion rings. Serve at once.

Russian Salt Herring

Russkaia selodka

1 kg (2 lb) large herring
1 kg (2 lb) coarse salt
1 1/2 teaspoons coarsely ground black pepper or crushed peppercorns
60 bay leaves
2 bulbs garlic
1 tablespoon whole black peppercorns
1 litre (1 3/4 pints) water

Wipe the herring with absorbent kitchen paper, but do not gut them. In a large shallow bowl, mix the coarse salt with the ground black pepper and about 10 bay leaves. Add the herring, turning the fish until well covered in the salt mixture. Separate the fish so that they do not touch each other. Cover the bowl and set aside for 2 or 3 days in a cool place.

Place the remaining bay leaves in a saucepan. Break the bulbs of garlic into cloves, peel them and add them to the pan with the peppercorns. Add the water, bring to the boil, lower the heat and simmer for 45 minutes. Cool. Add 2 to 3 tablespoons of coarse salt from the herring dish and 1 tablespoon of liquid from the herring.

Remove the fish from the salt mixture, dusting off the excess, and arrange them in a rectangular non-metallic dish. Cover generously with the marinade.

On serving, remove the fish one at a time, rinse and gut them, and remove the backbone. If they are too salty, rinse or soak them in milk. The traditional way of serving them is to lay them on a bed of bay leaves and decorate them with peppercorns.

Note: The herring may be eaten the next day but will keep for 10 to 14 days in the refrigerator.

Gherkins

Ogurtsi

12 Russian cucumbers, washed and trimmed
5 blackcurrant leaves
3 sprigs dill
3 cloves of garlic, peeled but left whole
3 oak leaves
2 bay leaves
20 peppercorns
600 ml (1 pint) hot water
2 tablespoons coarse salt

Stand the cucumbers up in a large preserving jar. Add the blackcurrant leaves, the dill, garlic, oak leaves, bay leaves and peppercorns. Mix the water with the salt, pour it over the cucumbers and seal the jar.

Note: The cucumbers may be eaten 2 to 3 days later and will keep for about 1 1/2 months in a sealed jar.

Fish Zakuski

1 loaf of rye bread, light or dark
150 g (5 oz) butter
a few fillets of smoked herring, smoked eel or smoked sturgeon
1 tin of sprats
1 tin of pilchards
gherkins or pickled cucumber, sliced
sprigs of dill, for decoration

Prepare 6–9 zakuski per person; each zakuska should be a single, appetizing mouthful. Trim slices of the loaf to neat squares then cut them diagonally to form triangles; or if it is a round loaf, trim to neat, mouthful-sized shapes. Butter each piece.

Cut the fish fillets into 4–6 pieces according to size, and place them on slices. The sprats are usually small enough for one whole fish to go on a slice. Remove the backbone and any other fish bones from the pilchards before cutting them into suitably sized pieces – one piece to make a zakuska.

Spread the dill and sliced gherkins between the zakuski and serve.

Russian Chicken Liver Pâté

Pashtety iz pechionok

100 g (4 oz) chicken livers
salt and pepper
200 g (7 oz) butter, in slivers
1 teaspoon brandy
1 truffle or 2–3 horns of plenty (optional)

Poach the livers in the top of a double boiler set over simmering water, turning them frequently until they are no longer red. Do not allow them to dry out.

Transfer the cooked livers to a bowl and immediately crush them with a fork. Alternatively put them through a food mill; do not use a blender as this would spoil the taste. Add salt and pepper to taste and incorporate the butter, crushing it with the fork. Add the brandy.

On a board, slice the truffle into tiny pieces. Add it to the liver mixture, with some of the truffle juice, or add the rinsed, blanched and finely sliced horns of plenty. Serve at once.

This pâté should be made just before the meal as it does not keep longer than a day. There is no need to refrigerate it.

Puff Pastry Pirozhki

Pirozhki iz sloiovavo testa

250 g (9 oz) plain flour
1 teaspoon salt
250 g (9 oz) butter
150 ml (1/4 pint) water
1 teaspoon lemon juice

Put the flour in a mixing bowl, make a well in the centre and add the salt with 25 g (1 oz) of the butter. Rub the ingredients together with your fingertips until they resemble breadcrumbs, then stir in the water and lemon juice to make a smooth dough. Knead the dough lightly on a floured board, transfer to a plate, cover with a cloth and leave in a cool place for 30 minutes. Meanwhile, soften the remaining butter.

Roll out the dough on a floured board to a thickness of 5 mm (1/4 inch) × 13 cm (5 inch) wide. Fold it in three by bringing one of the ends into the middle, and folding the other end over it. Leave the folded dough to rest for 15 minutes in a cool place, folding the other end over it. Then give the dough a quarter turn on the pastry board, roll it out and fold it in three again. Again, leave it to rest for 15 minutes in a cool place. Repeat the turning, rolling out and folding of the dough four more times, leaving it to rest for 15 minutes each time.

Roll out the dough for the last time. Cut out circles, filling and baking them as for the Yeast Dough Pirozhki.

Yeast Dough Pirozhki

Pirozhki iz testa na opare

butter and flour for greasing
20 g (3/4 oz) fresh yeast
1/2 teaspoon salt
120 ml (1/4 pint) milk
150 ml (1/4 pint) oil
500 g (1 lb) plain flour

Filling:
salt (see method)
1 medium cabbage, finely chopped
1 tablespoon oil
2 large onions, chopped
1 bunch dill, chopped
125 g (4 1/2 oz) salted butter, cubed

Grease and flour a large baking sheet. Combine the yeast, salt and milk in a mixing bowl. Add the oil and flour and knead for a few minutes by hand or in a food processor. Set aside.

Bring a saucepan of salted water to the boil. Add the cabbage and boil for exactly 10 minutes. Drain thoroughly and dry with a cloth or blot on absorbent kitchen paper.

Heat the oil in a large frying pan. Add the onions and sweat lightly. Tip the mixture into a bowl, stir in the eggs and dill and immediately add the butter, still stirring.

Roll out the dough on a floured board to a thickness of 3 mm (1/8 inch). Cut out shapes with a pastry cutter, or using a mug or bowl as a guide cut out rounds measuring 10 to 15 cm (4 to 6 inches) in diameter, depending on the size required. Put a little filling in the centre of each round. Fold it over and pinch the edges together to seal.

Place the pirozhki on the prepared baking sheet and bake in a preheated hot oven, 220°C (425°F), Gas Mark 7 for 5 to 7 minutes. Then reduce the cooking temperature slightly and cook for a further 5 to 7 minutes or until the pirozhki are golden brown.

Variations:
For a carrot filling, coarsely grate 4 or 5 large carrots, soften them in oil with a bay leaf and 2 chopped onions, then add 2 chopped hard-boiled eggs, 1 bunch of chopped dill and 125 g (4 1/2 oz) salted butter, in cubes. For a meat filling, substitute about 350 g (12 oz) minced meat or fish for the cabbage or carrots. Cooked chicken or red meat may also be used.

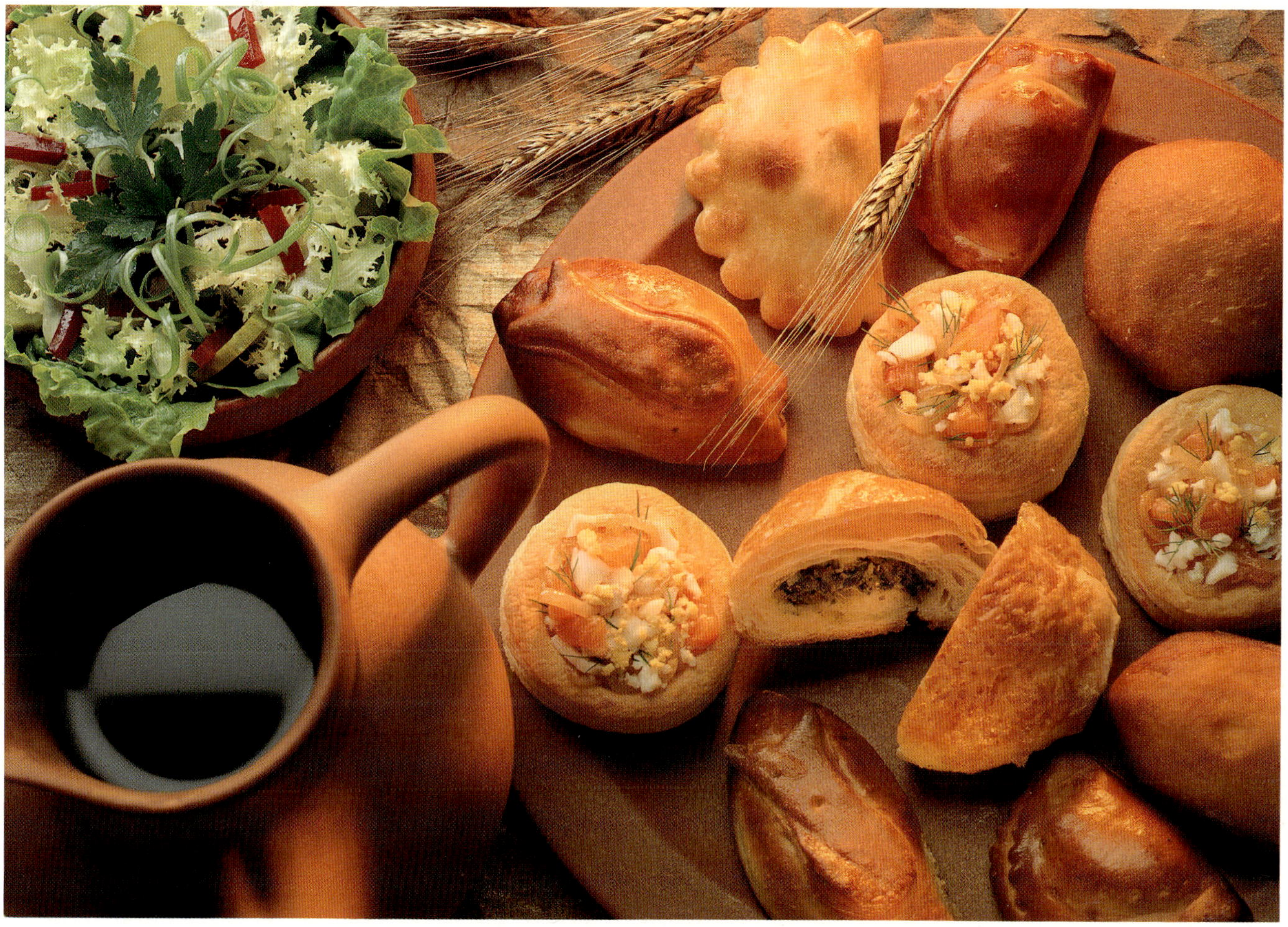

Pirozhki, little fish pies

Shortcrust Pirozhki

Pirozhki razsypchityie

250 g (9 oz) plain flour
a pinch of salt
100 g (4 oz) butter, cubed
1 egg
3 tablespoons water

Put the flour in a mixing bowl, make a well in the centre and add the salt and butter.

Rub the fat into the flour until the mixture resembles breadcrumbs, then stir in the water to make a smooth dough. Knead lightly on a floured board, cover with a cloth and leave to rest for 1 hour in a cool place.

Roll out the dough thinly on a floured board. Cut out circles, filling and baking as for the Yeast Dough Pirozhki.

Little Fish Pies

Rasstegai

Dough:
20 g (3/4 oz) fresh yeast
1/4 teaspoon salt
500 mg (1 lb) plain flour
150 ml (1/4 pint) oil
120 ml (4 fl oz) milk

Filling:
300 g (11 oz) cooked fish, chopped
2 hard-boiled eggs, chopped
1/2 bunch dill, chopped
2 onions, finely chopped
100 g (4 oz) salted butter, in small cubes
50 g (2 oz) cooked rice or cooked chopped fish cartilage (viziga)

Rasstegai are made with the same yeast dough as for pirozhki (recipe on p.16).

Mix the ingredients for the filling. Roll the dough out thinly. Using a mug or bowl cut out rounds and put a little filling in the centre of each, surrounded with a ring of pastry.

Bake at 200°C (400°F), Gas Mark 6, for 10 to 15 minutes or until golden. Serve hot.

Soft Roe Fritters

Oladii iz moloki

150 g (5 oz) plain flour
pinch of salt
150 ml (1/4 pint) milk, water or beer
1 egg, separated
1 1/2 tablespoons oil
300 g (11 oz) soft roe
oil for deep frying
chopped dill (optional)

Mix the flour and salt in a bowl. Gradually add the milk, water or beer, stirring with a wooden spoon, then mix in the egg yolk and the oil. If lumps form, use a whisk to eliminate them and strain the mixture through a sieve into a jug. Set aside to rest for at least 1 hour in a cool place.

In a clean, grease-free bowl, whisk the egg white to stiff peaks and fold it into the flour mixture.

Heat the oil in a deep fat fryer or a deep saucepan. Using a tablespoon, scoop up a portion of the soft roe. Dip the roe into the batter and fry immediately in oil.

Drain the cooked fritters in absorbent kitchen paper and serve hot, sprinkled with chopped dill if liked.

Stuffed Peppers

6 medium-sized green peppers
1 kg (2 lb) carrots, scraped
4 large onions, peeled
1 bay leaf
3 tablespoons sunflower oil
1 kg (2 lb) tomatoes
salt, pepper
50 g (2 oz) butter
200 ml (7 fl oz) crème fraîche
dill, chopped

Cut the peppers in two lengthwise and carefully remove all the seeds. Blanch the peppers for 10 minutes in boiling water, then strain them gently.

Grate the carrots and one onion, and mix together thoroughly. Cook the mixture gently in oil in a covered saucepan for 20 minutes, then fill the pepper halves with it.

Blend together the tomatoes and remaining onions, in a mixer. Place them in another saucepan, well salted and peppered, and reduce them in the butter on a low heat, stirring occasionally, until you have a fairly thick tomato sauce. Add the cream and dill when it is fully cooked.

Place the stuffed peppers into the saucepan, coating them with the sauce on top, and simmer them very gently for about 15 minutes. Serve hot.

Note: You can also stuff peppers with rice and chopped meat fried with chopped onions. Choose different coloured peppers for a colourful presentation.

Taramasalata

1 sac of smoked cod's roe, about 300 g (11 oz) in weight
1 small onion, finely grated
150 ml (5 fl oz) ground nut or sunflower oil
1–2 tablespoons lemon juice (optional)

Working over a bowl, slit the cod's roe membrane widthways. Allow the eggs to fall into the bowl. Discard the membrane. Add the onion and gradually incorporate the oil, stirring constantly with a wooden spoon. Do not use a whisk as this would break the eggs. The mixture should puff up like mayonnaise. Its consistency should be that of a thick dough. Add lemon juice to taste. Serve with buttered bread or blini.

Note: Choose a sac of cod's roe that is soft to the touch, not too pale and not too dark.

Taramasalata with Cream

1 sac of smoked cod's roe, about 300 g (11 oz) in weight
250 ml (8 fl oz) double cream
1 bunch of chives, chopped

Working over a bowl, slit the cod's roe membrane widthways. Allow the eggs to fall into the bowl. Discard the membrane.

Add the cream, mixing thoroughly but not too roughly with a fork. Stir in the chives. Refrigerate for 2 to 3 hours and serve cold, with toast.

Cucumbers with Cream

Ogurets so smitanoi

1 large cucumber or 2 medium ones
1 tablespoon coarse salt
100 ml (3 1/2 fl oz) crème fraîche
a few drops of vinegar or lemon juice
pepper
2 sprigs of dill, chopped

Peel the cucumber, then cut it into very thin slices and sweat them in a bowl with the coarse salt for 30 minutes. Remove them from the salt and place them in a salad bowl. Whisk the cream lightly with the vinegar and add it to the cucumber. Add the pepper, mix well, and sprinkle with dill.

Soups

Soups have been part of Russian cuisine for centuries. Shchi, based on cabbage, is a northern speciality, while borshch, made from beetroot, is very popular in the central and southern regions. Soups may be served as a main course as they often include meat or fish. They are accompanied by bread or pirozhki.

Fresh Cabbage Shchi

Shchi

2 large carrots
2 onions
2 turnips
1 medium white or Savoy cabbage, sliced
25 g (1 oz) butter
1.5 litres (2½ pints) beef stock
1½ teaspoons coarse salt
freshly ground black pepper
3 sprigs dill
3 sprigs parsley
1 bay leaf
2 cloves
500 ml (18 fl oz) double cream

Cut the carrots, onions and turnips into 2.5 cm × 5mm (1 × ¼ inch) matchsticks. Bring a large saucepan of water to the boil. Add the cabbage, allow the water to return to the boil, and drain immediately.

Melt the butter in a large saucepan and sauté all the vegetables for 15 minutes over moderate heat. Add the stock with salt and pepper. Bring the mixture to the boil, lower the heat and simmer for 10 minutes.

Stir in the dill, parsley, bay leaf and cloves and simmer for a further 10 minutes. Remove the herbs with a slotted spoon and serve. The cream is served separately.

Green Shchi with Nettles

Zelonyeshchi

750 g (1½ lb) shoulder or topside of beef
2 litres (3½ pints) water
2 onions, quartered
1 bay leaf
1 clove
salt and pepper
500 g (1 lb) young nettle or spinach shoots
3 large potatoes, peeled and cut into rounds
6 eggs
250 ml (8 fl oz) crème fraîche

Put the meat into a large saucepan. Add the water, onions, bay leaf and clove, with salt and pepper to taste. Cover the pan and simmer the meat gently for 1½ to 2 hours or until tender.

Using a slotted spoon, remove the meat from the pan and cut it into 1 cm/½ inch cubes. Set aside. Add the nettles and potatoes to the saucepan and cook for 30 minutes.

Put the soup through a vegetable mill or purée in a food processor or blender. Return it to the clean saucepan, add the cooked beef cubes and bring the liquid gently to the boil.

Meanwhile, soft boil the eggs. Shell them carefully and place 1 egg in each of 6 soup plates. Pour the hot soup into a tureen and serve immediately, ladling it into the bowls on top of the eggs, and adding a generous spoonful of *crème fraîche* to each portion.

Borshch

750 g (1½ lb) middle or best rib of beef
a few bones
2 litres (3½ pints) water
1 bay leaf
1 clove
salt and pepper
2 large onions
2 large carrots, peeled
1 turnip, peeled
1 cabbage, sliced
1 beetroot, cooked
1 tablespoon vinegar
6 frankfurters, in thick slices
few sprigs of dill, chopped
600 ml (18 fl oz) fresh double cream

Put the meat and the bones in a large saucepan with the measured water. Add the bay leaf and clove with salt and pepper to taste. Cover the pan and simmer the meat gently for 1½ hours or until tender.

Cut the onions, carrots and turnip into 2.5 cm (1 inch) matchsticks. Bring a second saucepan of water to the boil. Add the cabbage and cook for 10 minutes, then drain it and add it to the meat, with the onions, carrots and turnips. Cook for a further 10 minutes.

Working over a small saucepan, coarsely grate the beetroot into it. Add the vinegar and three ladlefuls of stock. Cover and heat through, but do not boil.

Add the sausage slices to the meat and heat for 10 minutes more.

Just before serving, remove all the meat from the pan. Slice the meat from the bones, cut it into 1 cm (½ inch) cubes, and put it into a hot soup tureen. Pour over the stock and vegetables and add the beetroot and its juice. Stir gently and sprinkle with dill. Serve the cream separately.

Variations: There are many variations on this traditional dish. You can add smoked bacon, smoked sausage or 125 g (4½ oz) black olives. Soured cream may be used instead and the dish served with kasha or pirozhki. For a lighter stock, use topside beef instead of rib.

Borshchok

1 large beetroot, cooked
1 tablespoon vinegar or lemon juice
2 litres (3½ pints) beef stock
blini to serve

Peel the beetroot, coarsely grate it and put it into a large saucepan. Pour over the vinegar or lemon juice to preserve its colour. Add the hot stock. Simmer for 10 minutes.

Strain the contents of the saucepan through a sieve into a clean pan. Serve in bowls, accompanied by blini (page 24).

Giblet Soup

Rassolnik

1 goose, duck or chicken carcass with giblets
5–6 chicken, duck or preferably goose giblets
salt and pepper
1 bay leaf
2 large potatoes, peeled and diced
2 onions, diced
3–4 tablespoons pearl barley
4 gherkins or salted cucumbers, sliced
1 bunch dill, finely chopped
200 ml (7 fl oz) crème fraîche

Put the poultry carcass and giblets into a large saucepan, omitting the livers, which give a bitter taste. Add water to cover, salt and pepper to taste and the bay leaf. Bring the liquid to the boil, lower the heat and simmer for 1 hour.

Remove the carcass and giblets and cut the giblets and pieces of meat into tiny cubes. Add the potatoes, onions and pearl barley to the stock in the pan. Cook for 5 minutes.

Add the sliced cucumbers and dill. Serve hot, handing the cream separately.

Fish Soup

Ukha

1 kg (2 lb) assorted freshwater fish of own choice, gutted and cleaned
2 litres (3½ pints) cold water
3 sprigs parsley
2 onions, sliced
salt and pepper
1 bay leaf
1 clove
1 bunch dill, chopped

Cut the large fish into small pieces. Leave the others whole. Place in a large saucepan or fish kettle with water to cover. Bring to the boil, skimming off the scum as it rises in the pan.

Add the parsley, onions, salt and pepper and cook over a gentle heat for 40 to 50 minutes.

Add the bay leaf and clove and sprinkle with dill. Simmer for 15 minutes more, then strain the stock into a tureen. Serve with Rasstegai (page 17) or Koulibiaca (page 27).

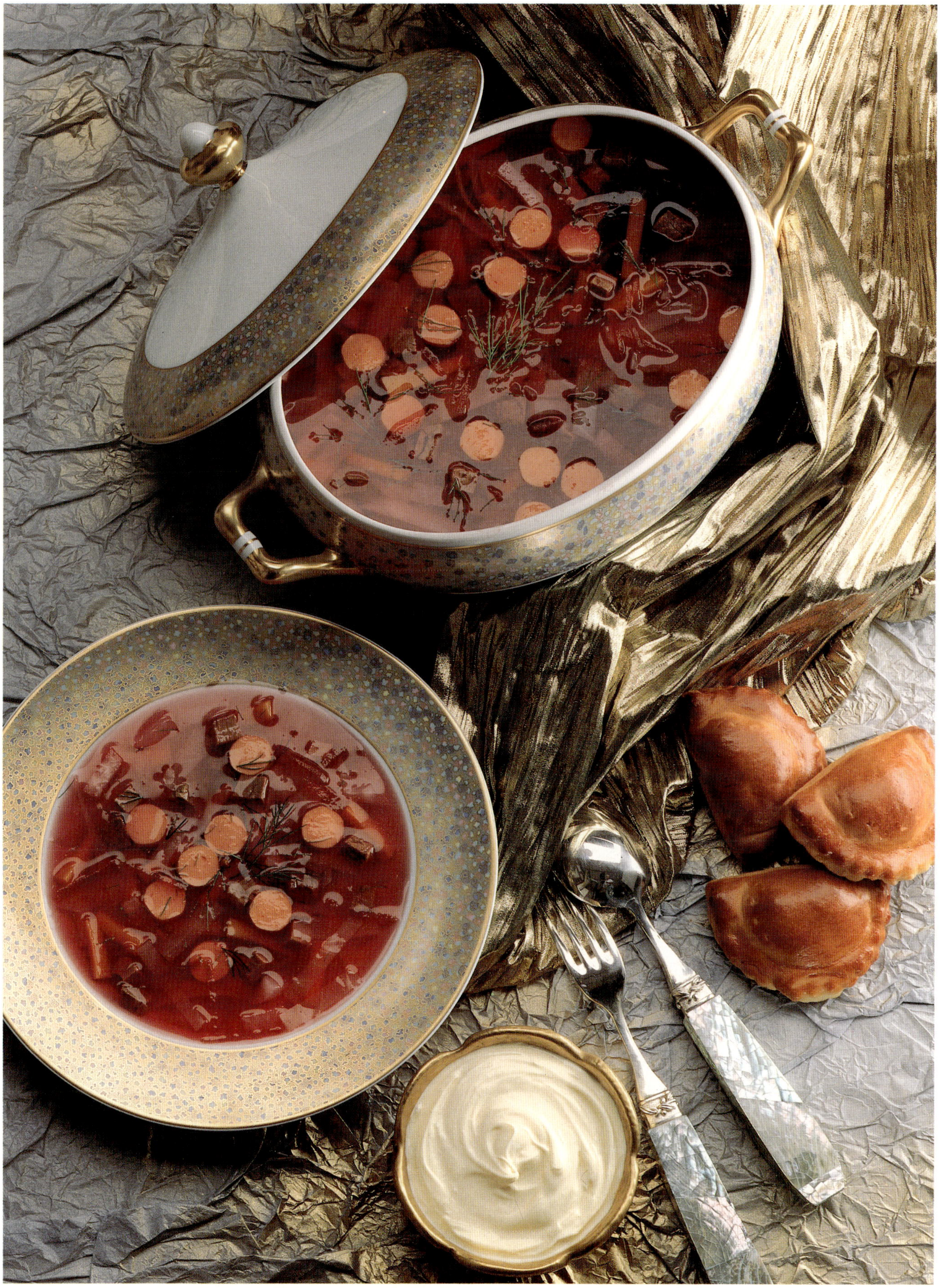

Borshch

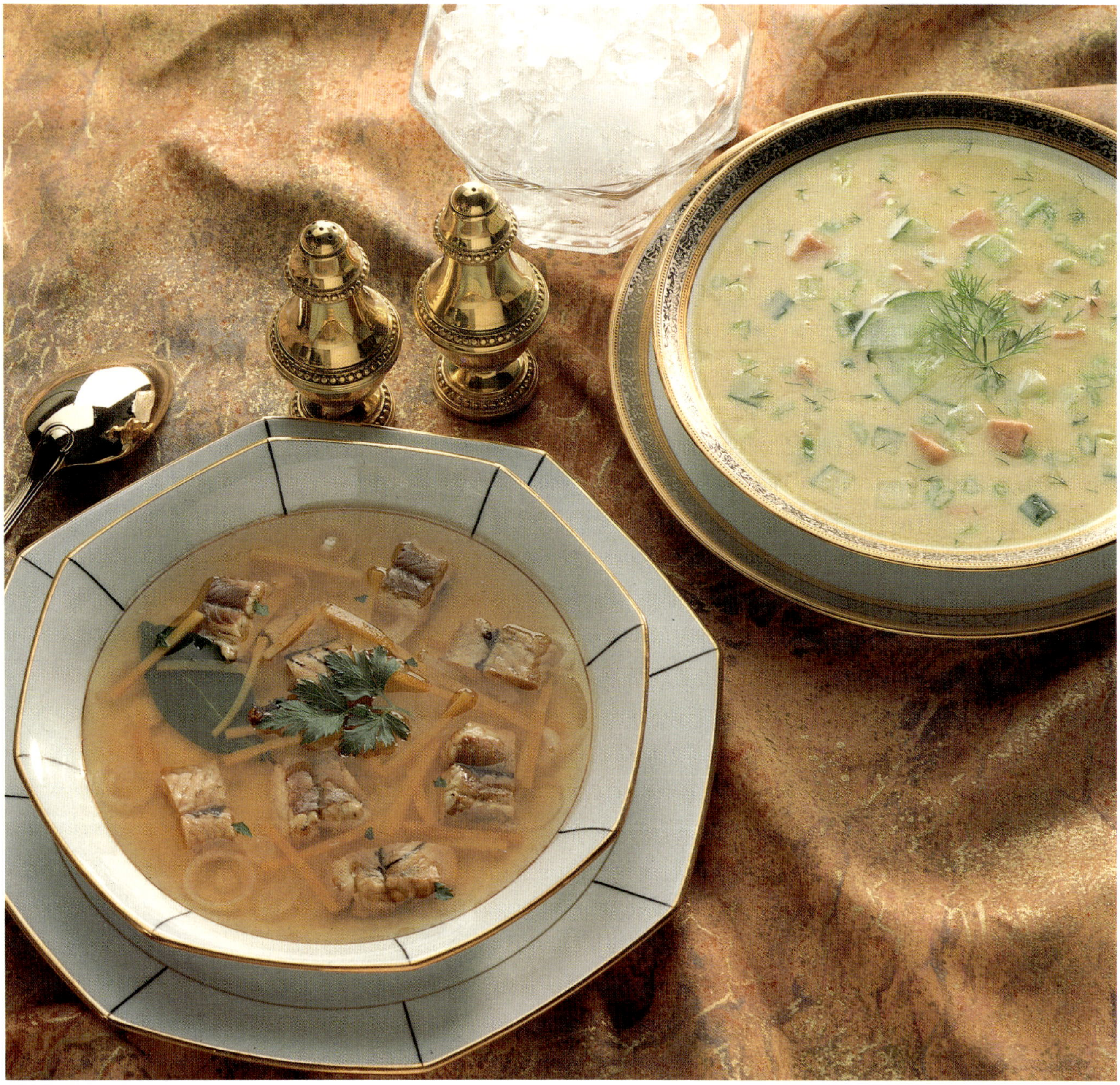

Eel Ukha; Iced Soup

Iced Soup

Okroshka

3 hard-boiled egg yolks
1½ tablespoons English mustard
salt
½ teaspoon sugar
2 litres (3½ pints) kvas or dry cider
1½ hard-boiled egg whites, cubed
200 g (7 oz) cooked beef, diced
200 g (7 oz) cooked veal, diced
1 thick slice ham, diced
1 large potato, cooked and diced
1 large cucumber, diced

To serve:
4-5 chive stalks
salt
1 bunch dill, chopped
500 ml (18 fl oz) cream
ice cubes

Place the egg yolks in a bowl with the mustard, a pinch of salt and the sugar. Mash lightly, gradually adding 250 ml (9 fl oz) of the kvas or cider, then pour in remaining kvas or cider. Cover the bowl and refrigerate for a few hours.

Just before serving combine the diced egg white, meat, potato and cucumber in a big soup tureen. Pour over the chilled kvas mixture.

Crush the chives with a pestle and mortar and add salt to taste. Stir into the soup and sprinkle with dill. Serve the ice cubes and cream separately.

Mushroom Soup

Gribnaia pokhliobka

250 g (9 oz) large ceps, sliced
(or 1 packet of dried ceps)
1.5 litres (2½ pints) water
4 large potatoes, quartered and sliced
2 onions, sliced
2 tablespoons pearl barley
salt and pepper

Put the sliced ceps into a saucepan with the measured water. Bring to the boil, lower the heat and simmer for 20 minutes. Add the potatoes, onion and pearl barley to the pan and cook for a further 25 minutes. Serve immediately.

This is an ideal recipe for using up mushroom stalks left over after the preparation of another dish, such as Mushroom Caviar (page 13) or Creamed Ceps (page 14). If you have made Marinated Ceps (page 14) use the stalks for this recipe and use some of the water used for blanching the ceps.

Eel Ukha

Ukha iz ugoria

1 kg (2 lb) eels
1 bay leaf
1 clove
1 onion, sliced
50 g (2 oz) butter
3 carrots, peeled and grated

Stock
a few small freshwater fish, cleaned and gutted
2.5 litres (4½ pints) water
salt and pepper

Start by preparing the stock. Put fish into a large saucepan or fish kettle. Add the water with salt and pepper to taste, and cook for 4 minutes over moderate heat. Strain the stock into a large jug.

Skin the eels. Gut them, remove the livers and thoroughly rinse the insides. Cut the eels into bite-sized pieces. Put the pieces of eel into a cast iron pot or saucepan. Pour over the stock and add additional salt and pepper if required. Add the bay leaf, clove and onion. Bring the stock to the boil, lower the heat and simmer gently for 25 minutes skimming from time to time to remove the scum but leaving the fat.

Meanwhile, melt the butter in a frying pan, add the carrots and sauté for 15 to 20 minutes. On serving, add the carrots but not the melted butter to the soup. Serve in a tureen.

Botvinia

250 g (9 oz) spinach, washed
salt and pepper
250 g (9 oz) sorrel, washed
25 g (1 oz) butter
1 teaspoon sugar
1 tablespoon English mustard
2 litres (3½ pints) kvas or dry cider
1 cucumber, sliced
75g (3 oz) chive stalks, snipped into short lengths
1 bunch dill, finely chopped
50 g (2 oz) grated horseradish
250 g (9 oz) cooked fish (pike or perch, for example), cut into bite-sized pieces

Remove the stalks from the spinach and sorrel leaves. Bring a saucepan of water to the boil. Add the spinach and cook for a few minutes. Drain. Melt the butter in a second saucepan, add the sorrel leaves and cook for 2 to 3 minutes until wilted. Transfer the sorrel leaves with the melted butter to the bowl of a food processor. Add the spinach and process to a fine purée. Alternatively, use a vegetable mill. Transfer the purée to a soup tureen and add the sugar and mustard. Dilute with kvas or cider, then add the cucumber, chives and dill. Check the seasoning and add salt and pepper as required.

To serve, put a little horseradish in each soup plate with some fish pieces. Pour over the cold soup.

Savoury Pastries

To the Russians, bread and salt are twin symbols of hospitality; the many ways of garnishing flaky pastry, shortcrust or yeast pastry show the importance of these dishes in Russian cuisine. Yeast pastry is by far the most popular and is often used in combination with leftover vegetables, meat or fish to make an original and tasty dish.

Blini, as typically Russian as vodka and caviar, have become part of the cuisine of the western world, perhaps introduced by nostalgic Russian émigrés.

Blini

Blini

1.75–2 litres (3–3½ pints) milk
600 g (1 lb 5 oz) plain white flour
60 g (2½ oz) butter, melted
20 g (¾ oz) fresh yeast
1 teaspoon salt
200 g (7 oz) buckwheat flour
3 eggs, separated
½ teaspoon sugar
butter for greasing

Warm 750 ml (1¼ pints) of the milk in a small saucepan. Put 400 g (14 oz) of the white flour into a deep mixing bowl and gradually stir in the warm milk and butter, using an electric whisk, if liked, to prevent the formation of lumps.

Crumble in the yeast and add half the salt. Cover the bowl and put it in a warm place for 1 hour or until the dough has doubled in bulk.

Warm a further 750 ml (1¼ pints) milk in a small saucepan. Work the rest of the white flour into the dough, also incorporating the buckwheat flour, the egg yolks and the warm milk. Add a little extra warm milk, if necessary, to create a thick pancake batter. To avoid the formation of lumps, add the flour and milk alternately.

Stir in the rest of the salt and the sugar. Cover the bowl and leave the batter to rise for 1 to 2 hours more.

An hour before cooking, heat 300 ml (½ pint) of the remaining milk to just below the boiling point. Whisk the hot milk into the batter. Finally, whisk the egg whites in a clean bowl until stiff. Fold them gently into the batter. Set the batter aside for 10 minutes. Do not stir the batter again.

Grease a cast-iron frying pan or heavy-bottomed pan with a little melted butter. The easiest way to do this is by using a pastry brush. Place the pan over moderate heat. When it is hot, drop in the batter, a tablespoon at a time, to form the blini. Do not be tempted to use more batter; blinis swell as they cook. Cook the blini for 2 to 3 minutes on each side.

Keep the cooked blini hot in a covered dish in a preheated moderate oven, 160°C (325°F), Gas Mark 3.

Serve on hot plates with melted butter, *crème fraîche*, smoked fish, sweet herring, taramasalata (page 18), salmon or – for a luxury touch – caviar.

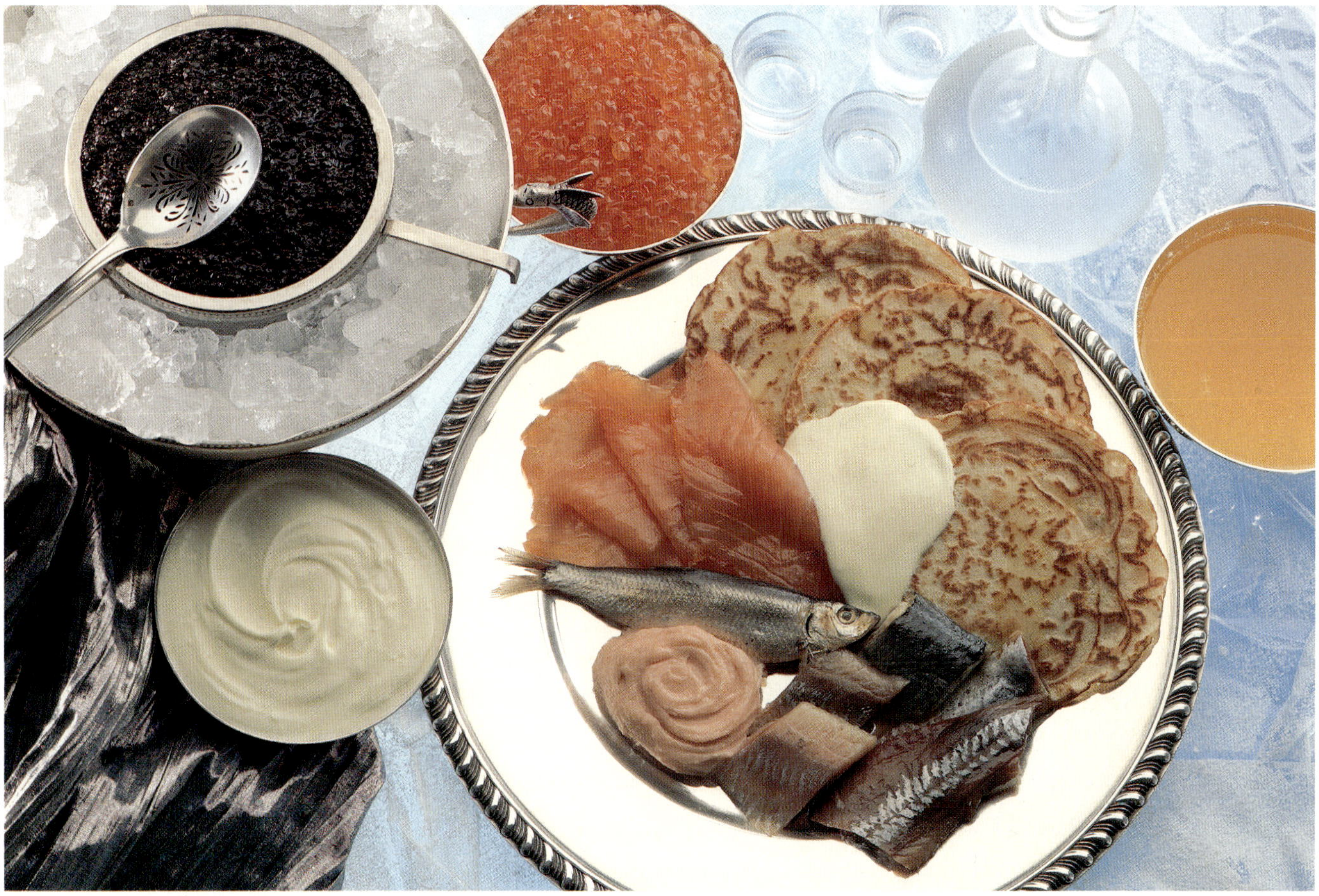

Blini

Quick Blini

Blini skorospelye

1 kg (2 lb) plain white flour, sifted
300 ml (1/2 pint) water
40 g (1 1/2 oz) fresh yeast
1 1/2 teaspoons salt
2 tablespoons sugar
1.2 litres (2 pints) milk
3 tablespoons oil
3 eggs, separated

Warm a mixing bowl. Sift the flour. Warm the water in a saucepan. It should be at about 38°C (100°F).

Dissolve the yeast, salt and sugar in the water. Pour the mixture into the warm bowl and whisk in the flour, milk, oil and egg yolks.

Whisk the egg whites in a clean bowl until stiff. Fold them into the batter, which should have the consistency of thick cream. If time permits, leave the batter to stand in a warm place; the longer it rests, the better it will rise.

Cook the blini as in the previous recipe, and serve very hot with melted butter, *crème fraîche* and smoked fish.

Mushroom Tart

Tort s gribami

Puff pastry:
220 g (9 oz) plain flour
120 g (4 oz) butter, in small cubes
1 egg
3 tablespoons water

Filling:
750 g (1 lb 10 oz) field mushrooms
100 g (3 1/2 oz) butter
2 large onions, sliced
500 ml (1 pt) crème fraîche
salt, pepper, nutmeg
100 g (3 1/2 oz) cheese, grated

Prepare the pastry according to the pirozhki recipe (page 16). Lay it in a flan tin, prick it over with a fork, and bake it for 15 minutes (heat no. 6–7, 220°C).

Slice the mushrooms and sauté them with the onions in 50 g (2 oz) of butter for 10 minutes, until the water has evaporated. Add the cream, salt, pepper and grated nutmeg, and spread the mixture evenly into the tart. Sprinkle the cheese and remaining butter over it and heat it in the oven for a further 5 minutes before serving.

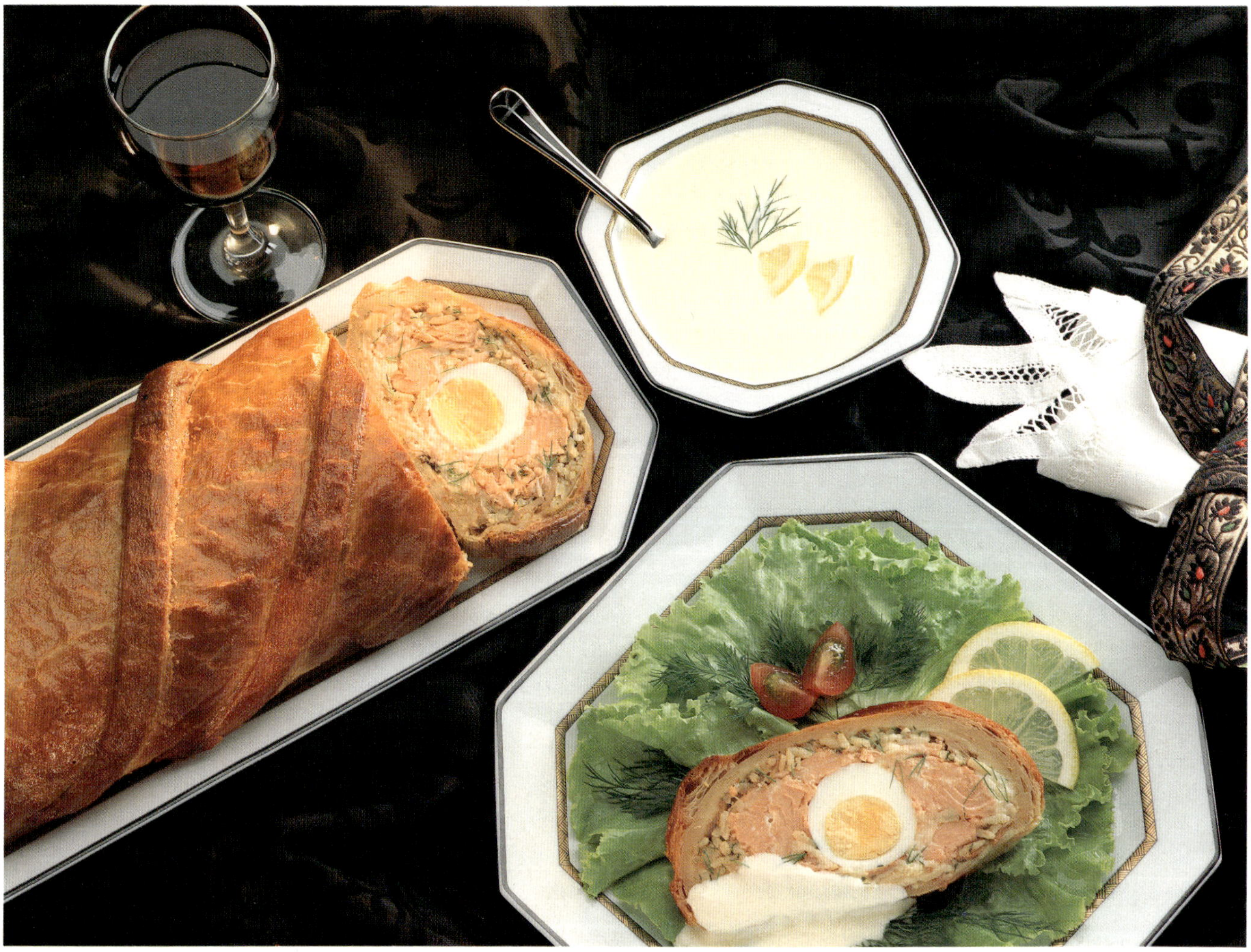

Salmon Koulibiaca

Stuffed Pancakes

Farshirovanii blinchiki

Batter:
120 g (4 oz) plain flour
1/2 teaspoon salt
250 ml (9 fl oz) water
2 egg yolks
cooking oil

Filling:
1/4 cabbage, thinly sliced
1 small onion, chopped
1 teaspoon oil
1 egg, hard boiled
2-3 sprigs of dill, chopped
35 g (1 1/4 oz) salted butter, in small cubes

1 egg white
30 g (1 oz) butter, in small cubes
50 g (1 3/4 oz) cheese, grated

This recipe will make about 12 pancakes.

Mix the salt and flour in a mixing bowl. Gradually add the water and egg yolks, whisking vigorously to prevent lumps. Let the batter rest for 45 minutes.

To make the filling, boil the cabbage in salted water for 10 minutes, then drain it well. Fry the onion lightly in oil to soften it, then thoroughly mix the cabbage, onion, egg, dill and butter together.

Lightly oil the pan and heat it up. Whisk the batter again briefly, then cook thin pancakes with it, frying them lightly on each side as described in the recipe for blini (page 24). Place them aside as you make them.

On each pancake spread a thin layer of the filling, then fold it in half and roll it very lightly. Brush a little of the egg white inside the corners of each pancake and pinch to seal them. Lightly sprinkle them with the butter and cheese and heat them in the oven until ready.

Note: You can also use the fillings used with pirozhki (see page 16). Serve the pancakes with a tomato or mushroom sauce (see page 50) or simply with cream.

Salmon Koulibiaca

Kulibiaka

Flaky Pastry:
350 g (12 oz) plain flour
½ teaspoon salt
250 g (9 oz) butter
200 ml (7 fl oz) water
1 teaspoon lemon juice
butter and flour for greasing and dusting
1 egg, beaten, to glaze

Filling:
750 g (1½ lb) fresh or drained canned salmon
2 litres (3½ pints) court bouillon *(see page 38)*
125 g (4½ oz) butter
200 g (7 oz) warm cooked rice
2–3 sprigs dill, chopped
salt and pepper
5 hard-boiled eggs, shelled but left whole

Make the pastry as for the Puff Pastry Pirozhki (see page 16). Divide the pastry into two balls, one slightly larger than the other, wrap separately and refrigerate.

Prepare the filling. If using fresh salmon, poach it gently in the *court bouillon* in a fish kettle or saucepan for 15 minutes. Drain the fish carefully and flake it, removing skin and bones. If using canned salmon, pick it over in the same way.

Put the hot rice into a bowl, add the butter and stir lightly until melted. Add the salmon and dill, with salt and pepper to taste. Set the filling aside.

Grease a large baking sheet generously with butter and dust with flour. On a floured surface, roll out the smaller of the balls of dough to a rectangle that will fit the baking sheet. Lop the pastry over the rolling pin and gently transfer it to the baking sheet, taking care not to stretch it.

Heap the salmon filling on to the pastry to within 2.5 cm (1 inch) of the edge and arrange the hard-boiled eggs in a row down the centre. Brush the exposed pastry border with some of the beaten egg.

Roll out the remaining pastry to a slightly larger rectangle and place it on top of the filling. Seal the edges. Make three diagonal cuts in the top of the pie. Roll out the pastry trimmings and cut decorations for the top of the pie. Fix these in place with the beaten egg and then glaze the completed koulibiaca with the remaining beaten egg.

Bake in a preheated moderately hot oven, 200°C (400°F), Gas Mark 6 for 40 to 50 minutes or until golden. If the pastry overbrowns, cover the pie with foil towards the end of the cooking time, removing the covering for the final 5 minutes' cooking. Serve with melted butter.

Kurnik

Pastry:
500 g (1 lb) plain flour
250 g (9 oz) butter
3 teaspoons salt
1 egg, beaten, to glaze

Filling:
4 eggs
2 onions, finely chopped
2 tablespoons oil
500 g (1 lb) roast chicken, diced
400 g (14 oz) warm cooked rice
1 bunch dill, finely chopped
100 g (4 oz) butter, in small cubes

Hard boil 2 of the eggs for the filling. When cold, shell the eggs, dice them and set them aside.

Make the pastry by hand or in a food processor by mixing all the ingredients together quickly. Divide the pastry into 2 balls, one a third of the size of the other, wrap separately and refrigerate for at least one hour.

Sweat the onion in the oil. Remove the pan from the heat and gently stir in the chicken, hard-boiled eggs, rice and dill. Add the butter and salt and pepper to taste. Beat the remaining eggs in a small bowl and use sufficient beaten egg to bind the filling.

On a floured surface, roll out the smaller of the balls of dough and line a 23 cm (9 inch) pie dish. Make a conical heap of the filling on the pastry, leaving a 2.5 cm (1 inch) border all around. Brush the border with a little of the beaten egg.

Roll out the remaining pastry and cover the filling, keeping the hat shape. Seal the edges well. Roll out the pastry trimmings and cut into decorative shapes, fixing these to the pastry 'hat' with beaten egg. Finally glaze the pie with the remaining beaten egg.

Bake in a preheated hot oven, 230°C (450°F), Gas Mark 8 for 25 to 30 minutes. Serve at once.

Pirog with Pancakes

Pirog blinchatii

butter for greasing
2 tablespoons fresh white breadcrumbs
250 g (9 oz) plain flour
½ teaspoon salt
2 eggs
100 ml (3½ fl oz) milk
1 tablespoon oil

Filling:
2 onions, finely chopped
3 tablespoons oil
500 g (1 lb) minced meat (see note below)
3 sprigs parsley or 2 sprigs dill
salt and pepper
50 g (2 oz) butter, in small cubes

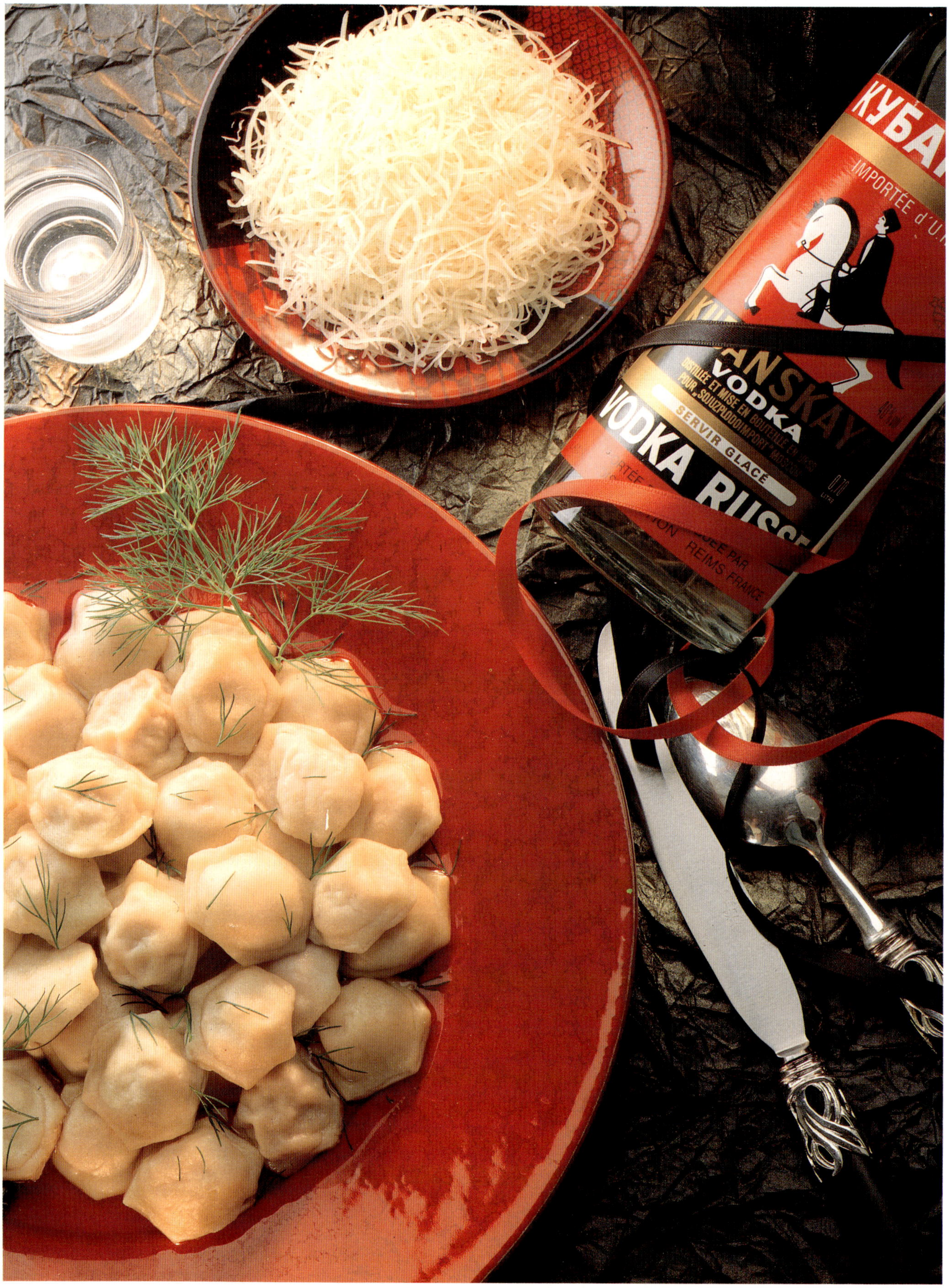

Siberian ravioli

Generously grease an 18 cm (7 inch) soufflé dish with butter and line it with breadcrumbs. Set aside.

Put the flour and salt into a deep mixing bowl and gradually beat in the eggs, milk and oil to make a smooth pancake batter. Whisk the batter vigorously, let it rest for 3 to 4 hours, then whisk again.

Meanwhile make the filling. In a saucepan, sweat the onions in the oil, add the minced beef and fry, stirring frequently, until cooked. Add the parsley or dill, with salt and pepper to taste.

Grease an 18 cm (7 inch) pancake pan with butter and, using about 1 tablespoon of the batter at a time, make a batch of pancakes. Place a pancake in the prepared soufflé dish and top with a layer of filling. Repeat the layers until the dish is full, ending with a pancake. Dot with the butter cubes, cover the dish with a lid or foil and place the dish in a roasting pan. Add hot water to the outer pan to a depth of about 5 cm (2 inches).

Bake the pirog in this water bath (bain-marie) in a preheated moderate oven, 180°C (350°F), Gas Mark 4 for 40 minutes. Serve with a mushroom or tomato sauce, if liked.

Note: Choose meat that is slightly fatty for this dish. Minced stewing beef is ideal.

Siberian Ravioli

Pelmeni

Dough:

575 g (1¼ lb) plain flour
25 g (1 oz) butter, diced
2 eggs
150 ml (¼ pint) water
½ teaspoon salt
Pepper

Filling:

350 g (12 oz) stewing steak, finely minced
350 g (12 oz) loin of pork, finely minced
1 onion, finely chopped
4–5 sprigs dill, snipped
salt and pepper

To Cook and Serve:

2.5 litres (4½ pints) beef stock
150 ml (¼ pint) crème fraîche
150 ml (¼ pint) vinegar
250 g (9 oz) Gruyère cheese, grated

Set aside 50 g (2 oz) flour in a small bowl. Put the rest of the flour in a mixing bowl and add the remaining ingredients. Working quickly, mix to a fairly firm dough, like that used for fresh pasta.

In a bowl, combine the meats, onion and dill with salt and pepper to taste. Flour a work surface with the reserved flour and roll out the dough as thinly as possible. It should be transparent but not so thin that it tears. Using a small glass, cut out as many 5 cm (2 inch) rounds as possible. Place ½ teaspoon of filling in the centre of each round and fold over to form a half moon shape, moistening the edges lightly with water to seal.

Bring the stock to the boil in a large saucepan. Add the pelmeni to the stock. As soon as they float to the surface, they are ready. Pour the soup and pelmeni into a soup tureen and serve at once accompanied by jugs of *crème fraîche* and vinegar and the bowl of cheese.

Yeast Dough Pirog

Pirog iz drozhdevovo testa

Dough:

20 g (¾ oz) fresh yeast
½ teaspoon salt
120 ml (4 fl oz) milk
150 ml (¼ pint) oil
500 g (1 lb) plain flour
butter for greasing
1 egg, beaten, to glaze

Filling:

salt (see method)
1 large white cabbage, sliced
2 onions, chopped
1 tablespoon oil
2 hard-boiled eggs, chopped
1 large bunch dill, chopped
125 g (4½ oz) salted butter, in cubes

Prepare the dough as for Yeast Dough Pirozhki (see page 16). Set it aside.

Make the filling. Bring a saucepan of salted water to the boil. Add the cabbage and cook for 10 minutes. Drain thoroughly and blot dry with absorbent kitchen paper. Heat the oil in a large frying pan, add the onions and sweat lightly. Tip the mixture into a bowl and stir in the cabbage, eggs and dill. Immediately stir in the butter, which should melt in the hot filling.

Grease a round dish, 20 cm (8 inches) in diameter and about 5 cm (2 inches) deep. On a floured board, roll out half the dough and line the dish. Spread the filling on top. Roll out the remaining dough to make a top crust for the pie, tucking the edges of the pastry under the bottom crust. If there is any dough left over, make decorations, fixing these to the pie with a little of the beaten egg. Glaze with the remaining beaten egg.

Bake the pirog in a preheated oven, 200°C (400°F), Gas Mark 6 for about 20 minutes or until golden. Serve with melted butter or beef stock.

Variation: Vary the filling by substituting 1 kg (2 lb) cooked diced carrot, or 1.5 kg (3¼ lb) chopped cooked beef for the cabbage, or add rice and slivers of leftover fish or meat.

Meat & Poultry

Pork and poultry are extensively used in Russian cuisine, but beef, mutton, game and offal are also found in many dishes and prepared in many different ways. The meat is generally well cooked. It is often minced or cut into pieces and served with thick cream-based sauces. Roast suckling pig is a classic dish, traditionally associated with Easter, and poultry, including turkey, is also considered an Easter dish.

Kholodets

½ pig's head
2 calf's feet, washed
1 veal bone
250 g (9 oz) veal tendons
salt
15 peppercorns
2 large carrots
2 onions, sliced
1 stick celery, sliced
1 bouquet garni
oil for greasing
cold horseradish sauce (see page 51)

Put the pig's head, calf's feet, veal bone and tendons into a big saucepan and add cold water to cover. Heat slowly until the water begins to boil and carefully skim off the scum that rises to the surface. Add a little salt, the peppercorns, the vegetables and the bouquet garni. Cook for 1½ hours.

With a slotted spoon, remove the carrots and meat from the pan. Slice the meat and cut the carrots into rounds. Bone the meat and remove the skin. Return the bones and skin to the pan and cook for 1 hour more or until the stock has reduced and becomes gelatinous. Strain and leave to cool.

Oil the base of a fairly deep dish and line with the gelatinous stock. Refrigerate to set the aspic, then add the sliced meats and the carrots. Cover with stock and refrigerate for several hours.

Turn the kholodets out of the dish onto a platter. Serve with the horseradish sauce to bring out the flavour.

Beef Croquettes

Kotlety

125 g (4½ oz) bread, crusts removed, or slices of Melba toast
1 kg (2 lbs) braising steak, minced
2 eggs
1 onion, grated
2 tablespoons finely chopped dill
100 g butter, softened
salt and pepper
3 tablespoons oil
300 ml (½ pint) crème fraîche *(optional)*

Soak the bread or Melba toast in water and squeeze them out rapidly. Place in a bowl with the meat, eggs, onion and dill. Add half the softened butter, season with salt and pepper and knead the mixture thoroughly. The more the mixture is kneaded, the better the results will be.

Form the mixture into oval croquettes, each about 10 cm (4 inches) long and 4–5 cm (1½–2 inches) wide.

Melt the remaining butter in the oil in a large frying pan. Add the croquettes and fry for about 10 minutes or until the meat is cooked through. Using a slotted spoon, transfer the cooked croquettes to a serving dish and keep warm.

Add the *crème fraîche* to the pan and warm gently, stirring to incorporate any sediment on the base of the pan. Pour the sauce into a sauce boat and serve with the croquettes.

Note: The proportions given in this recipe are generous as this dish is very popular, especially with children. Small round meatballs can also be made in this way. These are usually served cold with tomato sauce, mayonnaise, cream flavoured with dill, or simply with mustard.

Variation: tefteli
Using the croquette ingredients, make small meatballs and sauté them in the pan. Keep them hot. Fry in a saucepan a finely sliced onion using 50 g (2 oz) of butter. Add in a little sugar, 70 g (3 oz) of tomato concentrate, one bay leaf and a tablespoon of *crème fraîche*, and cook together on a low heat for 10 minutes.

Put the tefteli into the sauce, ladling it over them if necessary, and cook gently for a further 15 minutes. Serve immediately with potatoes or rice.

Beef Croquettes

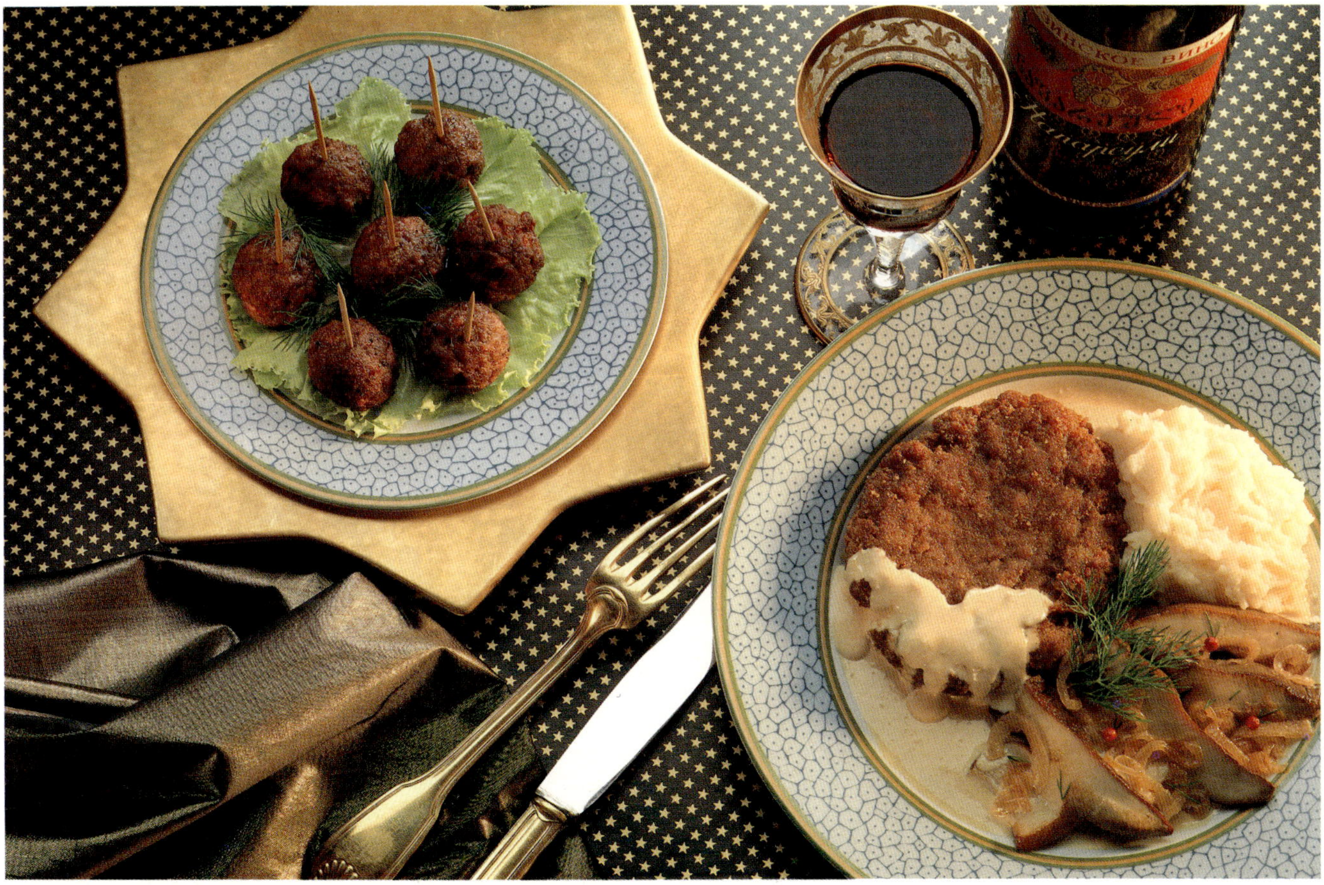

Beef Stroganoff

5 tablespoons oil
50 g (2 oz) butter
2 large onions, sliced
1 kg (2 lb) topside or neck of beef
3 tablespoons plain flour
2 tablespoons English mustard
1 bay leaf
salt and pepper
200 ml (7 fl oz) crème fraîche

Melt the butter in the oil in a large frying pan. Sweat the onions in the pan but do not allow them to brown.

Cut meat into thin strips about 3 cm (1¼ inches) long. Spread the flour in a shallow dish and toss the meat until well coated. Add them to the pan containing the onions and brown swiftly.

Add the mustard and bay leaf to the pan, with salt and pepper to taste, and sufficient boiling water to cover all the ingredients. Stir well and bring to the boil over a high heat, then lower the heat and simmer for 1 hour 20 minutes, stirring occasionally to prevent the sauce catching.

Add the *crème fraîche*, mix well, bring to the boil again and remove from the heat immediately.

Decorate the meat with parsley and serve with sauté potatoes.

Beef Stroganoff

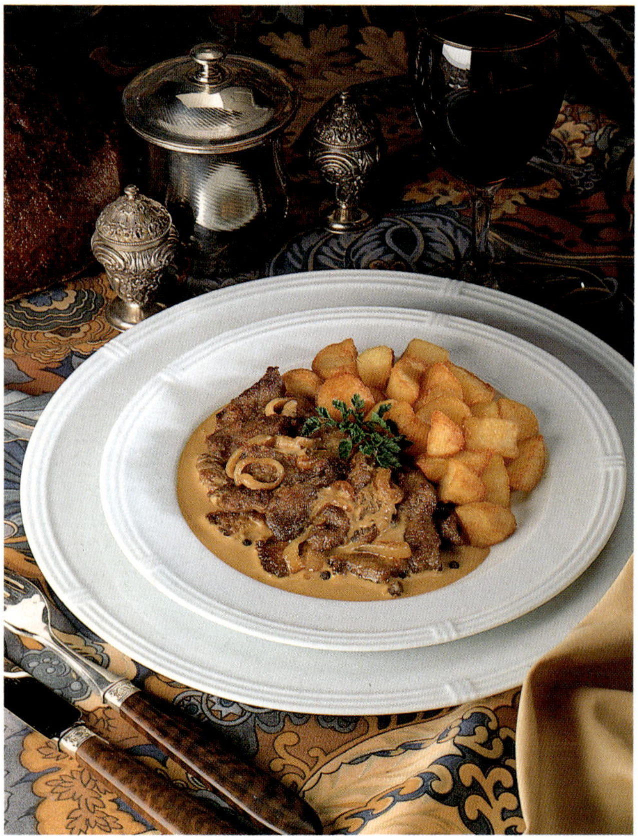

Pozharski Cutlets

Pozharski kotlety

125 g (4½ oz) white bread, crusts removed or Melba toast
200 ml (7 fl oz) crème fraîche
750 g (1½ lb) chicken breasts, finely chopped
1 egg, beaten
90 g (3½ oz) butter
100 g (4 oz) fresh white breadcrumbs
3 tablespoons oil

Soak the bread in the *crème fraîche*. Add the chicken and egg with 40 g (1½ oz) of the softened butter, and knead all the ingredients together by hand.

Form little balls, about 5 cm (2 inches) in diameter, roll them in the breadcrumbs and flatten them by hand to make flat cakes 2 cm (¾ inch) thick.

Fry them in the remaining butter and oil until golden brown on both sides, then cook them on a low heat for 10 to 15 minutes more. Serve immediately.

Kiev Cutlets

Kievskie kotlety

350 g (12 oz) butter
salt and pepper
6 chicken breasts and 6 wings
125 g (4½ oz) plain flour
2 eggs, beaten
oil for deep frying

These cutlets have a delicious butter filling which may spurt out when they are pierced. Take care when eating them.

Cut the butter into 6 sticks of 50 g (2 oz) each Season the butter sticks with salt and pepper and wrap each in foil. Chill until firm.

Slit the chicken wings and carefully bone them with a very sharp knife. Remove all meat from the bones and set them aside. Remove the fat from the chicken breasts. Place a breast between 2 sheets of greaseproof paper and flatten it evenly with a rolling pin until it is very thin. Repeat with the remaining chicken breasts.

Season the chicken breasts. Quickly unwrap the butter sticks. Stick a chicken bone in each butter stick allowing about 2.5 cm (1 inch) to protrude. Tightly roll a chicken fillet around each butter stick, folding over the end like an envelope. If necessary, tie with string.

Dip the cutlets in a shallow bowl containing the flour, then in a similar bowl of egg and finally in breadcrumbs. Heat the oil and deep fry the crumbed cutlets for about 10 minutes. When they are golden brown, remove them with a slotted spoon, drain on kitchen paper and serve at once on a preheated dish, accompanied by rice and mixed vegetables.

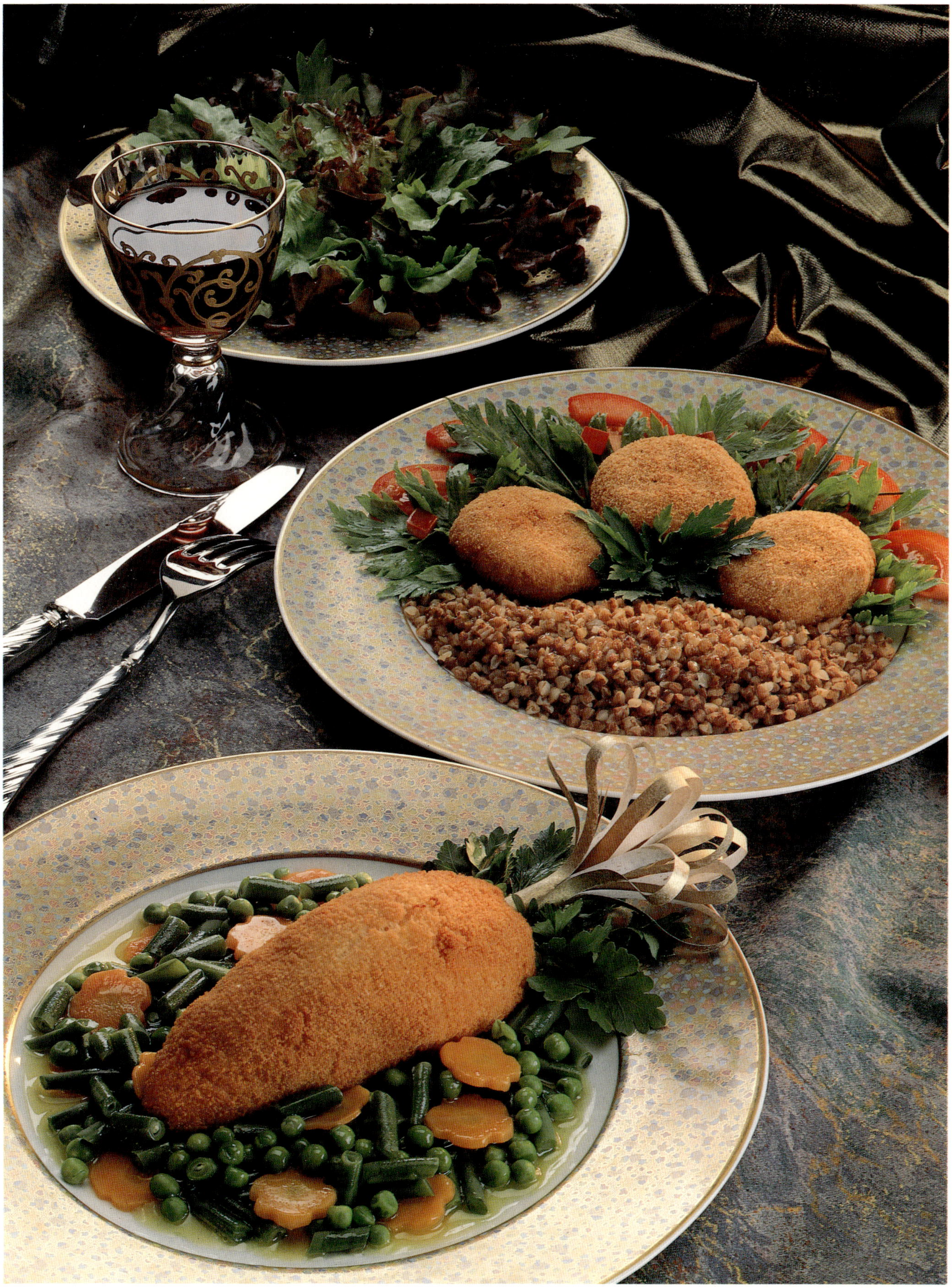

Kiev cutlets, pozharski cutlets

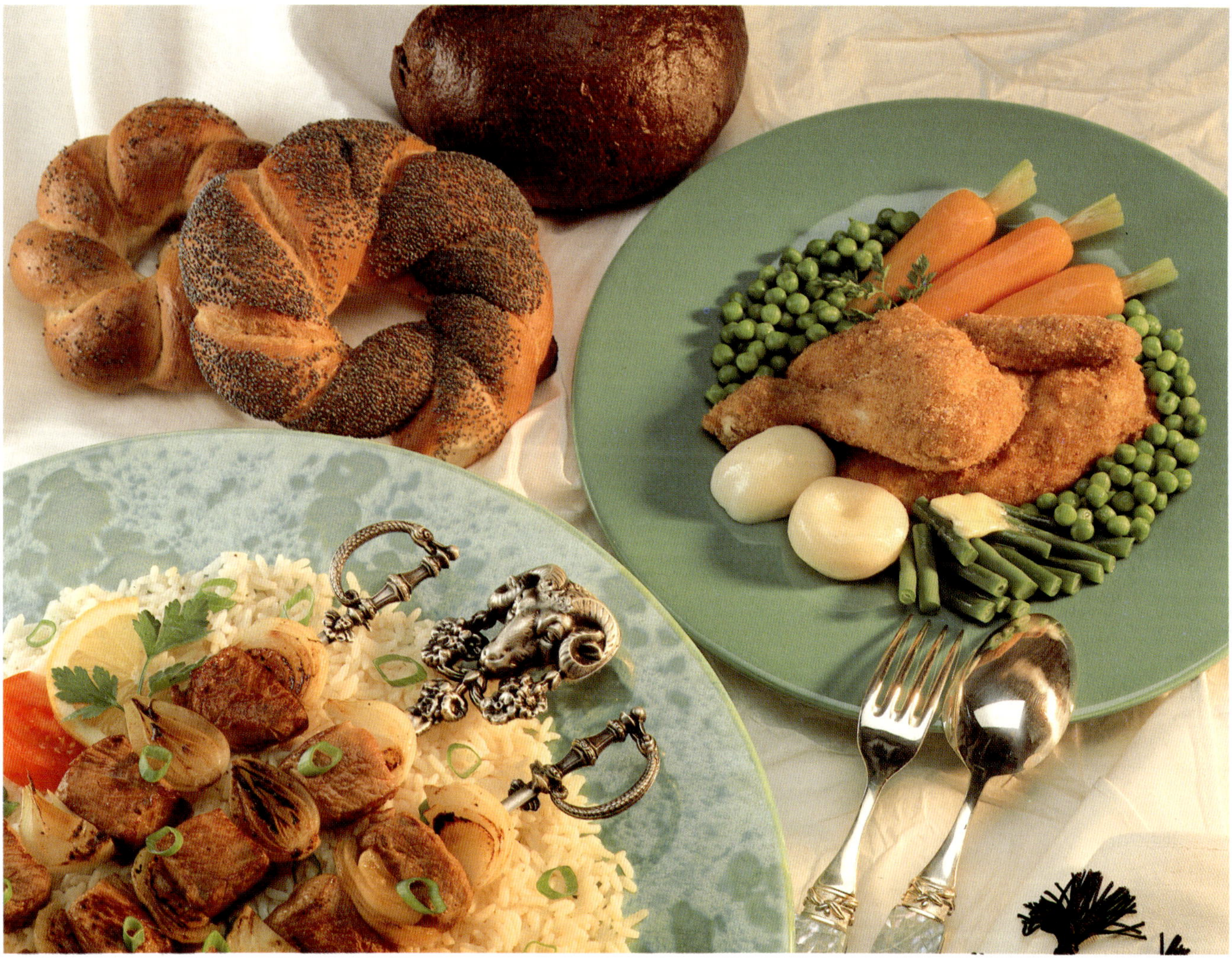

Caucasian Shashlik; Cockerel in Breadcrumbs

Cockerel in Breadcrumbs

Tsipliati v sukhariakh

salt and pepper
3 oven-ready cockerels
75 g (3 oz) plain flour
2 eggs, beaten
75 g (3 oz) fresh white breadcrumbs
oil for shallow frying

Bring a large saucepan of salted water to the boil. Add the cockerels, immersing them in the water, and simmer for 20 minutes.

Drain the cockerels well and cut them in half. Season the flour with salt and pepper and put it in a shallow bowl. Have the beaten eggs and breadcrumbs ready in similar bowls. Dip the cockerels in the flour, then in the egg and finally in breadcrumbs, coating them all over. Heat the oil in a large frying pan and fry the crumbed cockerels for about 5 minutes on each side, or until cooked. Drain on kitchen paper and serve piping hot with a jardinière of vegetables.

Caucasian Shashlik

Shashlik

1 kg (2 lb) boned leg of lamb cut into 4 cm
(1½ inch) cubes
salt and pepper
4 small onions
2 tablespoons vinegar or lemon juice
2 tablespoons oil
2 tablespoons melted butter
2 spring onions, green part only, chopped
500 g (1 lb) small, firm tomatoes, quartered
2 lemons, sliced

Put the lamb into a dish and sprinkle with salt and pepper. Finely chop 2 of the onions and add them to the dish with the vinegar or lemon juice. Mix well. Cover the dish and marinate for 2 to 3 hours in a cool place.

Drain the meat and put on skewers, alternating with slices of raw onion. Brush with oil and grill over charcoal embers for 15 to 20 minutes or fry in oil.

Serve with melted butter and garnish with the green spring onion, the tomatoes, and lemon slices with rice if liked.

Fried Liver

Zharenaia pechen

800 g (1¾ lb) calf's or lamb's liver, sliced
50 g (2 oz) butter
salt and pepper
2 large onions, sliced
200 ml (7 fl oz) double cream

Sauté the liver in the butter in a very hot frying pan then lower the heat and cook gently for 10 to 12 minutes. Salt and pepper them and keep them warm.

Sweat the onions in the same pan. Transfer them to the dish containing the liver.

Add the cream to the pan, bring it to the boil and pour this sauce over the liver and onions. Serve with steamed or mashed potatoes.

Brains with Morels

Mozgi so smorchkami

6 lambs' brains or 3 calves' brains rinsed
salt and pepper
5–6 peppercorns
1 tablespoon vinegar
1 bay leaf
1 packet of dried morels
4 tablespoons fresh white breadcrumbs
200 g (7 oz) butter
1 lemon, sliced to garnish

Put the brains in a saucepan with a little salt. Add the peppercorns, vinegar and bay leaf. Cover with cold water. Bring gently to the boil and simmer for 15 minutes over a low heat. Drain.

Meanwhile, soak the morels in water, following the instructions on the packet. Spread out the bread-crumbs in a shallow dish.

Cut each brain in two, sprinkle with salt and pepper and roll in the breadcrumbs. Melt 50 g (2 oz) of the butter in a large, shallow frying pan, add the crumbed brains and fry over a gentle heat for 5 minutes until golden brown. Meanwhile, in a second pan, sauté the drained morels in 50 g (2 oz) of the remaining butter.

Serve the brains with the rest of the melted butter, the morels, and slices of lemon, accompanied by steamed vegetables.

Stuffed Goose with Apple

Gus farshirovannyi iablokami

1 oven-ready goose about 4 kg (9 lb)
150 ml (¼ pint) oil or 75 g (3 oz) butter
salt and pepper
3 kg (7 lb) cooking apples, cut into small pieces
150 ml (¼ pint) water
250 ml (9 fl oz) chicken stock or stock made from the goose giblets

Ideally, use a free-range goose which is much tastier and which has less waste than the equivalent bird from a commercial producer. Keep the giblets to make rassolnik soup (see page 20), and use the liver to make pâté. Save the goose fat dripping for other dishes, such as casseroles.

Oil or butter the goose. Season it inside and out then stuff with the apples, sewing up the opening.

Pour the measured water into a large roasting pan. Place the goose on its back in the pan and roast in a preheated hot oven, 230°C (450°F), Gas Mark 7 for about 45 minutes. Lower the oven temperature to moderately hot, (375°F), Gas mark 5. Cover the bird with a tent of foil and cook for another 2¼ hours. Baste frequently with the pan juices, adding a little additional water if necessary. To test whether the goose is cooked all the way through prick the flesh at the chest part with a fork; the juices should no longer be pink.

To serve, cut the thread and spoon the apple stuffing onto a hot serving dish. Carve the goose and arrange the pieces on top of the apple. Pour away most of the fat from the roasting pan. Add the stock and heat gently on top of the stove, stirring to incorporate the sediment on the base of the pan. Serve this gravy with the goose.

Stuffed Duck with Apple

Farshirovannaia utka

1 oven-ready duck, about 3 kg (7 lb)
150 ml (¼ pint) oil or 75 g (3 oz) butter
salt and pepper
1.5 kg (3¼ lb) cooking apples, cut into small pieces
150 ml (¼ pint) water
250 ml (8 fl oz) stock

Proceed as for stuffed goose with apple, reduce the initial cooking time to 20 minutes and the total cooking time to 1–1¼ hours.

Roast Suckling Pig with Kasha

Porosionok s krashoi

1 × 5 kg (11 lb) suckling pig, or the saddle and hind legs of a larger suckling pig
500 ml (18 fl oz) double cream
salt and pepper

Coat the pig with cream, sprinkle with salt and pepper and roast in a preheated moderately hot oven, 200°C (400°F), Gas Mark 6 for about 40 minutes or until the skin is golden and crisp.

Lower the oven temperature down to moderate, 180°C (350°F), Gas mark 4 and bake for about 2 hours more, basting frequently to ensure that the meat is tender inside. For a larger suckling pig, over 6 kg (14 lb), allow 2½ hours and for over 8 kg (18 lb) allow 2½ to 3 hours. Serve with Kasha (see page 46).

Suckling Pig with Horseradish

Porosionok s khrenon

4 kg (9 lb) suckling pig
2 carrots, peeled
2 onions
1 stick celery
bouquet garni
salt
15 peppercorns
hot horseradish sauce (see page 51)

Wrap the meat in a clean dishcloth and tie it in such a way as to enable you to slide a long wooden spoon through the bindings horizontally to form a string cradle. Place the spoon horizontally over a large saucepan so that the pig is suspended inside the pan without touching the base.

Roast Suckling Pig with Kasha

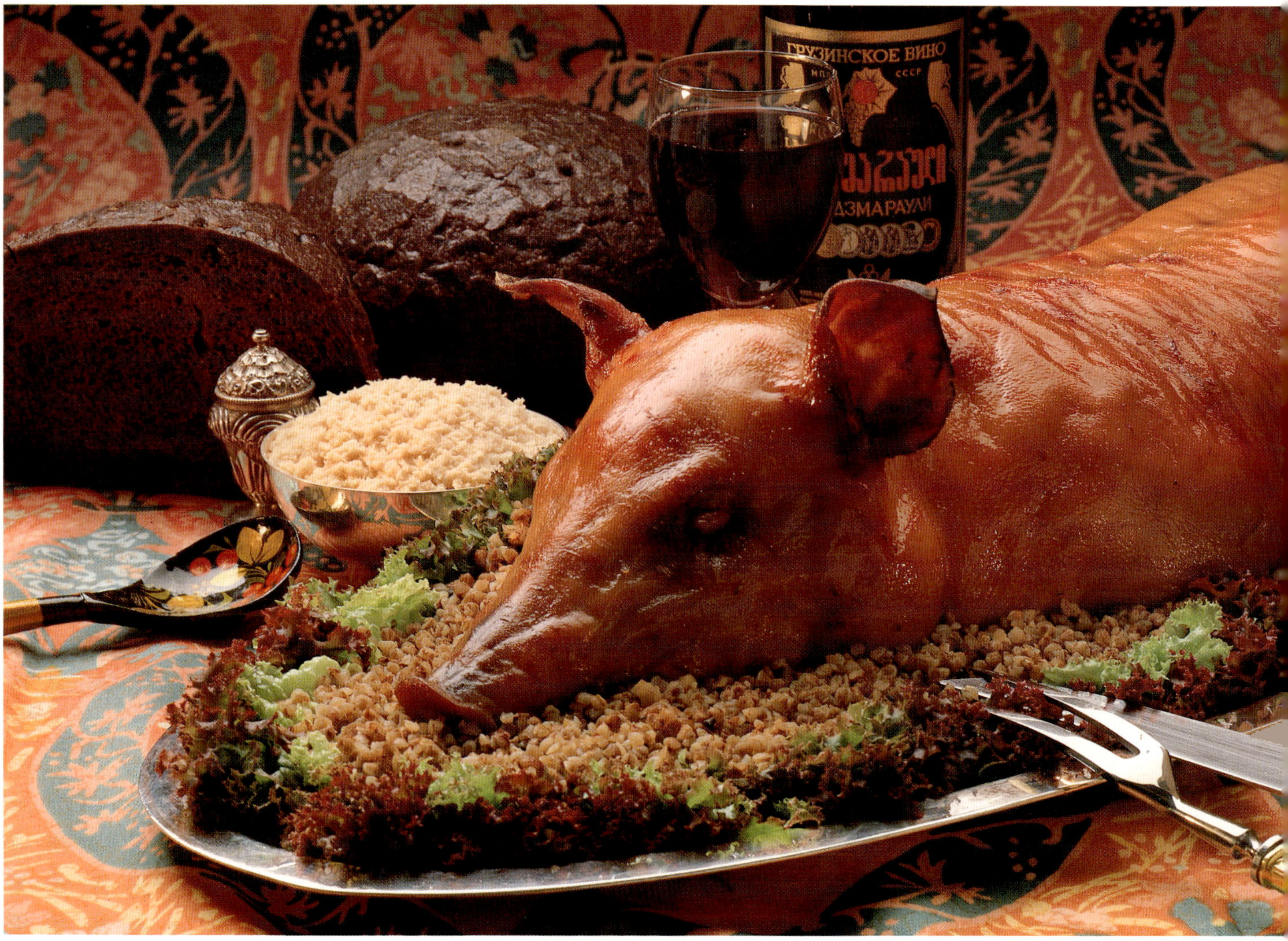

Pour cold water into the pan to cover the pig. Add the vegetables and bouquet garni, with salt and pepper to taste.

Bring to the boil then lower the heat and simmer for 1½ hours. Remove the pan from the heat and leave the pig to cool in the stock.

When the pig is cold, remove it from the stock. Cut the strings and remove the dishcloth, then place the suckling pig on a large platter. Serve with the horseradish sauce.

Variation:
For suckling pig in aspic follow the recipe above, but add 2 pig's trotters, 1 veal bone and 300 g (11 oz) cartilage (tendons, for example) to the stock.

Remove the pig after cooking but leave the remaining meat to simmer in the stock for 2 hours more. Strain the stock and leave to cool. Pour one third of the stock into the bottom of a big shallow dish, refrigerate to set the aspic then place the suckling pig on top. Pour over the rest of the cold stock. Refrigerate and serve when the aspic has set.

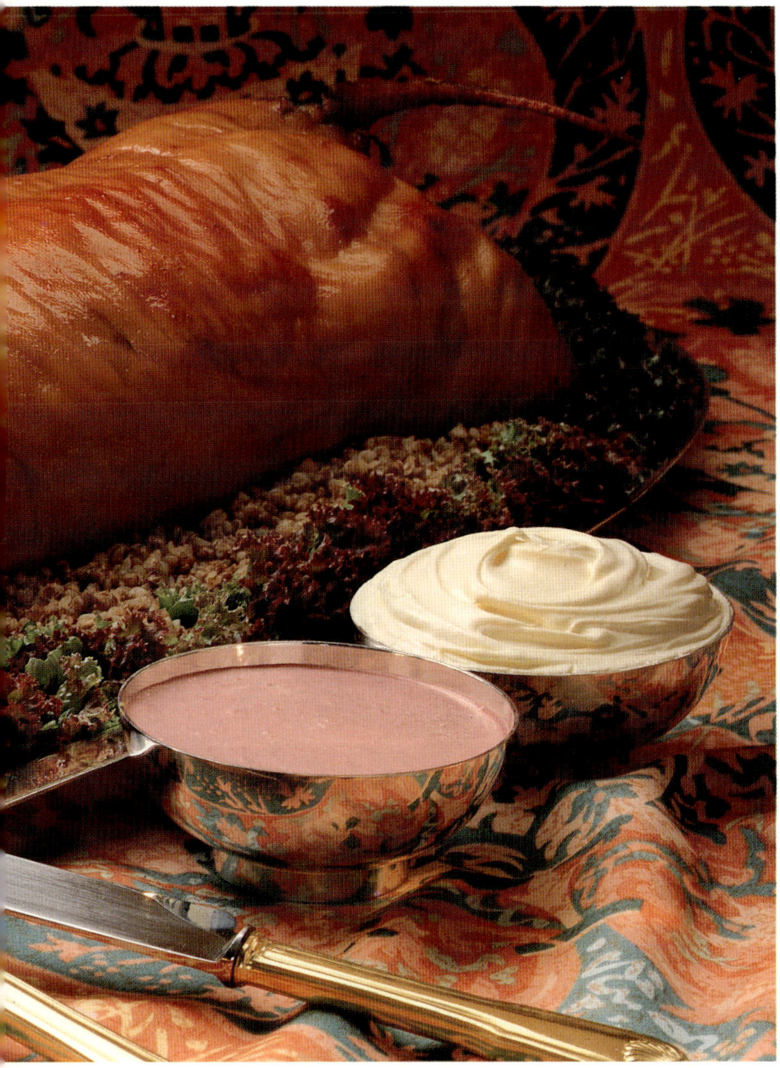

Marinated Roast Pork

Svinina marinovanaia

1 pork roasting joint, about 1.5 kg (3¼ lbs)
2 onions, sliced
1 clove garlic, crushed
2 bay leaves
1½ teaspoons peppercorns
2 cloves
1 litre (1¾ pints) kvas or dry cider
1 tablespoon coarse salt
125 g (44 oz) butter or 150 ml (¼ pint) oil

To serve:
steamed potatoes
grated horseradish
sliced gherkins

Place the pork joint in an earthenware or oven-proof glass roasting dish. Add the onions, garlic, bay leaves, peppercorns and cloves. Pour over the kvas and marinate for 1 hour in a cool place.

Remove the meat, dry it, rub it with coarse salt. Strain the marinade into a jug. Roast in a preheated oven, 200°C (400°F) Gas mark 6 for 1 hour basting the meat frequently.

When the pork is cooked, slice it, putting the slices in a large frying pan. Add the butter and pour over the strained marinade. Bring to the boil, then serve with steamed potatoes, grated horseradish and gherkins. Pork fillet, shoulder of pork or loin are suitable for this recipe.

Bitki with Pork and Beef

Bitki

5 slices Melba toast
250 g (9 oz) minced pork
250 g (9 oz) minced beef
500 ml (18 fl oz) milk
2 eggs
1 onion, finely chopped
salt and pepper
100 g (4 oz) fresh white breadcrumbs
50 g (2 oz) butter
3 tablespoons oil
300 ml (½ pint) crème fraîche *(optional)*

Soak the slices of Melba toast in water, then squeeze them out rapidly, and mix with the pork, beef, milk, eggs and onion. Add salt and pepper to taste. Mix well, then knead vigorously.

Sprinkle the breadcrumbs over a chopping board. Form the meat mixture into rounds, each weighing about 50 g (2 oz). Flatten the meat balls by hand, roll them in the breadcrumbs, and fry them for about 7 minutes on each side in a mixture of oil and butter. When the meatballs are cooked, remove them.

Add the *crème fraîche* to the pan and warm gently. Pour the mixture over the meatballs and serve.

F i s h

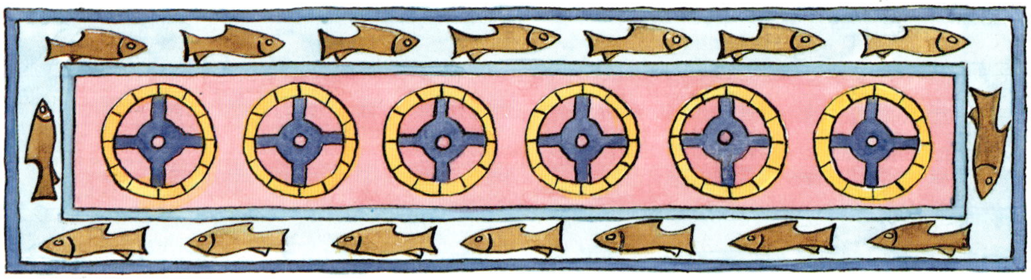

Fish has always played a major economic role in Russia. Seas, lakes and rivers provide an abundant supply of fish, which are cooked in numerous ways. Certain varieties are baked, others are poached in court bouillon or fried. Some fish are smoked and their eggs preserved according to age-old methods which have become famous all over the world. The smaller fish are popular for smoking – herring, pilchards, and sprats. From carp and eel to salmon and sturgeon, all occupy a prominent place in Russian gastronomy.

Salmon in Court Bouillon

Lossos

1 salmon, about 1 kg (2 lb) cleaned and gutted

Court bouillon:
2 litres ($4\frac{1}{2}$ pints) water
50 ml ($\frac{1}{4}$ pint) white wine or 5 tablespoons vinegar
2 large onions, sliced
1 large carrot, peeled and cut into four sticks
2 bay leaves
1 clove
salt
15 peppercorns

To garnish:
100 g (4 oz) butter, melted
juice of 1 lemon
2–3 sprigs dill, chopped

First make the *court bouillon*: put the water in a saucepan and add the other ingredients. Bring to the boil and cook for about 30 minutes until the vegetables are tender. Leave to cool.

Put the court bouillon in a fish kettle and add the whole salmon, immersing it completely. Bring slowly to the boil, lower the heat and simmer for 15 to 20 minutes. Turn off the heat, leaving the fish in the stock for 5 minutes more.

Carefully remove the salmon, keeping it intact. Remove the skin. Serve on a platter with melted butter flavoured with lemon juice, salt and pepper and dill.

This recipe could also be used with other fish, including for example pikeperch. It is a traditional Russian way with freshwater fish, but can also be used with white fish such as cod and halibut.

Pike Loaf

Pate iz shchuki

1 pike, about $2^1/_2$–3 kg ($5^1/_2$–6 lb), skinned
250 g (9 oz) bread, crusts removed
300 ml ($^1/_2$ pint) milk
1 clove of garlic, crushed
1 onion, chopped
2 eggs
salt and pepper
softened butter for greasing

Fish fumet:
2 litres ($3^1/_2$ pints) court bouillon *(page 38)*
1 kg (2 lb) fish trimmings (heads, bones, skin)

Start by making the *fumet*: Put the *court bouillon* into a large saucepan. Add the fish trimmings, including the skin from the pike, and cook for 1 hour. Strain through a fine sieve into a large jug.

Fillet and finely chop the pike. Soak the bread in the milk in a shallow bowl, then squeeze it out thoroughly. Put the bread into a large bowl and add the chopped pike, garlic, onion and eggs. Mix well, add salt and pepper to taste and form into a sausage 7.5 cm (3 inches) in diameter.

Butter a fine cloth and wrap it around the sausage, tying the ends. Place on the rack of a fish kettle and pour over the fish stock. Simmer for 25 minutes.

Remove the sausage to a dish, carefully remove the cloth and slice the sausage. Arrange the slices on a hot platter and serve at once with a complementary sauce.

Pike Loaf

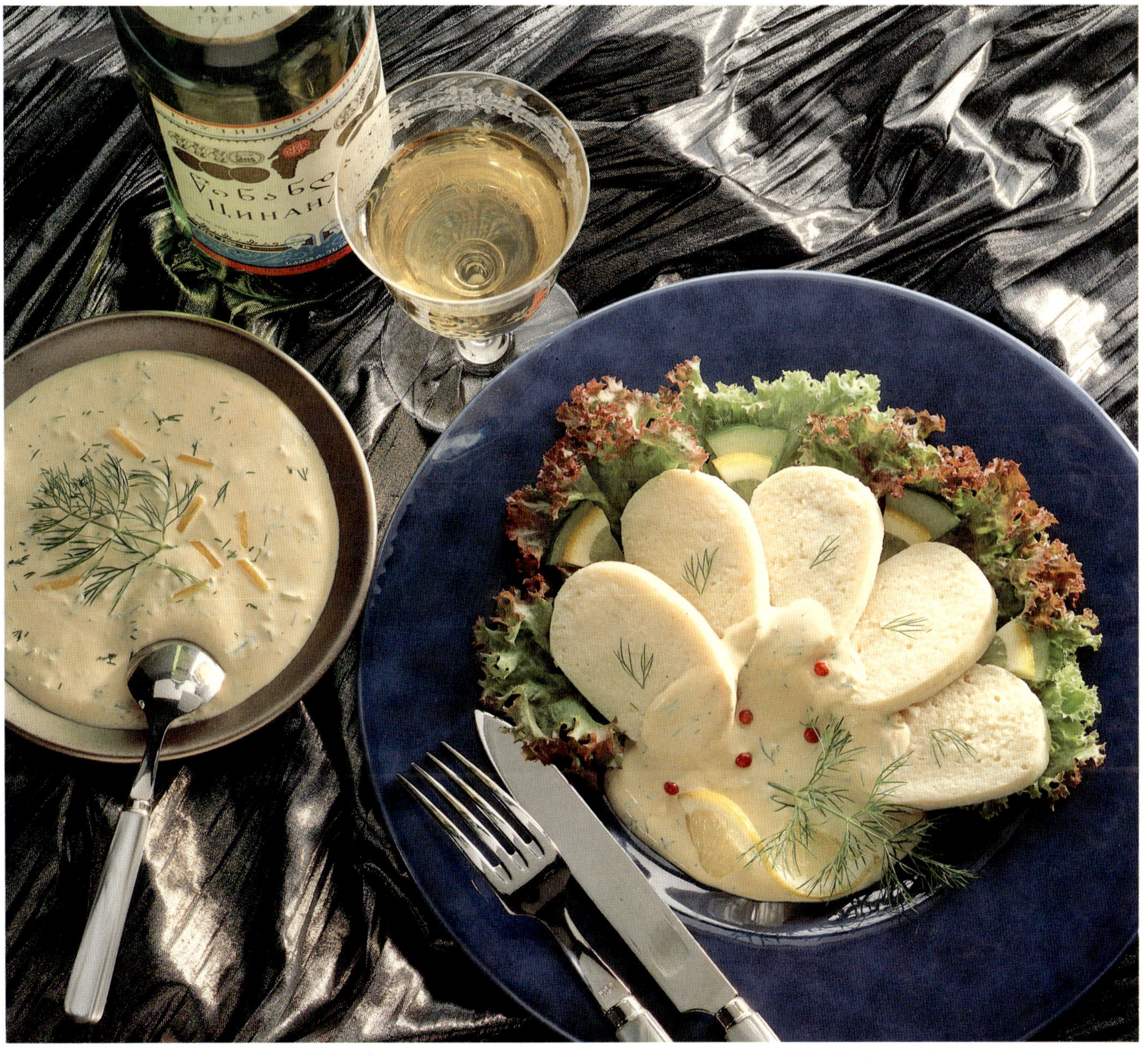

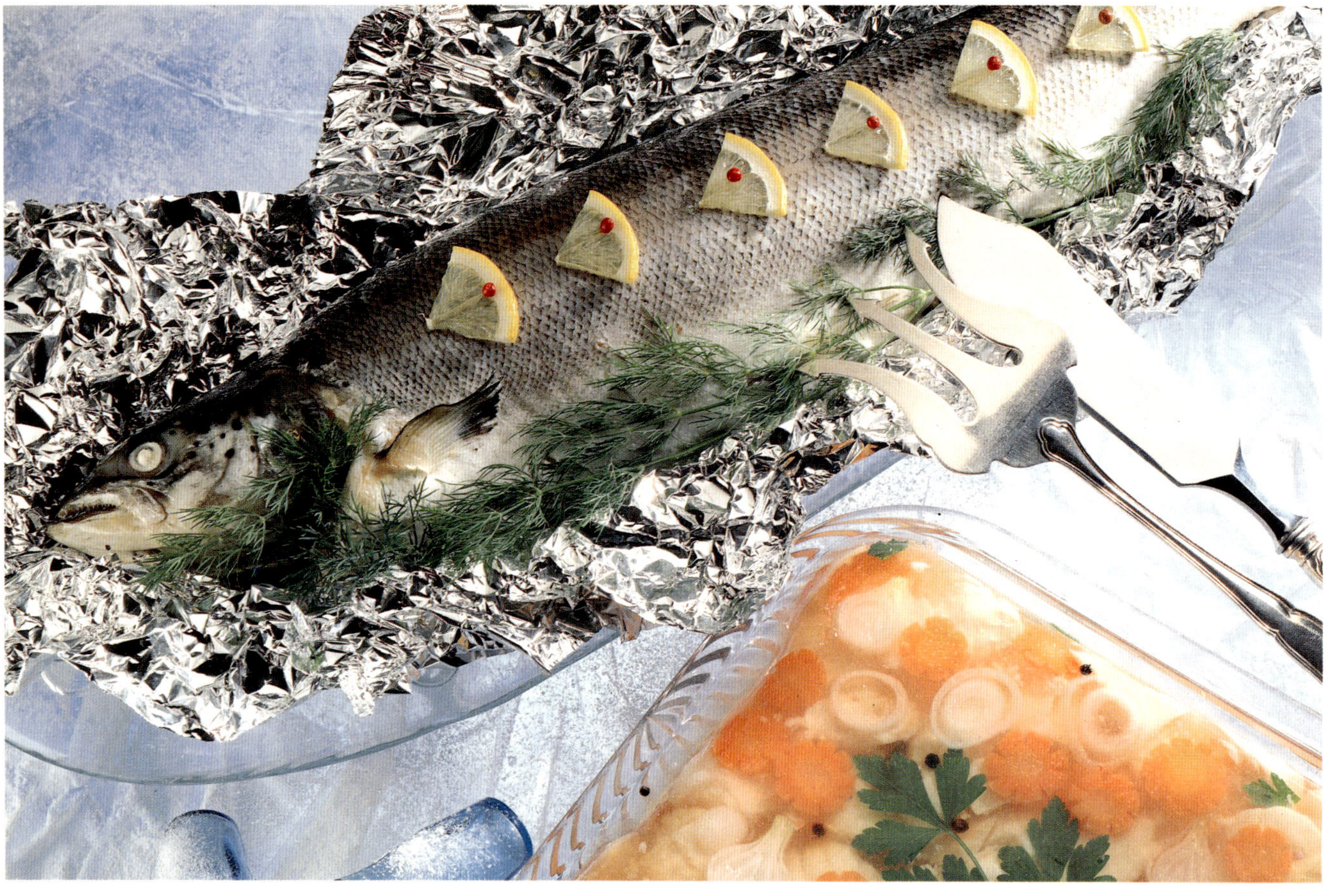

Baked Pikeperch; Studen

Sautéed Eel

Ugor

1.5 kg (3¼ lb) eel, gutted and skinned
3 tablespoons plain flour
2 eggs plus 3 egg yolks
salt and pepper
75 g (3 oz) butter
3 shallots, finely chopped
300 ml (½ pint) fish fumet *(see page 38)*
½ lemon, finely sliced
chopped parsley to garnish

Cut the eels into slices and wipe them thoroughly with kitchen paper, then dip them first into flour, then into beaten egg. Sprinkle with salt and pepper and roll them in the flour. Set aside.

Melt 50 g (2 oz) of the butter in a large frying pan and fry the eel slices for about 5 minutes or until cooked.

Make the sauce: melt the remaining butter in a saucepan. Add the shallots and remaining flour. Cook for 1 minute, stirring, then add the fish stock and the lemon slices, with salt and pepper to taste.

Bring the sauce slowly to the boil, stirring constantly. Strain into a jug and add the yolks. Mix well.

When the eel slices are cooked pour the sauce over the top, sprinkle with chopped parsley and serve with steamed potatoes.

Cod au Gratin

Treska

2 large onions, sliced
6 tablespoons oil
750 g (1½ lb) fresh cod steaks
salt and pepper
300 g (11 oz) tomatoes, sliced
750 g (1½ lb) potatoes, peeled and sliced
3–4 tablespoons water
100 g (4 oz) butter, melted

To garnish:
10 sprigs parsley, finely chopped
10 chive stalks, finely chopped

Sauté the onions in 1 tablespoon of the oil. Line the base of a gratin dish with the onions and cover with the steaks. Add salt and pepper to taste. Put a layer of tomatoes on top of the fish. Sprinkle lightly with more salt and pepper.

Heat the remaining oil and fry the potatoes for about 25 minutes, until they are golden brown, and place them on top of the tomatoes. Add the water to the dish. Drizzle the melted butter over the top.

Cover the dish and bake in a preheated oven, 230°C (450°F), Gas Mark 8 for 20 to 30 minutes. Garnish with the herbs and serve.

Muscovite Solianka

Moskovskaia solianka

6 onions, chopped
4 carrots, peeled and chopped
6 tomatoes, chopped
7–8 tablespoons oil
2 bay leaves
salt and pepper
1 teaspoon sugar
200 g (7 oz) Russian sauerkraut (see page 45)
6 gherkins
250 ml (9 fl oz) fish fumet *(see page 39)*
1.5 kg (3¼ lb) conger eel, coley, or cod filleted and cut into small pieces
100 g (4 oz) butter
50 g (2 oz) fresh white breadcrumbs
lemon slices to garnish

Sauté the onions, carrots and tomatoes in 3 tablespoons of the oil in a large saucepan. Add bay leaves, salt and pepper, and sugar. Cook for 5 minutes, stirring all the time. Add the sauerkraut. Slice 4 of the gherkins and add them to the pan. Stir gently and moisten with the stock. Cover the pan and simmer the vegetables for about 15 minutes or until tender.

In a separate pan, sauté the fish in the remaining oil.

Using half the butter, grease a deep oven-proof dish and sprinkle with half the breadcrumbs. Line the base with a layer of vegetables, followed by a layer of fish. Repeat the layers until all the ingredients have been used ending with a layer of vegetables.

Sprinkle the remaining breadcrumbs over the top layer. Melt the remaining butter in a small saucepan and drizzle it over the breadcrumbs. Bake in a preheated oven, 200°C (400°F), Gas Mark 6 for 10 to 15 minutes. Serve garnished with gherkins.

Fish Fricassee

Zharenie ryby v smetane

1.5 kg (3¼ lb) small fish (dabs, small sea bream) gutted and cleaned but left whole
salt and pepper
40 g (1½ oz) plain flour
25 g (1 oz) butter
200 ml (7 fl oz) single cream

Rinse the fish and dry. Sprinkle with salt and pepper. Put the flour in a shallow bowl, add the fish and coat well. Melt the butter in the oil in a large pan and fry the fish on both sides for a few minutes. Pour over the cream and cook for 10 minutes more over very gentle heat.

Transfer the fish and sauce to a warm platter and serve immediately, with kasha, if liked.

Baked Pikeperch

200 g (7 oz) butter
salt
1 small bunch dill
1 pikeperch, about 2 kg (4½ lb) cleaned and scaled
2 hard-boiled eggs, finely chopped

Soften 50 g (2 oz) butter with 1 teaspoon salt in a small bowl. Add a sprig of dill. Use the flavoured butter to line the inside of the fish with this.

Wrap the fish in foil and bake in a preheated moderately hot oven, 200°C (400°F), Gas Mark 6 for 20 minutes. Switch off the oven and allow the fish to continue cooking for 10 minutes more.

Meanwhile, melt the rest of the butter in a saucepan. Tip it into a bowl, add salt to taste and lightly stir in the chopped hard-boiled eggs. Chop the remaining dill finely and stir it into the egg mixture. Serve with the fish.

Studen

2 litres (3½ pints) court bouillon *(see page 38)*
1 large sturgeon head
salt
1 carrot, sliced
1 bunch small onions
cold horseradish sauce (see page 51)

Put the *court bouillon* in a large saucepan, add the fish head and cook over gentle heat for 1½ hours. Using a strainer, carefully transfer the fish head to a board.

Bring a saucepan of salted water to the boil, add the carrot and onions and cook for 15 to 20 minutes until tender. Drain and reserve.

Skin the fish and remove the flesh from the bones, not forgetting the cheeks. Arrange the fish pieces in a serving dish with the carrot and onions.

Heat the fish stock remaining in the saucepan, skim off any scum, then strain into a jug. Pour the hot stock over the fish and vegetables. When cool, refrigerate for a few hours until set. Serve with the horseradish sauce.

Variation:
Instead of sturgeon, use 1.5 kg (3¼ lb) cod. Cook the whole fish in the *court bouillon* until the flesh flakes off in large pieces. With a slotted spoon, remove the bones and cartilage and continue cooking the fish for 1 hour, adding 1 kg (2 lb) fish trimmings for extra flavour. Discard the trimmings when serving the cod and vegetables with the strained stock.

Fish au Gratin

Zapechonie ryby

butter for greasing
500 g (1 lb) potatoes, peeled and sliced
about 200 ml (7 fl oz) oil
1.5 kg (3¼ lb) firm-fleshed fish or 1 fillet per person
4 onions, sliced
500 g (1 lb) button mushrooms, wiped and sliced
4 hard-boiled eggs, quartered

Béchamel sauce:
75 g (3 oz) butter
1 tablespoon plain flour
250 ml (8 fl oz) fish fumet *(see page 39)*
salt and pepper
125 g (4½ oz) Cheddar cheese, grated
100 ml (3½ fl oz) crème fraîche

Heat 5 tablespoons of the oil in a large frying pan and fry the potatoes for 20 minutes. Grease a gratin dish generously with butter. Line the gratin dish with the potatoes. If using a whole fish, cut it into 6 or 12 pieces. Add a further 5 tablespoons of the oil to the frying pan and cook the fish pieces or fillets for 15 minutes. Using a slotted spoon, arrange them on the bed of potatoes in the gratin dish.

Add the onions to the pan, with more oil if necessary and fry for 10 minutes. Cover the fish with the fried onions.

Add about 2 tablespoons of oil to the frying pan and sauté the mushrooms for 5 minutes. Put them on top of the onions and add the eggs.

Make a light Béchamel sauce. Melt the butter in a saucepan and stir in the flour. Cook, stirring, for 1 minute, then add the fish stock, with salt and pepper to taste. Cook over low heat stirring constantly for about 15 minutes, then stir in the cheese. Remove the pan from the heat and add the cream.

Pour the sauce over the fish mixture and bake in a preheated hot oven 230°C (450°F) Gas mark 8 for 15 minutes. Serve piping hot.

Fish Croquettes

Rybnye kotlety

1 kg (2 lb) fish fillets
300 g (11 oz) bread, crusts removed
300 ml (½ pint) milk
1 onion, finely grated
1 egg
80 g (3¼ oz) butter, softened
about 25 g (1 oz) fresh white breadcrumbs
2 tablespoons oil
mushroom sauce (see page 50)

Fillet and finely chop the fish, or put them through a food mill. A food processor may be used, but care should be taken not to overprocess the fish. Set aside.

Soak the bread in the milk in a shallow bowl. Squeeze out excess liquid and add the bread to the fish with the onion, egg and 50 g (2 oz) of the softened butter. Knead thoroughly by hand and roll into balls, each weighing about 75 g (3 oz). Spread the breadcrumbs in a shallow bowl, add the fish balls and coat well. Form the crumbed fish balls into an oval.

Heat the oil with the remaining butter in a large frying pan and fry the fish croquettes until they are golden brown. Serve at once with mushroom sauce.

For Stuffed Fish Croquettes, make the basic croquette mixture as in the recipe above. Prepare a stuffing by frying 500 g (1 lb) chopped fresh mushrooms for 4 to 5 minutes in 2 tablespoons oil, together with 1 large onion, chopped, and 2 to 3 tablespoons chopped parsley. Break off small balls of the croquette mixture. Flatten them out to rounds, about 1 cm (½ inch) thick. Place ½ teaspoon of stuffing on one half of each round. Fold it over carefully and pinch the edges together as for pirozhki. Dip into beaten egg, then into breadcrumbs and fry in oil. Remove carefully with a slotted spoon and serve at once.

Poached Pike

Shchuka

1.5 kg (3¼ lb) pike or salmon
4 tablespoons plain flour
50 g (2 oz) butter
10 onions, coarsely chopped
500 ml (1 pint) fish fumet *(see page 39)*
150 ml (¼ pint) white wine
200 g (7 oz) mushrooms, wiped and sliced (optional)
1 bay leaf

Skin and fillet the fish, and cut into large chunks. Roll these in the flour in a shallow bowl and set aside on a chopping board.

Melt the butter in a large frying pan and fry the onions. Add the fish and brown for a few minutes, then pour over the fish stock and white wine. Add the mushrooms and bay leaf.

Cook over a low heat for 20 minutes. Serve with steamed potatoes, if liked.

Fish Fritters

Rybny oladii

2 small fish fillets per person
fritter batter (see page 18)
oil for deep frying

Dip the fish fillets in the bowl of batter and fry quickly in hot oil. Serve hot.

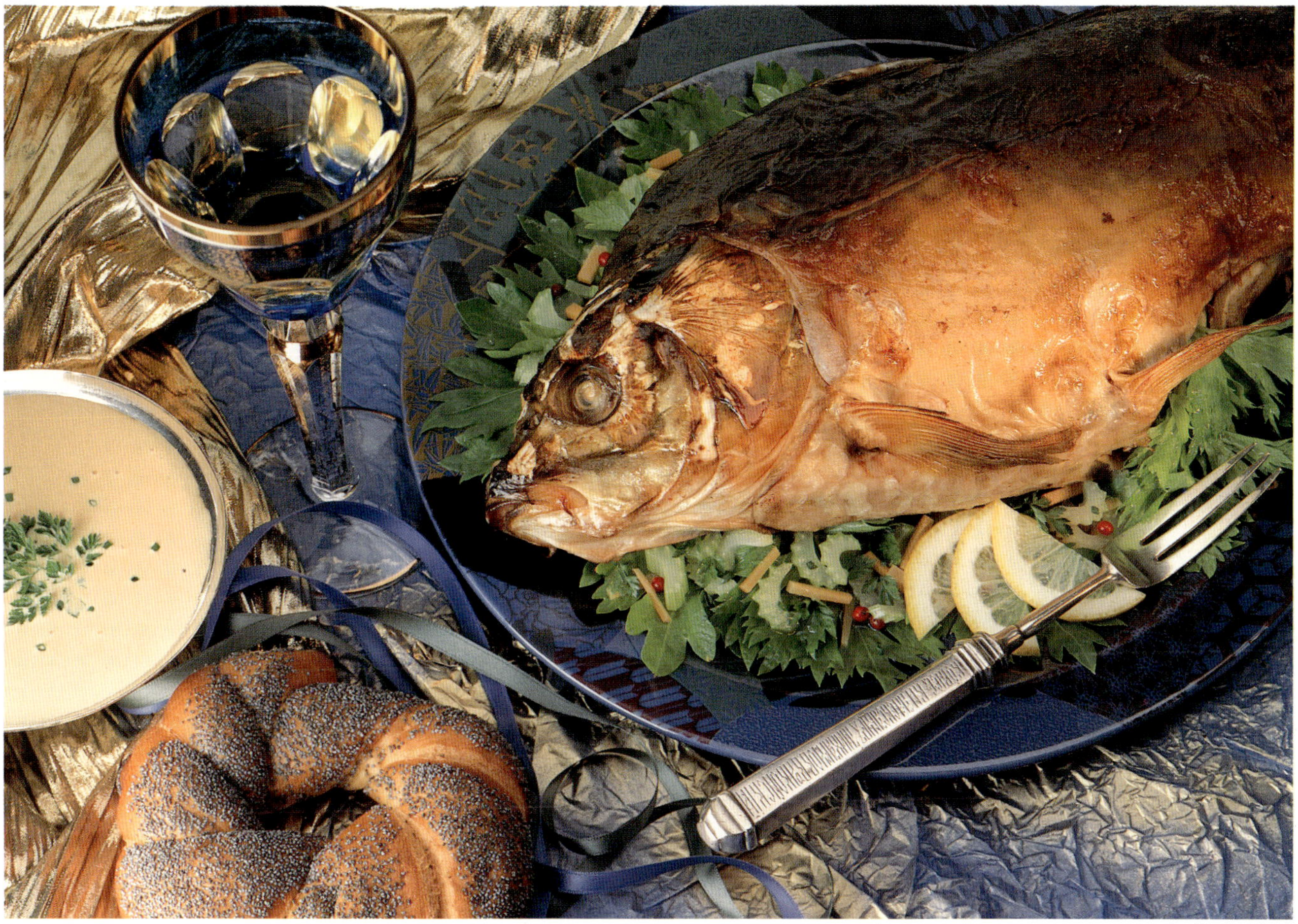

Stuffed Baked Carp

Baked Carp with Beer

Pechionyi karp v pive

3 carrots, finely sliced
3 onions, finely sliced
3 sticks celery, finely sliced
75 g (3 oz) butter
1 carp, about 1.5 kg (3¼ lb) scaled and gutted, roe (if any) reserved
salt
1 litre (1¾ pints) beer or kvas
2 tablespoons crème fraîche

Sweat the carrots, onions and celery in the butter in a large saucepan. Put the carp in a large flameproof dish and surround it with the vegetables. Sprinkle with salt, pour over the beer and bake in a preheated moderately hot oven for 30 minutes, basting frequently.

Transfer the fish on to a hot serving dish and keep warm. Place the flameproof dish over moderate heat and cook the sauce until it has reduced by two thirds. Strain the sauce, bind it with the cream and pour it over the carp. If the carp contained any soft roe, slice and use as a garnish.

Stuffed Baked Bream

Farshirovanyi lieshch

1 tablespoon oil
1 onion, chopped
2 eggs
200 g (7 oz) buckwheat (raw weight)
1 bream, about 1.5 kg (3¼ lb) scaled and gutted
150 ml (¼ pint) crème fraîche
salt

Heat the oil in a small frying pan, add the onion and fry until golden. Tip the contents of the pan into a bowl and set aside. Hard-boil one of the eggs.

Cook the buckwheat according to the recipe on page 46. Add it to the onion and stir in the hard-boiled egg and the raw egg. Mix well. Stuff the fish with the mixture.

Put the fish in a shallow baking dish and cover with the *crème fraîche*, seasoned with a little salt. Bake in a preheated moderately hot oven; 250°C (400°F), Gas Mark 6 for 30 minutes, basting frequently. Serve hot.

Vegetables

Served solo or as an accompaniment, Russian vegetables typify a cold climate: buckwheat, potatoes and mushrooms are the most commonly used, but cabbage occupies a unique position in Russian cuisine. This vitamin-rich vegetable can be preserved in barrels for the long winter months, a fact which has made it very popular over the centuries.

Stuffed Cabbage Leaves

Golubtsy

1 large Savoy cabbage
salt and pepper
500 g (1 lb) minced braising steak
7 tablespoons oil
2 onions, finely chopped
125 g (4½ oz) long-grain rice
2 tablespoons chopped dill
250 ml (9 fl oz) crème fraîche
1 × 140 g (4½ oz) can concentrated tomato purée
1 teaspoon sugar
2 bay leaves

Remove the leaves from the cabbage one by one. Bring a saucepan of water to the boil, add 1 tablespoon salt, then add the cabbage leaves. Blanch them for 3 to 4 minutes, draining them carefully so as not to tear the leaves. Pat them dry. With a sharp knife, trim the stalks to the same thickness as the leaves. Leave to cool.

Heat 2 tablespoons of the oil in a frying pan. Add the minced beef and brown, stirring for 5 minutes. With a slotted spoon, transfer the mince to a bowl. Set aside. Add a further 1 tablespoon oil to the pan and sweat the onions. Mix them with the meat.

Bring a large saucepan of water to the boil. Add 1 teaspoon salt, with the rice. Boil the rice for 10 to 12 minutes or until cooked. Drain and add to the meat mixture. Stir in half the dill.

Place 2 tablespoons of stuffing on each cabbage leaf and wrap it up tucking in the sides to form a neat parcel. Heat the remaining oil in the clean frying pan and brown the cabbage parcels on all sides. Transfer them, in a single layer, to a baking dish.

In a bowl, mix the cream with the tomato concentrate and sugar. Pour the mixture into the frying pan, add the bay leaves and dill, with salt and pepper to taste. Place over gentle heat, removing the pan from the heat as soon as the sauce comes to the boil. Pour the sauce over the cabbage rolls and bake in a preheated oven, 180°C (350°F), Gas Mark 4 for 35 minutes. Serve at once.

Russian Sauerkraut

Skorospelaia kislaia kapusta

1 white cabbage, about 1 kg (2 lb), cut into quarters
5 anise seeds
5 cumin seeds
1 small sprig mint
1 litre (1¾ pints) boiling water
25 g (1 oz) coarse salt
1 black bread crust
2½ tablespoons sunflower oil
1 tablespoon sugar

Remove the cabbage stalk. Coarsely chop the leaves and put them in an earthenware pot. Add the herbs. Mix the boiling water and salt. Pour the mixture over the cabbage and cover with a plate and suitable weight to stop the cabbage floating to the top.

When the liquid has cooled, add the bread crust to initiate fermentation. Leave in a warm place for 3 days.

Stir in the oil and sugar to remove any bitter taste.

Note: This sauerkraut must be eaten quickly, as there is not enough salt to preserve it for long. It is sold ready made in all Russian shops and is considered an excellent source of vitamin C.

Sauerkraut

Kislaia kapusta

1 white cabbage, chopped
1 carrot, peeled and roughly grated
1½ tablespoons coarse salt
a few black bread crusts
2 tablespoons sunflower oil
½ tablespoon sugar

Mix the cabbage, carrot and salt in a large bowl. Line an earthenware container with the bread crusts, put in the cabbage and pack it down. Cover with a weighted plate and set aside at warm room temperature for 2 to 3 days.

Transfer the earthenware pot to the refrigerator. To serve, mix the cabbage with the oil and sugar.

Note: The cabbage will keep as long as it is covered in juice. Remove any mould that forms: it is harmless.

Stuffed Cabbage Leaves

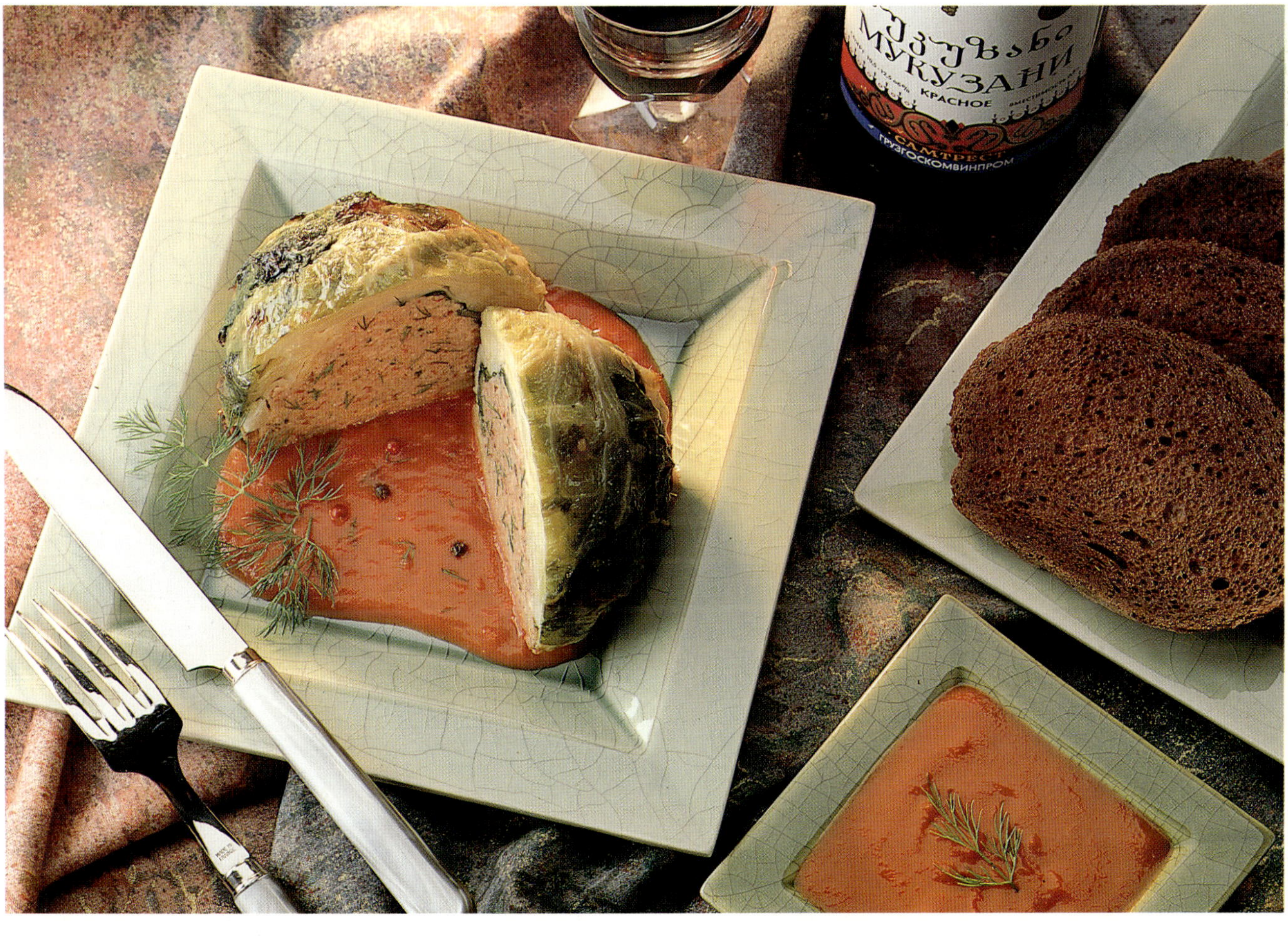

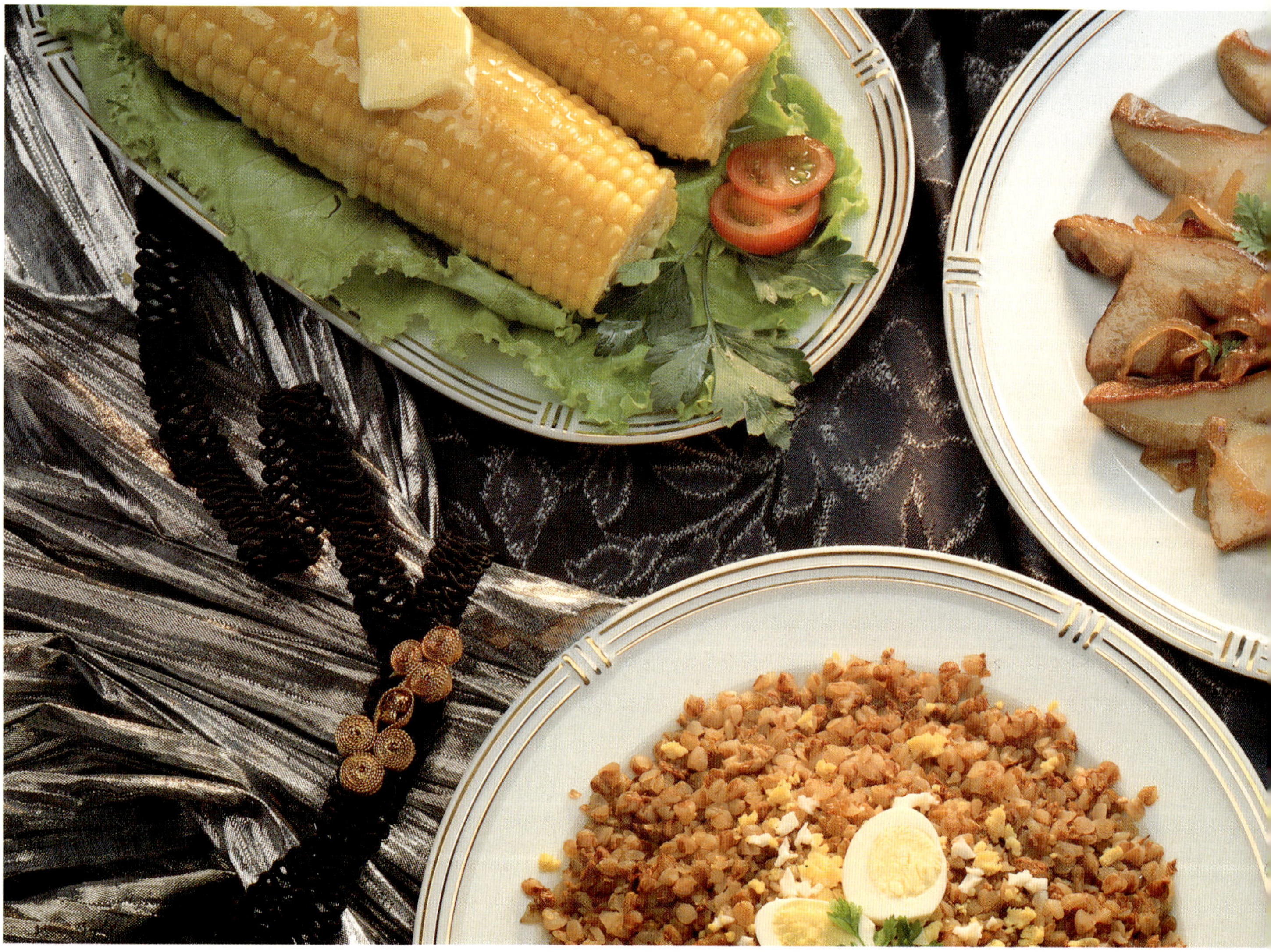

Corn on the Cob, Kasha, Fried Ceps

Kasha

350 g (12 oz) buckwheat groats
1 egg, beaten
750 ml (1¼ pints) very hot beef stock
50 g (2 oz) butter, diced

Put the buckwheat groats in an earthenware pot. Place on a heat diffuser over high heat and add the egg at once. Stir with a wooden spoon until the groats are dry and separate.

Pour over the stock and continue to stir for 2 minutes. Add the butter and cover.

Fold a blanket into four and place on it a newspaper folded in three and then in two. Stand the pot on the newspaper and fold over the sides of the blanket to envelop the pot. Place a pillow on top to keep the pot warm.

Leave the kasha to swell for 2 hours, then mix it with a spoon and serve with a meat dish or as a dish in its own right with hard-boiled eggs, onions and sautéed mushrooms.

Note: A more modern method is to toast the grains in a dry frying pan, then trickle them into a saucepan containing the boiling stock. Return to the boil and cook for 2 to 3 minutes until thick. Lower the heat, cover and simmer for 10 minutes. Remove the lid, fluff up with a fork and continue to simmer over the lowest possible heat for 1 hour, forking the mixture through at frequent intervals.

Corn on the Cob

Kukuruza

1 or 2 ears of corn per person, leaves removed
salt
butter to serve

Bring a large saucepan of water to the boil and add the corn. When the water returns to the boil cook the corn cobs for 3 to 5 minutes, depending on their size. Do not add salt as this would toughen the corn kernels. When tender, drain and serve hot with salt and butter.

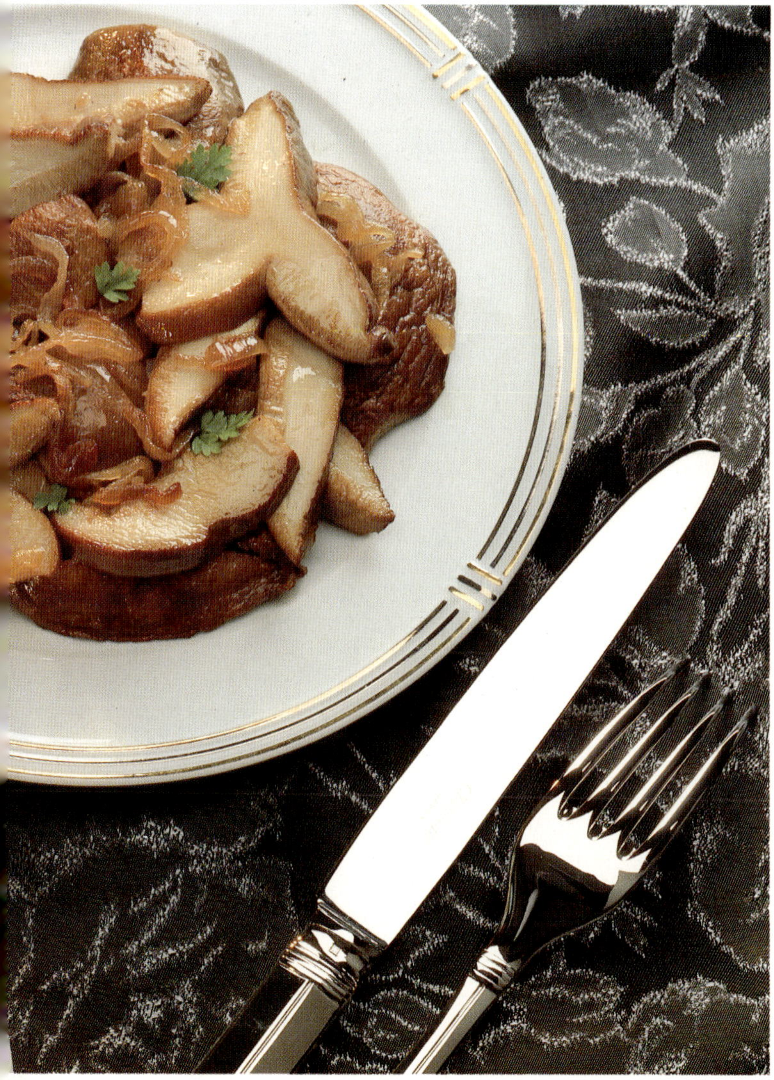

Fried Ceps

Belig griby

500 g (1 lb) ceps or boletus mushrooms
50 g (2 oz) butter
salt and pepper
200 ml (7 fl oz) crème fraîche
1 bunch parsley
1 sprig dill
1 bay leaf
2 cloves
4–5 peppercorns

Rinse, trim and cut the mushrooms into slivers, and sauté them lightly in butter. Add salt and pepper to taste and transfer them to an earthenware pot.

Variation: Pour over the *crème fraîche*. Tie the parsley, dill, bay leaf, clove and peppercorns in a muslin bag and suspend this bouquet garni in the pot. Cover and cook in a preheated moderate oven, 180°C (350°F), Gas Mark 4 for 1 hour. Remove the bouquet garni and serve straight from the cooking pot.

Kasha Croquettes

350 g (12 oz) buckwheat groats
1 litre (1¾ pints) very hot meat stock
salt
3 eggs
25 g (1 oz) fresh white breadcrumbs
75 g (3 oz) butter

Cook the groats with the stock according to the previous recipe. Left over kasha may be reheated with a little stock and stirred until smooth. Add salt if necessary. Spoon the kasha into a bowl and set aside until cold.

Stir the eggs into the cold kasha and form the mixture into long croquettes. Roll them in the bread-crumbs in a shallow bowl. Heat the butter in a large frying pan, add the croquettes and fry for 3 to 4 minutes until golden on all sides. Drain and serve with mushroom sauce or hot salted cream, if liked.

Stuffed Potatoes

Farshirovannii kartofel

9 large potatoes, or 12 medium ones
salt and pepper
150 ml (5 fl oz) thick crème fraîche
2 eggs, whisked
6 slices of bread
50 g (2 oz) cheese, grated
50 g (2 oz) dried breadcrumbs
50 g (2 oz) butter

Boil the potatoes in salted water but take them off the heat before they are completely cooked.

While they are boiling mix the cream and the eggs. Cut the crust off the slices of bread and soak them in the mixture.

Strain the potatoes, remove the skins, and cut them in halves. Hollow out the middle of each half and put this part in a mixer or blender together with the bread and the mixture of eggs and cream. Blend all together adding salt and pepper and put this filling into each half-potato. Sprinkle each with cheese and breadcrumbs topped with a knob of butter, and cook them in the oven (Gas Mark 3–4, 160°C) for 10 to 15 minutes until the potatoes have browned slightly on top.

Serve with a mushroom sauce (see page 50) or to accompany a meat dish.

Solianka with Mushrooms

Gribnaia solianka

1 kg (2 lb) Savoy cabbage, finely chopped
200 g (7 oz) butter
1 tablespoon vinegar
1 bay leaf
2 tablespoons tomato purée
1 pickled gherkin, cut into rounds
1 teaspoon sugar
salt and pepper
500 g (1 lb) button mushrooms, wiped
1 large onion, finely chopped
150 g (5 oz) black olives, stoned
25 g (1 oz) fresh white breadcrumbs
2 tablespoons melted butter

Melt 100 g (4 oz) of the butter in a large pan. Add the cabbage, vinegar and bay leaf, cover the pan and cook the mixture over a low heat for 45 minutes.

Stir in the tomato purée, gherkin and sugar into the cabbage mixture, with salt and pepper to taste, and cook for 15 minutes more.

Bring a saucepan of salted water to the boil and blanch the mushrooms for 5 minutes. Drain them, cut them into slivers, and sauté them in the remaining butter for 10 minutes. Transfer them to a bowl.

Add the onion to the oil remaining in the frying pan and sauté lightly. Stir it into the mushrooms and add the black olives. Put half the braised cabbage into a baking dish, add the mushrooms and cover with the rest of the cabbage. Sprinkle the surface with breadcrumbs. Melt the remaining butter in the frying pan and drizzle it over the breadcrumbs. Brown the dish in a preheated oven, 230°C (450°F), Gas Mark 8 for 10 minutes.

Variation: Solianka can also be made with braised Russian sauerkraut, in which case omit the vinegar.

Potato Croquettes

Kartofelnye kotlety

1 kg (2 lb) potatoes
2 eggs, beaten
25 g (1 oz) fresh white breadcrumbs or plain flour
150 ml (1/4 pint) oil or 75 g (3 oz) butter
mushroom sauce (see page 50)

Boil the potatoes in their jackets for 20 minutes. Peel them, place them in a bowl and mash with the eggs.

When the mixture is cool enough to handle, form it into small croquettes. Roll these in breadcrumbs.

Fry croquettes in oil or butter for 2 to 3 minutes until golden. Drain and serve at once, with the mushroom sauce.

Muscovite Solianka

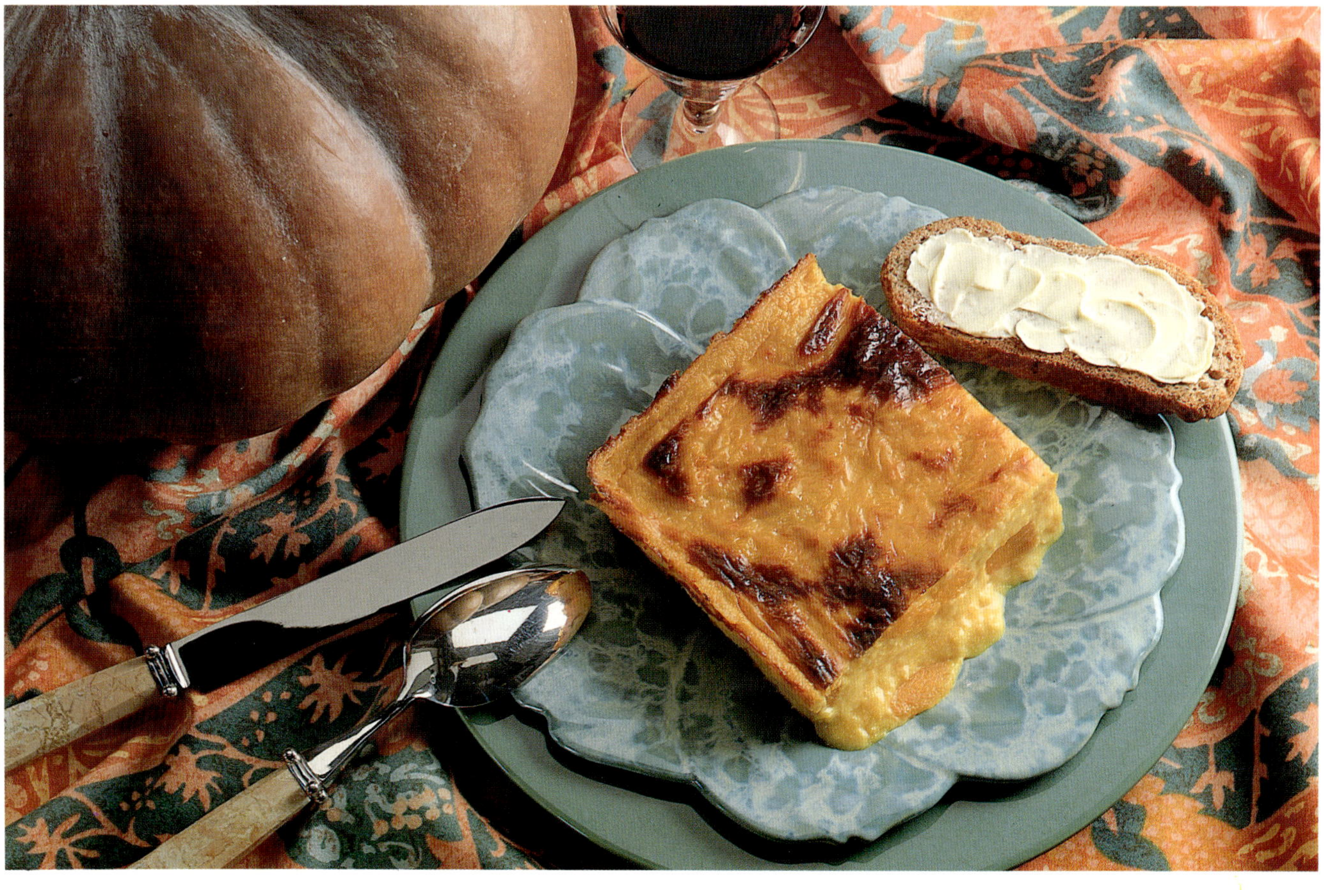

Potatoes with Cream

Kartofel s kremom

1 kg (2 lb) new potatoes, scraped
salt and pepper
200 ml (7 fl oz) thick crème fraîche
1 tablespoon finely chopped dill

Boil the potatoes, with salt to taste, for 20 minutes. Heat the *crème fraîche* in the top of a double boiler set over simmering water. Add salt and a little pepper.

Drain the potatoes, tip them into a bowl, pour over the seasoned *crème fraîche* and sprinkle with dill.

Fried Pumpkin

Zharenaia tykva

40 g (1½ oz) plain flour
salt and pepper
2 kg (4½ lb) pumpkin or squash, peeled, and cut into 5 cm (2 inch) cubes
150 ml (¼ pint) oil or 100 g (4 oz) butter
2 tablespoons chopped dill

Put the flour into a shallow bowl with salt and pepper to season. Add the pumpkin cubes and coat evenly on all sides, then fry in oil or butter for 10 to 15 minutes until cooked. Drain, sprinkle with dill and serve.

Pumpkin au Gratin

Zapekanka iz tykvy

2 kg (4½ lb) pumpkin or squash, peeled, deseeded, and cut into large cubes
salt
125 g (4½ oz) butter
5 tablespoons plain flour
1 litre (1¾ pints) milk
300 g (11 oz) Emmenthal cheese, grated
1 onion, finely grated
butter for greasing

Boil the pumpkin with salt to taste for 10 minutes, then drain the cubes and put them in a buttered ovenproof dish.

Melt 50 g (2 oz) of the butter in a saucepan. Stir in the flour and cook for 1 minute, then stir in the milk. Cook, stirring, until the sauce thickens, then add 200 g (7 oz) of the cheese, with the onion. Pour the sauce over the pumpkin and sprinkle with the remaining grated cheese. Dice the remaining butter and dot it over the surface of the bake.

Brown the dish in a hot oven, 230°C (450°F), Gas Mark 7 for 15 minutes.

Pumpkin au Gratin,

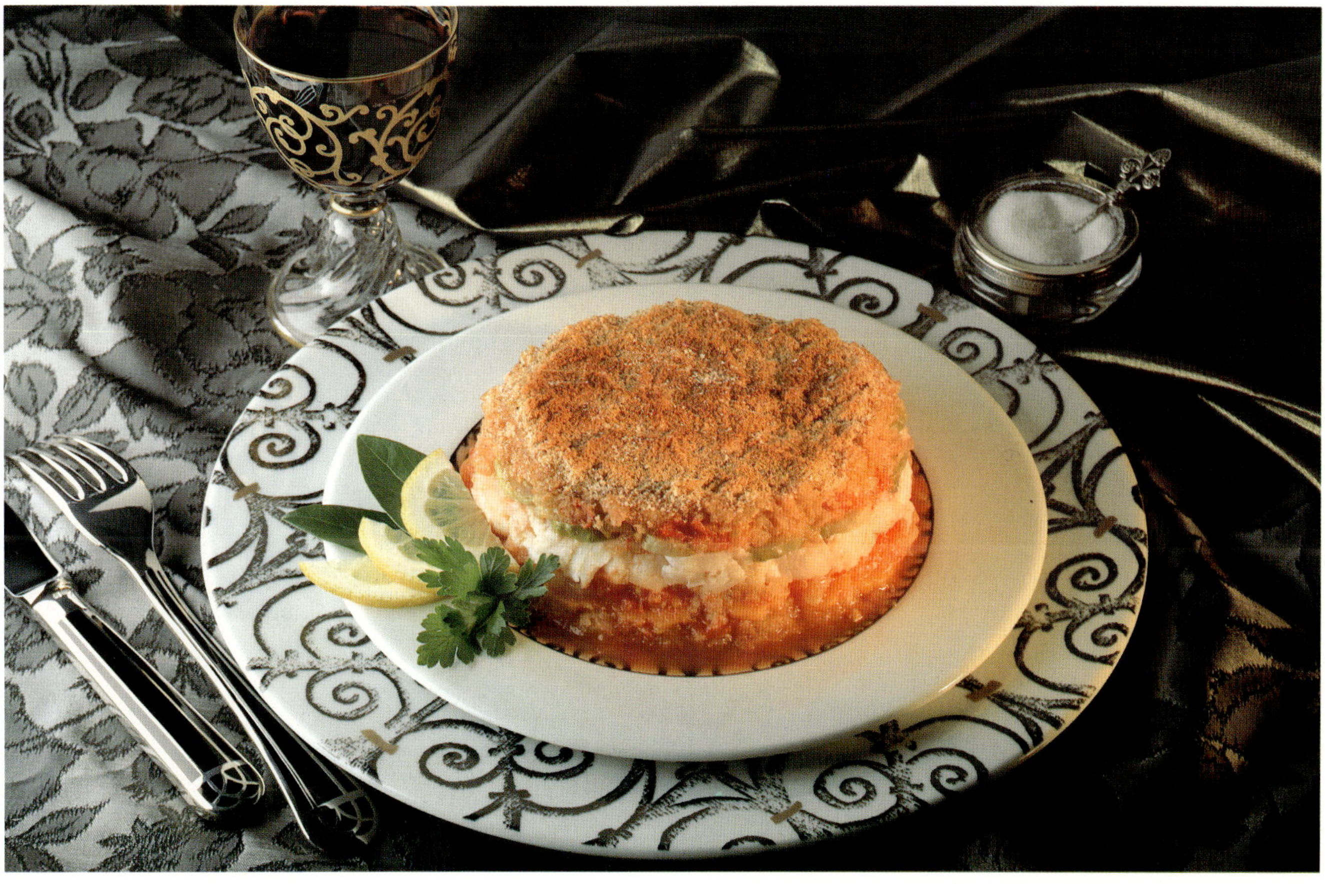

Sauces

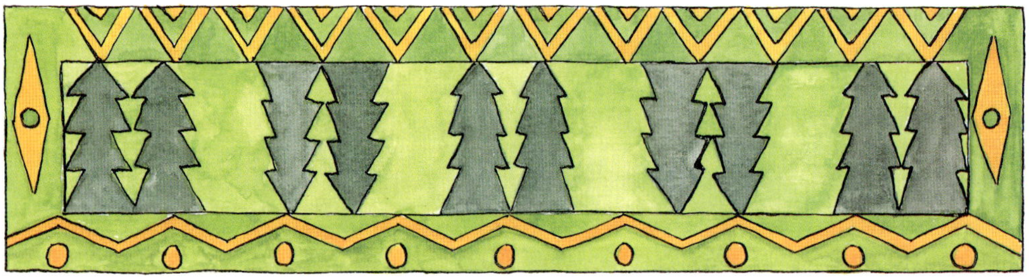

Elaborate sauces made their appearance in Russian cuisine at the court of Peter the Great under the influence of French chefs. Family cooking favours smetana or cream. Melted butter flavoured with dill or the sweet and sour piquancy of gherkins is also popular, as are the traditional flavourings of wild mushrooms and horseradish.

Fish Sauce

Sous s ogurtsami

1 litre (1¾ pints) water
150 ml (¼ pint) dry white wine
1 onion
1bay leaf
2 sprigs parsley
1 kg (2 lb) fish trimmings (heads, skins, bones)
salt
50 g (2 oz) butter
1 tablespoon plain flour
4 gherkins, diced
150 ml (¼ pint) gherkin juice

Make a stock by heating the water, wine, onion, bay leaf, parsley and fish trimmings in a large saucepan. Add ½ teaspoon salt and cook for 1 hour, then strain.

Melt the butter in a saucepan over very low heat. Stir in the flour and cook for 1 minute. Moisten gradually with the stock and cook the sauce until it has the consistency of thick cream, stirring constantly. Add the gherkins and their juice. Serve hot with fish.

Variation: For a creamy fish sauce substitute 100 ml (3½ fl oz) *crème fraîche* for the gherkins and their juice. Bring slowly to the boil and remove from the heat at once. Serve with fish.

Mushroom Sauce

Sous s gribami

200 g (7 oz) fresh mushrooms
1 tablespoon oil
1 onion, finely chopped
50 g (2 oz) butter
1 tablespoon plain flour
300 ml (½ pint) milk
100 ml (3½ fl oz) crème fraîche

Rinse the mushrooms quickly under running water, drain thoroughly and chop finely. Heat the oil in a frying pan, add the mushrooms and onion and fry for 3 to 4 minutes.

Mix the butter and flour in a saucepan and slowly melt the butter over low heat stirring constantly. Gradually add the milk and *crème fraîche*, stirring the sauce until it thickens.

Pour the sauce over the sautéed mushrooms, mix gently and serve with meat or fish croquettes, kasha or potatoes.

Melted Butter Sauce

Rasstoplennii maslenii sous

250 g (9 oz) butter
3 hard-boiled eggs, finely chopped
juice of 1/2 lemon
salt and pepper

Melt the butter in a saucepan over low heat. Add the eggs and lemon juice. Season to taste. Serve with poached fish.

Hot Horseradish Sauce

Tioplii sous so khrenom

50 g (2 oz) butter
2 tablespoons plain flour
750 ml (1 1/4 pints) beef stock
1 200 g (7 oz) jar horseradish

Melt the butter in a saucepan. Stir in the flour, and cook for 1 minute, then gradually add the stock. Allow the sauce to thicken over low heat, stirring constantly, bring to the boil, cook for 3 minutes, then lower the heat and stir in the horseradish. Heat for a few minutes without boiling. Serve with a meat stew or tongue.

Cold Horseradish Sauce

Kholodnii sous so khrenom

200 ml (7 fl oz) single cream
4 tablespoons grated fresh or drained bottled horseradish
1 1/2 teaspoons vinegar (optional)
salt

Combine the cream and horseradish in a bowl. If the horseradish is fresh, add the vinegar. Flavour with salt and serve with cold fish or suckling pig.

Cold Sour Cream Sauce

Smetanii sous

500 ml (1 pint) cream
juice of 1/2 lemon
salt and pepper
sprigs of dill, chopped
1 carrot, cooked

This sauce goes well with meat and fish pâtés and with steamed potatoes.

Whisk the cream with the lemon juice and add salt and pepper. Slice the carrot lengthwise into short, thin sticks and stir them into the mixture with the dill. Keep the sauce cold until you are ready to serve it.

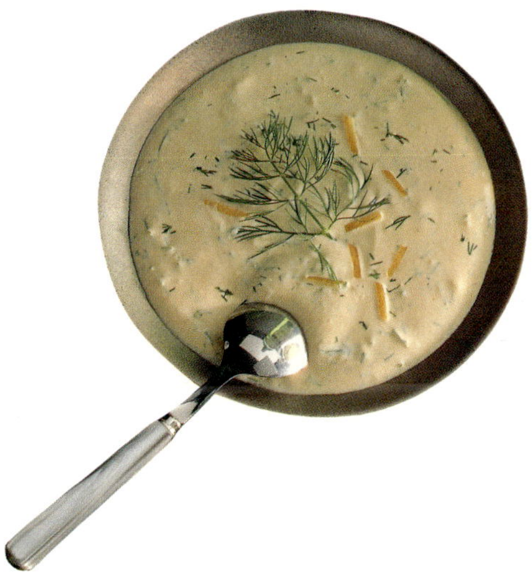

Cold sour cream sauce

Desserts

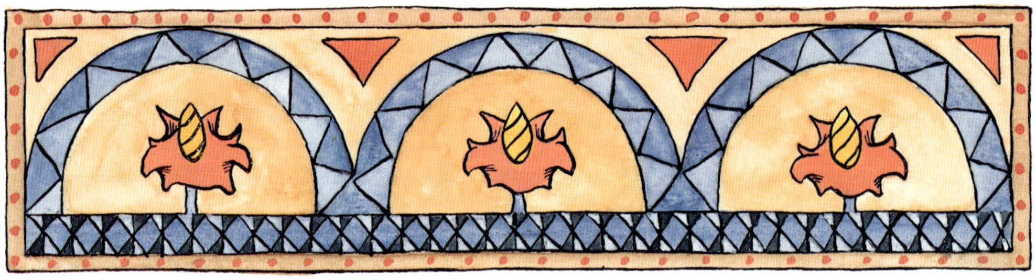

As in many other countries, the desserts popular in Russia are the expression of several centuries of tradition, as much through the ingredients used as through their composition. Lark cakes are made on the first day of spring, *pashka* and *kulich* are eaten at Easter and *kutia* at Christmas. Soft white cheese like *fromage blanc* is widely used, and so is cream, but equally popular is fresh or candied fruit. There are many other popular traditional flavourings – walnuts and hazelnuts, honey, aniseed, caraway seeds, poppy seeds, lemon – which are widely used.

Pashka with Candied Fruit

Pashka s tsukatami

6 egg yolks
375 g (13 oz) caster sugar
250 ml (9 fl oz) milk or 1 × 400 g (14 oz) can unsweetened condensed milk
½ vanilla pod, cut lengthways
250 g (9 oz) butter, in slivers
1 kg (2 lb) fromage blanc
125 g (4½ oz) candied fruit, diced
100 g (4 oz) ground or flaked almonds

This recipe requires a special conical mould, with a hole in the tip for drainage. A new, unused flowerpot may be used instead, or a shaped oil or cardboard container with a hole in the base.

Put the egg yolks in a large enamel saucepan. Add the sugar and mix well; then stir in the milk and add the vanilla pod. Heat slowly, stirring constantly with a wooden spoon. Bring to the boil and immediately remove from the heat. Stir in the butter.

Put the fromage blanc through a fine mill or sieve it into a large bowl. Add it to the saucepan with the candied fruit and almonds and mix vigorously.

Return the pan to a low heat and stir until the mixture begins to steam. Remove from the heat and pour the mixture into an earthenware bowl, continuing to stir until it has completely cooled. Remove the vanilla pod.

Line the mould with a clean muslin cloth and pour in the mixture. Pack it down firmly, folding the muslin over the top. Place the tip of the mould over a jar to allow the excess liquid to drain. After a few hours, put a board covered with a weight on top of the pashka to pack it down firmly so it will keep its shape once it is turned out. Refrigerate for 12 to 24 hours then turn out on to a round plate to serve.

Note: At Easter you can buy very dry *fromage blanc* in Russian shops. As an alternative use *fromage blanc* with 40% fat, straining it for at least 24 hours in a cloth placed over a sieve, with a weight on top.

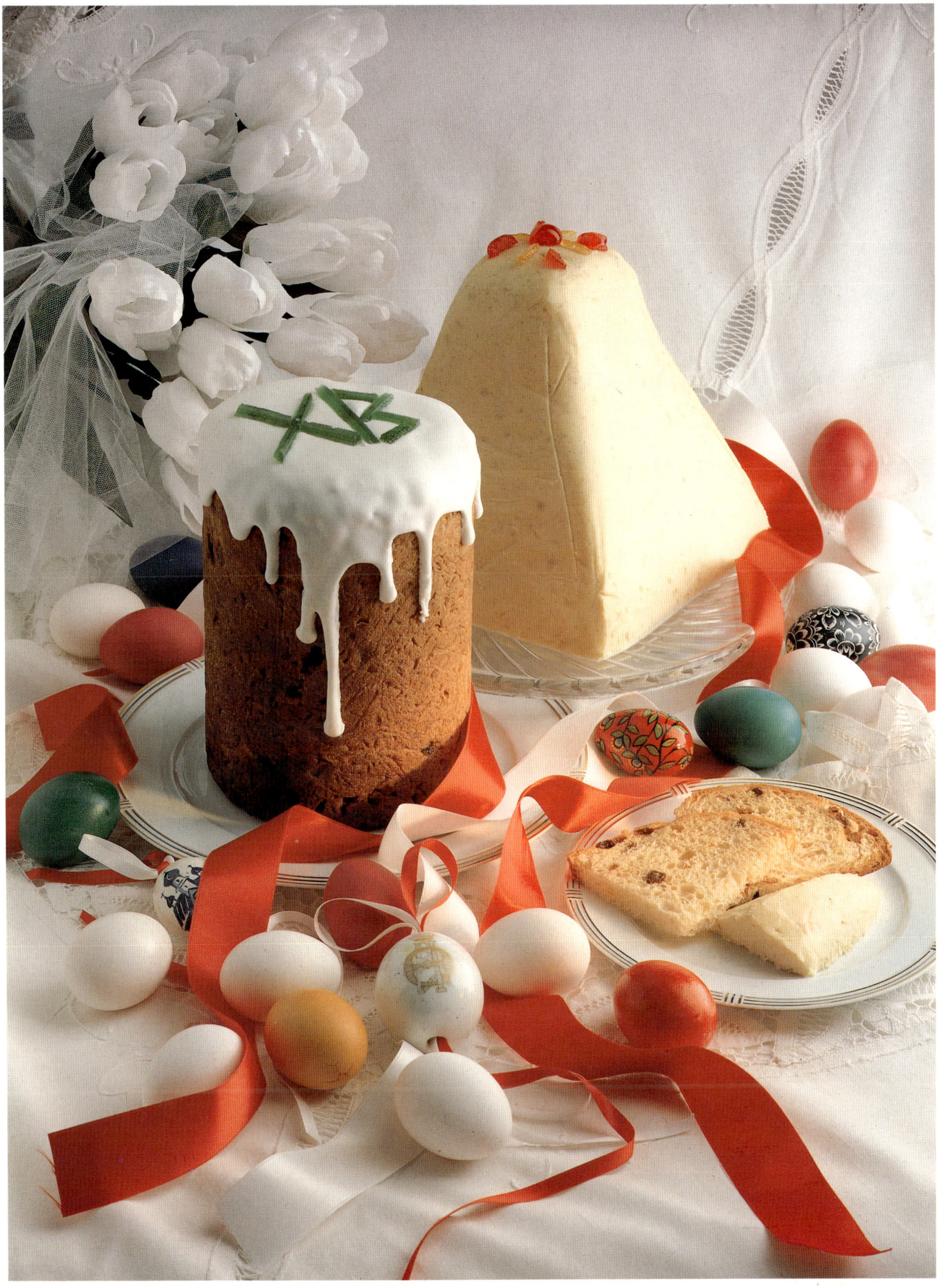

Kulich (page 55); Pashka with Candied Fruit

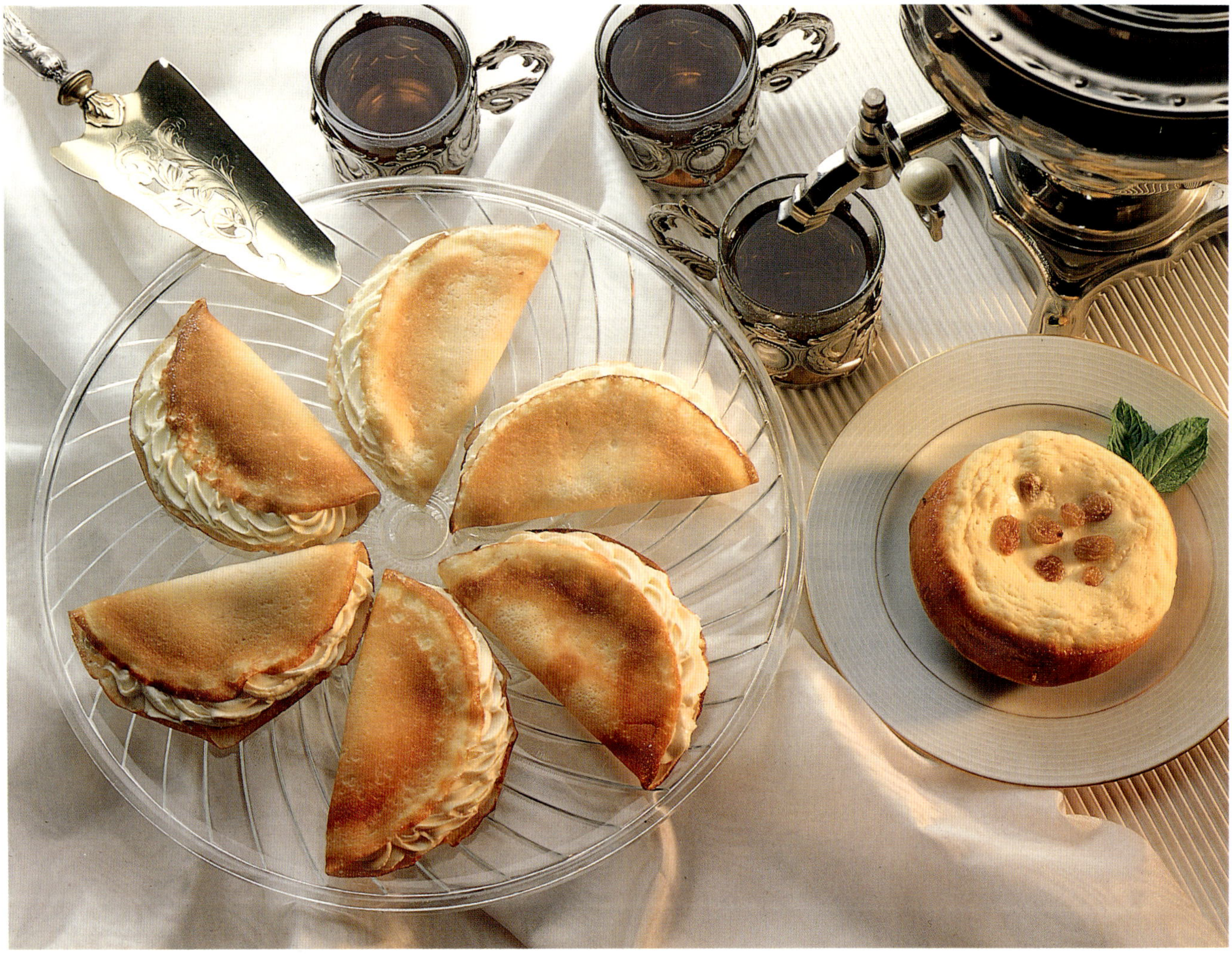

Pancakes Stuffed with Fromage Blanc, *Vatrushka*

No-cook Pashka

Syraia paskha

100 g (4 oz) sultanas
1 kg (2 lb) strained fromage blanc *(see note page 52)*
500 g (1 lb) butter, melted
500 ml (18 fl oz) 9 crème fraîche
350 g (12 oz) sugar
½ teaspoon vanilla essence
150 g (5 oz) ground almonds or almond flakes

Prepare a conical mould as in the previous recipe.

Soak the sultanas in a bowl with water to cover for 15 minutes.

Meanwhile mill the *fromage blanc* or sieve it into a bowl. Add the butter, *crème fraîche*, sugar and vanilla essence. Drain the sultanas and add them to the bowl with the almonds, mixing vigorously with a wooden spoon for about 1 hour.

Fill the prepared mould and proceed as in the previous recipe; refrigerate.

Almond Pashka

Paskha s mendaliom

1 kg (2 lb) strained fromage blanc *(see note on page 52)*
350 g (12 oz) butter, in slivers
1 × 400 g (14 oz) can unsweetened condensed milk
3 eggs, beaten
500 g (1 lb) caster sugar
1 vanilla pod, split
100 g (4 oz) ground almonds

Finely mill the *fromage blanc* or sieve into a large bowl. Stir in butter and the condensed milk. Put the mixture in a large enamel saucepan. Stir in the eggs and sugar, mixing vigorously to obtain a smooth cream. Add the vanilla pod and the almonds.

Heat very gently, preferably on a heat on a diffuser, stirring constantly until the mixture begins to boil. Remove from heat at once. Off the heat, continue stirring until the mixture has cooled completely. Remove the vanilla pod. Fill a prepared mould as described in Pashka with Candied Fruit and refrigerate.

Stuffed Pancakes with Fromage Blanc

Blinchiki s tvorogom

6 eggs
350 g (12 oz) plain flour
500 ml (18 fl oz) milk
1 teaspoon salt
2 tablespoons oil
butter for greasing
200 ml (7 fl oz) crème fraîche
50 g (2 oz) caster sugar

Filling:
500 g (1 lb) strained fromage blanc *(see note, page 52)*
2 egg yolks
3 tablespoons sugar
1 × 7 g (1/4 oz) sachet vanilla sugar or 1/2 teaspoon vanilla essence

Whisk together the eggs, flour and milk. Add the salt and oil. Leave to rest for 2 to 3 hours. Grease an 18 cm (7 inch) crêpe pan with butter and using about 1 tablespoon of batter at a time, make a batch of thin pancakes. Keep them hot on a plate over a saucepan of simmering water. Mix all ingredients for the filling.

Place one tablespoon of filling on each pancake. Roll up the pancakes and put them in a baking dish. Pour over the *crème fraîche*, sprinkle with caster sugar and brown in a preheated hot oven 230°C (450°F), Gas Mark 8 for 15 minutes. Serve immediately.

Vatrushka

Pastry:
250 g (9 oz) plain flour
1/4 teaspoon salt
125 g (4 1/2 oz) butter, diced
1 egg
3 tablespoons water

Filling:
500 g (1 lb) fromage blanc
2 large egg yolks
100 g (4 oz) caster sugar
1 × 7 g (1/4 oz) sachet vanilla sugar or 1/2 teaspoon vanilla essence

Make the pastry by hand or in a food processor by mixing all the ingredients together quickly. Leave to rest for 1 hour, then roll out on a floured board and line a 23 cm (9 inch) flan dish. Bake blind in a preheated hot oven, 230°C (450°F), Gas Mark 8 for 10 minutes.

In a bowl, beat the *fromage blanc* with the egg yolks and sugar. Spread the mixture over the base of the pastry case and return it to the oven. Bake for 15 to 20 minutes or until golden brown. Serve hot or cold.

Kulich

butter or breadcrumbs for lining moulds
40 g (1 1/2 oz) fresh yeast
1 teaspoon salt
250 ml (9 fl oz) hot milk
3 sugar lumps or 1 tablespoon granulated sugar
1 kg (2 lb 3 oz) plain flour
6 egg yolks plus 2 whites
250 g (9 oz) butter, melted
175 g (6 oz) sultanas
125 g (4 1/2 oz) candied fruit, finely diced
300 g (11 oz) ground almonds
50 g (2 oz) blanched almonds

Icing:
3 egg whites
500 g (1 lb) icing sugar
juice of 1/2 lemon
candied fruit to decorate

Butter 2 deep round moulds, or sprinkle them with breadcrumbs. In a warm bowl, mix the yeast and salt, then add the crushed sugar lumps and enough of the flour to make a thick cream. Cover with a cloth or polythene bag and leave in a warm place for about 1 hour. The mixture should double in bulk.

In a large mixing bowl, whisk the egg yolks and caster sugar thoroughly, adding the vanilla essence. Add the yeast mixture, mixing well. Gradually stir in the rest of the flour with the butter, sultanas, candied fruit and almonds.

Whisk the egg whites in a clean, dry bowl to stiff peaks. Fold them into the yeast dough. Knead the dough by hand or in a mixer or food processor until it comes away from the sides of the bowl. This may take quite a long time. Cover the bowl and leave the dough to rise in a warm place.

Divide the dough between the prepared dishes, filling them no more than one-third full. Leave to rest again in a warm place until well risen.

Bake in a preheated moderate oven, 180°C (350°F), Gas Mark 4 for about 1 hour, or until a skewer inserted in the kulich comes out clean. If the dough looks as though it is going to spill over, cover the top of the dishes with foil. Turn the cooked kulich out on to wire racks to cool.

Make the icing. In a clean, dry bowl, whisk the egg whites until stiff, then gradually beat in the sugar and lemon juice. Coat the tops of the cakes with this icing, decorate with candied fruit and set aside for 3 to 4 hours until the icing has hardened.

Thrifty Kulich

Ekonomicheskii kulich

butter or breadcrumbs for lining dishes
40 g (1½ oz) fresh yeast
1 teaspoon salt
250 ml (8 fl oz) milk
50 g (2 oz) caster sugar
1 kg (2 lb 3 oz) plain flour
2 eggs, separated
1 × 7 g (¼ oz) vanilla sugar or ½ teaspoon vanilla essence
200 g (7 oz) butter or margarine, melted
100 g (4 oz) sultanas
50 g (2 oz) orange peel
100 g (4 oz) ground almonds

Working the dough very thoroughly, follow the process given on the previous page.

Sweet Ravioli

Varenniki

575 g (1¼ lb) plain flour
pinch of salt
2 eggs
150 ml (¼ pint) milk
20 g (¾ oz) butter
cream and sugar to serve

Filling:
500 g (1 lb) strained fromage blanc *(see page 52)*
1 egg
50 g (2 oz) sugar
1 teaspoon salt

Combine the flour, salt, eggs, milk and butter in a bowl. Mix swiftly and thoroughly to a dough. Cover and leave to rest for 1 hour in a cool place.

Meanwhile make the filling. Rub the *fromage blanc* through a fine sieve into a second bowl. Stir in the egg, sugar and salt.

On a floured board, roll out the dough very thinly (it should be transparent) and using a glass as a guide cut out circles. Place 1 teaspoon of filling in the centre of each circle. Moisten the edges with water, fold over to half-moon shapes and pinch the edges to seal.

Bring a large saucepan of lightly salted water to the boil. Toss in the varenniki. As soon as they rise to the surface, they are ready. Drain and serve with sugar and cream.

Variation: 500 g (1 lb) stoned fresh cherries may be substituted for the filling.

Sochni

20 g (¾ oz) fresh yeast
120 ml (4 fl oz) warm milk
1 teaspoon salt
25 g (1 oz) sugar
500 g (1 lb) plain flour
175 g (6 oz) butter
100 ml (3½ fl oz) single cream
cream to serve

Filling:
300 g (11 oz) strained fromage blanc (see page 52)
2 eggs, beaten
25 g (1 oz) sugar

In a warm bowl, dissolve the yeast in the milk with the salt and sugar. Beat enough of the flour to make a thick cream. Cover the bowl and leave to rise in a warm place until the mixture has doubled in bulk. Add 50 g (2 oz) of the butter and cream and knead the mixture until it no longer sticks. Cover and leave to rise again.

Roll out the dough on a floured board to a thickness of 5 mm (¼ inch) and cut out circles, using a large glass as a guide.

Make the filling by mixing the *fromage blanc*, eggs, and sugar in a bowl. Put 1 teaspoon of filling in the middle of each circle of dough. Fold each dough circle in half, moisten the edges with water or milk, then pinch them together to seal in the filling. Leave to rest for a few minutes.

Melt the remaining butter in a large frying pan, add the filled dough crescents and fry for 4 to 5 minutes. Transfer the cooked crescents to a hot platter and serve at once, with the cream.

Fromage Blanc Croquettes

Sirniki

1 kg (2 lb) fromage blanc, *40% fat*
3 eggs
6 tablespoons plain flour
¼ teaspoon salt
4 tablespoons sugar
100 g (4 oz) butter
cream and sugar to serve

Wrap the *fromage blanc* in a muslin cloth and put it in a strainer. Put a weight on top and set the strainer over a bowl for several hours.

When the *fromage blanc* is dry, tip it into a bowl. Add the eggs with 4 tablespoons of the flour. Stir in the salt and sugar and mix together thoroughly.

Form the mixture into round croquettes. In a shallow bowl roll the croquettes in the remaining flour and flatten them. Melt the butter in a large frying pan, add the croquettes and fry for 3 to 4 minutes. Serve hot with cream and sugar.

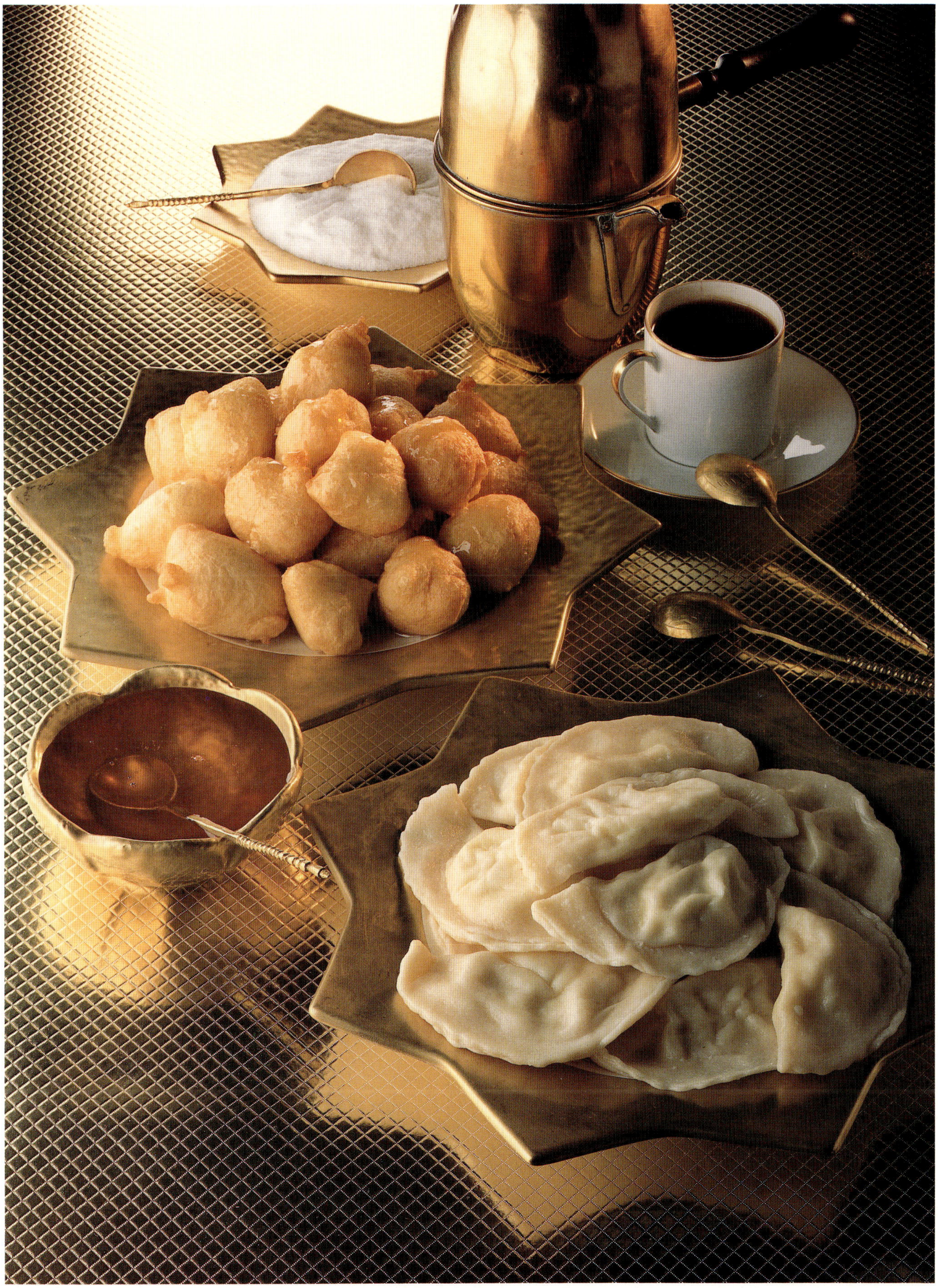

Doughnuts, Sweet Ravioli

Doughnuts

Oladii

25 g (1 oz) fresh yeast
250 ml (9 fl oz) milk, warmed
½ teaspoon salt
1 tablespoon sugar
2 eggs, beaten
500 g (1 lb) plain flour
350 ml (12 fl oz) sunflower oil
clear honey, to serve

In a mixing bowl, dissolve the yeast in the warm milk with the salt and sugar. Add the beaten eggs and beat in the flour, using an electric whisk, if liked, to avoid the formation of lumps. The batter should have the consistency of thick cream. If it is too thick, add warm milk or a little water. Leave to rest for 1 hour.

Heat the oil in a large deep frying pan or deep fat fryer to a temperature of 190°C (375°F) or until a cube of bread browns in 30 seconds. Carefully drop 1 tablespoon of the batter into the oil and let it brown for a few minutes on each side. Remove, drain and keep hot. Continue to make oladii until all the batter has been used. Serve hot with honey.

Lazy Varenniki

Lenivye varenniki

500 g (1 lb) strained fromage blanc *(see note page 52)*
250 g (9 oz) plain flour
pinch of salt
50 g (2 oz) sugar
cream and sugar to serve

Rub the *fromage blanc* through a sieve into a large bowl. Add the flour, salt, eggs and sugar and mix to a dough. Shape the dough into a long sausage as thick as your thumb and cut it into fat slices.

Bring a saucepan of lightly salted water to the boil. Toss in the varenniki. As soon as they rise to the surface they are ready. Drain and serve at once with cream and sugar.

Krupennik

500 ml (18 fl oz) milk
200 g (7 oz) buckwheat groats
200 g (7 oz) strained fromage blanc *(see note page 52)*
2 eggs, beaten
½ teaspoon salt
2 tablespoons sugar
100 ml (3½ fl oz) double cream
50 g (2 oz) butter
2 tablespoons fresh white breadcrumbs
cream and sugar

Bring the milk to the boil in a large saucepan. Pour in the buckwheat groats and put the pan over a low heat until the groats swell. Finely sieve the *fromage blanc* into a bowl, and add it to the buckwheat with the eggs, and the sugar. Stir in half the cream and mix well.

Using about three quarters of the butter generously grease a 20 cm (8 inch) baking tin. Pour in the buckwheat mixture and sprinkle with the breadcrumbs. Pour over the rest of the cream. Melt the remaining butter and drizzle it over the top.

Bake in a hot oven, 230°C (450°F), Gas Mark 8 for 40 minutes. Turn out on to a platter and serve with cream and sugar.

Christmas Kasha

Kutia

350 g (12 oz) hulled corn or coarse semolina
300 g (11 oz) honey
125 g (4½ oz) raisins
5 tablespoons rum
125 g (4½ oz) dried apricots
200 g (7 oz) shelled walnuts

Kutia is a traditional Christmas Eve dessert. Put the corn in a sieve and rinse it, then simmer it over very low heat for several hours, until it swells and becomes soft, but not sticky. Drain the corn and return it to the clean pan. In a measuring jug, mix the honey with 250 ml (8 fl oz) boiling water. Stir well, then add to the corn. Bring the mixture to the boil, then leave to cool.

Put the raisins in a small bowl with the rum, and the apricots in a separate bowl with 300 ml (½ pint) water. Leave to stand until plump, then add the dried fruit to the corn mixture with the walnuts. Stir well, then leave in a cool place for several hours.

Ponchiki with Jam

Ponchiki

20 g (¾ oz) fresh yeast
5 tablespoons warm milk
pinch of salt
about 250 g (9 oz) plain flour
3 egg yolks
65 g (2½ oz) sugar
1 × 500 g (1 lb) jar whole-fruit jam
350 ml (12 fl oz) oil

In a mixing bowl dissolve the yeast in the warm milk with the salt. Add 240 g (8½ oz) of the flour. In a second bowl beat the egg yolks with the sugar. Add the eggs to the mixing bowl, stirring well with a wooden spoon, then cover the dough and leave to rise for 1 hour in a warm place.

Roll out the dough on a floured board to a thickness of about 5 mm (¼ inch). Cut the dough in half to form 2 rectangles. Spoon out the fruit from the jar of jam, and place it at regular intervals on one of the rectangles of dough. Try to avoid taking too much of the liquid jam

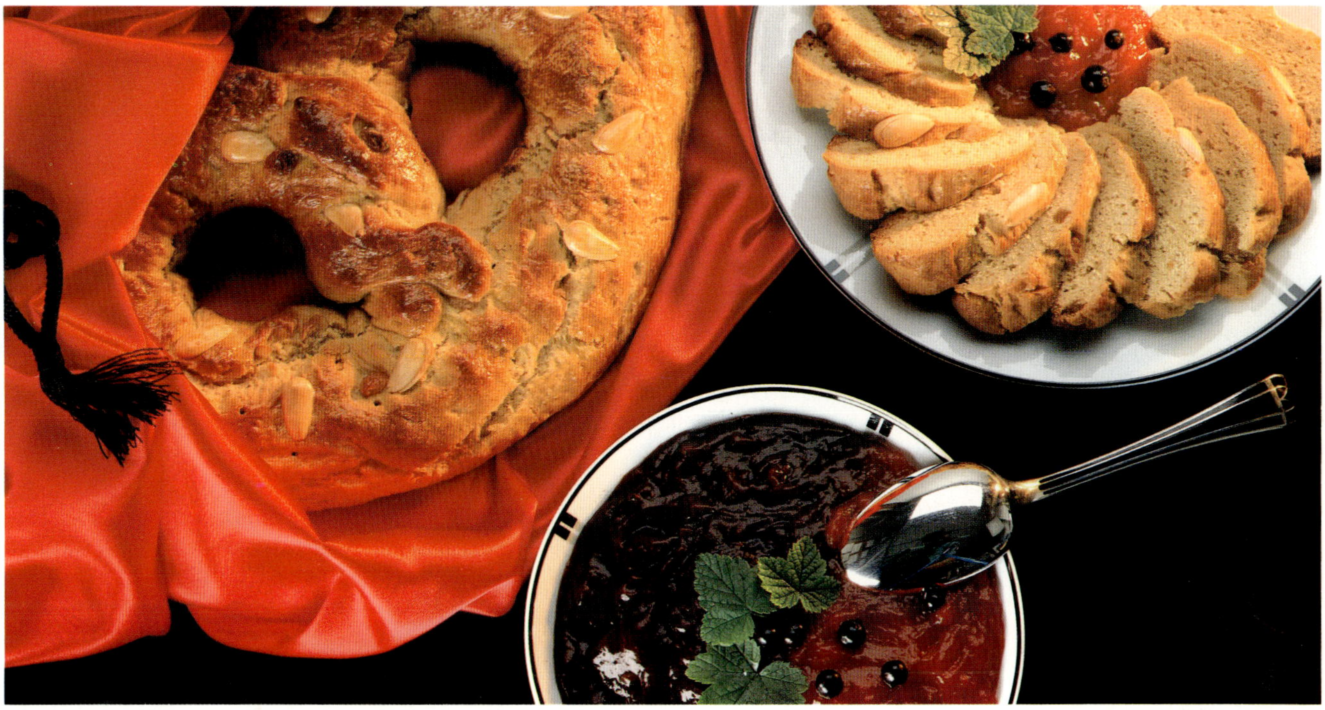

Krendel, fruit juice purée

with the chunks of fruit. Cover with the second dough rectangle. Cut out circles around each piece of fruit and form them into balls. Arrange the jam-filled balls on a board and leave them to rise for 30 minutes.

Heat the oil in a large deep frying pan or deep fat fryer to a temperature of 190°C (375°F). Add the ponchiki to the oil and fry for 2 to 3 minutes, turning them to ensure even browning. Remove with a slotted spoon and drain on absorbent kitchen paper. Serve at once.

Fruit Juice Purée

Kissel

1.5 kg (3¼ lb) soft fruit (blackcurrants, redcurrants, raspberries or strawberries)
1 litre (1¾ pints) water
45 g (1½ oz) potato flour
sugar (optional)

This cream, which children love, will keep for about a week.

Clean and prepare the fruit and simmer it gently for about 15 minutes until tender. Sieve the fruit into a bowl, using a wooden spoon to crush the berries to extract the juice. Leave to cool.

Put the potato flour into a cup and add enough of the cold fruit juice to make a cream. Bring the rest of the juice to the boil in a saucepan. Remove the pan from the heat and add the potato flour cream, mixing vigorously to prevent the formation of lumps. Taste and add sugar if necessary.

Pour the cream into a bowl and chill until required. Serve with single cream, if liked.

Lark Cakes

Zhavoronki

25 g (1 oz) fresh yeast
120 ml (4 fl oz) warm milk
½ teaspoon fine salt
1½ sugar lumps or 1½ teaspoons granulated sugar
500 g (1 lb 3 oz) plain flour
4 egg yolks
100 g (4 oz) caster sugar
1 teaspoon vanilla essence
125 g (4½ oz) butter, softened
50 g (2 oz) raisins or currants
1 beaten egg, to glaze

In a warm bowl, dissolve the yeast in the milk, with the salt and crushed sugar lumps. Beat in enough of the flour to make a thick cream. Cover the bowl and leave to rinse for 30 minutes to 1 hour.

Whisk the egg yolks with the caster sugar and the vanilla essence until they are pale and thick. In a separate bowl, beat butter until creamy, then add it to the yeast mixture with the egg and sugar mixture.

Mix in the rest of the flour and knead the dough thoroughly. Leave to rise for about 1 hour.

Cut the dough into several sausages of about 100 g (4 oz). Divide each sausage into 2 pieces, one half the size of the other, and assemble them to make a bird shape. Use two raisins or currants for the eyes.

Place the zhavoronki on greased baking sheets, brush with beaten egg to glaze and bake in a preheated oven, 220°C (425°F), Gas Mark 7 for 15 to 20 minutes. Cool slightly, then transfer the cakes to wire racks to cool completely.

Red Fruit Compote

Kompot iz krasnikh iagod

1 kg (2 lb) red fruit
575 g (1¼ lb) sugar
500 ml (18 fl oz) water
juice of ½ lemon (optional)

In this recipe, the fruit is not cooked, so the flavour is fully preserved.

Put the fruit in a large bowl. Add 300 g (11 oz) of the sugar. Set the bowl aside for about 1 hour to draw out the fruit juice.

Meanwhile, make a syrup by mixing the remaining sugar with the water in a saucepan. Bring to the boil, stirring until the sugar has dissolved, then lower the heat and simmer for about 20 minutes.

As soon as the syrup thickens, pour it over the fruit. Stir and leave to cool. Taste the compote: if it is too

Semolina Fruit Mousse

Shliopannaia kasha

1 kg (2 lb) berry fruit (blackcurrants, redcurrants, bilberries)
600 ml (1 pint) water
sugar to taste
75 g (3 oz) semolina

Clean and prepare the fruit. Put it into a saucepan with the water and simmer gently for about 15 minutes until tender. Sieve the fruit into a bowl, using a wooden spoon to crush the berries against the sides of the sieve to extract the juice.

Return the fruit juice to the clean saucepan, stir in the sugar and sprinkle the semolina on top of the liquid. Cook over a gentle heat for 15 to 20 minutes, stirring constantly until thick and smooth. Pour the semolina mixture into a bowl and cover the surface with a piece of damp greaseproof paper to prevent the formation of a skin.

Put the bowl of semolina into a larger bowl filled with ice. Whisk with an electric whisk until the semolina mousse is firm, then pour it into a serving bowl or into individual ramekins. Refrigerate for a few hours before serving.

Prianiki with Honey

Medovie prianiki

butter and flour to line moulds
1 kg (2 lb) clear honey
1 kg (2 lb 3 oz) plain flour
4 eggs, separated
5 bitter almonds, ground
grated zest of ½ lemon
nutmeg to taste

Moulds with a Christmas theme are traditionally used for this dessert. Stars, fir trees, and bells are typical shapes. Prepare the moulds by buttering them generously and dusting them with flour.

Warm the honey over gentle heat in a large saucepan. Whisk it by hand or with an electric whisk, then remove from the heat and stir in the flour, egg yolks, almonds and lemon zest.

In a clean, dry bowl whisk the egg whites to stiff peaks. Fold them into the honey mixture with a little grated nutmeg. Pour into the prepared moulds.

Bake the prianiki in a preheated hot oven, 230°C (450°F), Gas Mark 8 for 5 minutes, then lower the oven temperature to moderately hot, 190°C (375°F), Gas Mark 5 and bake for 10 to 15 minutes more. Cool the prianiki for 10 minutes in the moulds before turning them out on to wire racks to cool completely.

Prianiki with Honey and Coffee

Medovi prianiki s kofeem

butter and flour for lining moulds
190 g (6½ oz) clear honey
5–6 tablespoons strong black coffee
120 ml (4 fl oz) sunflower oil
125 g (4½ oz) soft brown sugar
2 eggs, beaten
1 teaspoon ground cinammon
2 teaspoons baking powder
275 g (10 oz) plain flour

Put all the ingredients, except the flour in a large mixing bowl. Using a whisk beat the mixture well. Gradually add the flour, whisking well after each addition. Cover the bowl and refrigerate overnight.

Next day, spoon the dough into the tins, filling them no more than half full. Bake in a preheated hot oven, 230°C (450°F), Gas Mark 8 for 5 minutes, then lower the oven temperature to moderately hot, 190°C (375°F), Gas Mark 5 and bake for 20 to 30 minutes more or until a skewer, inserted in the spiced honey bread, comes out clean. Turn the loaves out on wire racks to cool.

Milk Curds

Prastakvasha

Use milk straight from the cow, neither sterilized nor pasteurized. Put the milk in glasses or earthenware bowls. Cover the containers of milk and leave in a warm place for 24 hours at summer temperatures. The cream will rise to the surface. When the milk curdles, refrigerate it. Seve chilled. It will only keep for 2 days.

Sweets & Cakes

Baranki

120 ml (4 fl oz) warm milk
15 g (½ oz) fresh yeast
½ teaspoon salt
250 g (9 oz) plain flour
7 tablespoons oil
1 egg, beaten, to glaze
100g (4 oz) poppy seed or cumin

In a warm bowl, dissolve the yeast thoroughly in the warm milk with the salt. Stir in about 50 g (2 oz) of the flour to create a thick cream. Cover with a cloth and leave to rise in a warm place for 1 hour, until the mixture doubles in bulk.

Add the rest of the flour and knead the dough until it no longer sticks to your hands. Form into a ball, cover and leave to rise in a warm place for 1 hour.

Knead the dough again, then work it into rings 15 cm (6 inches) in diameter and 2 cm (¾ inch) thick. Leave to rise for 1 hour more.

Bring a large saucepan of water to the boil and immerse the baranki, a few at a time. When they start to float to the surface remove them.

Drain them on kitchen paper, then transfer to a floured baking sheet. Brush the tops of the baranki with the beaten egg, to glaze. Sprinkle with poppy seed or cumin. Leave to rest for 15 minutes, then bake at 230°C (450°F), Gas Mark 8 for 10 minutes or until they are golden brown.

Khvorost

5–6 tablespoons milk
1 tablespoon single cream
3 eggs, yolks plus 1 white separated
20 g (¾ oz) sugar
pinch of salt
150 ml (¼ pint) brandy
675 g (1 lb 6 oz) plain flour
oil for deep frying

Mix the milk, cream, egg yolks, sugar, salt and brandy in a large bowl. Carefully stir in the flour to make a dough. Knead the dough, cover with a cloth and leave to rest for 1 hour.

Roll out the dough very thinly. Cut it into thin strips 10 to 13 cm (4–5 inches) long. Plait them in groups of 2 or 3, pinch the ends and brush them with the egg white to glaze.

Fry the khvorost in butter or oil, a few at a time, for 1 to 2 minutes or until well risen and golden brown.

Bublichki

100 ml (3½ fl oz) crème fleurette
(sweetened crème fraîche*)*
5 egg yolks
50 g (2 oz) butter, diced
2 teaspoons baking powder
240 g (8½ oz) plain flour
500 ml (18 fl oz) milk
3 tablespoons sugar

Quickly mix all the ingredients except the milk and sugar by hand or in a food processor to obtain a fairly firm dough, and shape it into rings 3 cm (1¼ inches) in diameter and 1 cm (½ inch) thick.

Bring the milk to the boil. Add the rings, a few at a time, removing them carefully with a slotted spoon as soon as they float to the surface.

Drain the bublichki on kitchen paper then transfer them to a floured baking sheet. Sprinkle them with sugar and bake at 220°C (425°F), Gas Mark 7 for 10 minutes.

Variation: To make savoury bublichki, substitute poppy seed or cumin for the sugar topping.

Krendel

250 ml (9 fl oz) hot milk
40 g (1½ oz) fresh yeast
¾ teaspoon salt
250 g (9 oz) sugar
1 kg (2 lb 3 oz) plain flour
12 egg yolks
3 × 7 g (¼ oz) sachets vanilla sugar or 1 teaspoon vanilla essence
300 g (11 oz) butter, softened, or margarine
200 g (7 oz) sultanas
250 g (9 oz) nibbed almonds
1 egg, beaten
1–2 tablespoons icing sugar

To make the dough, combine the milk, yeast and salt in a warm bowl. Add 1 tablespoon of the sugar and stir in enough flour to make a smooth cream. Mix until all the lumps have dissolved. Cover the bowl and leave to rise in a warm place for 30 minutes to 1 hour.

Meanwhile, whisk the egg yolks in a mixing bowl with the remaining sugar and vanilla sugar or essence until the mixture becomes thick and white.

In a separate bowl whisk the butter or margarine until light and fluffy. Carefully stir the whisked butter into the egg yolk mixture and add the risen dough.

Mix well, then knead by hand or in a food processor until the dough comes away from the sides and no longer sticks to the hands.

Add the sultanas with 200 g (7 oz) of the almonds. Knead again, cover the dough with a cloth and leave to rise in a warm place for 1 hour.

On a floured work surface, form the dough into a long sausage shape tapering at the ends. Fold these ends to the middle, crossing them over, and carefully transfer the folded dough to a floured baking sheet. Leave to rise again.

Brush the krendel with the beaten egg, sprinkle with the remaining nibbed almonds and bake at 200°C (400°F), Gas Mark 6 for 40 to 45 minutes.

Savoury Biscuits

Lepioshki

300 g (11 oz) plain flour
200 ml (7 fl oz) thick crème fraîche
1 tablespoon baking powder
½ teaspoon salt and pepper to taste

Mix all ingredients except the oil and butter rapidly by hand or in a food processor, without kneading the dough.

Roll the dough into a large sausage shape and cut it into thick slices. Flatten these by hand to form biscuit shapes 1 cm (½ inch) thick. Prick the biscuits with a fork and bake at 220°C (425°F), Gas Mark 7 for 15 minutes. Serve hot or cold with butter.

Apple Crunch

Pastila

10 cooking apples, peeled and cored
500 g (1 lb) caster sugar
1 egg white
butter for greasing
extra caster sugar for sprinkling

Bake the apples in a moderate oven, 150°C (350°F), Gas Mark 4 for about 15 minutes or until soft. Mash them with the sugar, then whisk the mixture until it is white and fluffy.

Whisk the egg white until stiff, fold it into the apple. Spread the mixture 1 to 2.5 cm (½ to 1 inch) thick on a baking sheet covered in buttered greaseproof paper.

Dry out in a very cool oven, 100°C (225°F), Gas Mark 1 for at least 2 hours, as for meringues, then sprinkle lightly with sugar. Cut into squares to serve.

Fudge with Cream

Tianushki

200 ml (7 fl oz) crème fraîche
500 g (1 lb) sugar lumps or granulated sugar
1 vanilla pod
butter for greasing

In an enamel or pyrex saucepan, combine *crème fraîche*, sugar and vanilla pod. Bring to the boil and cook for about 45 minutes until the mixture is thick and smooth, stirring constantly. Remove the vanilla pod.

Spread the mixture in a layer 2 cm (¾ inch) thick on a buttered marble slab.

When cool, cut the fudge into 5 cm (2 inch) sticks.

Korzhiki

165 g (5½ oz) plain flour
40 g (1½ oz) softened butter
5–6 tablespoons single cream
a pinch of salt
3 tablespoons sugar
½ teaspoon baking powder
2 eggs, beaten

Make a well in the flour, put in the butter, cream, beaten sugar, baking powder and half of the beaten eggs and mix to make a smooth dough.

Knead the dough well, then roll it out to a thickness of 5 mm (¼ inch) and cut out circles.

Place the korzhiki on a greased and floured baking sheet. Prick them with a fork and brush them with the remaining beaten egg. Bake at 220°C (425°F), Gas mark 7 for 15 minutes.

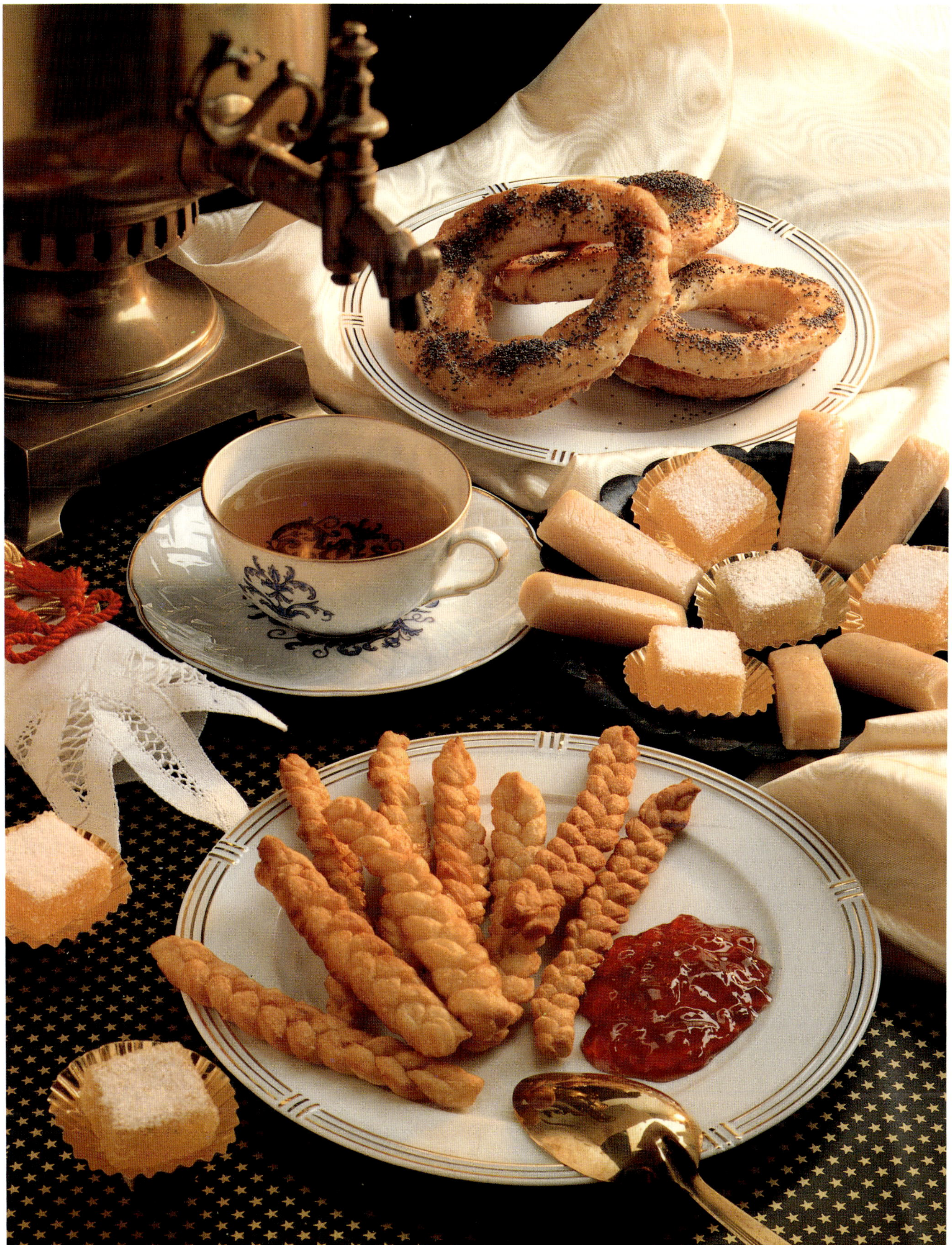

Baranki, Khvorost, apple crunch, fudge with cream

Index